全国高职高专专业英语规划教材

商务英语翻译教程
（第2版）

房玉靖　刘海燕　主　编
叶惠玲　樊文霞　副主编

清华大学出版社
北　京

内容简介

本书是专为高职高专英语翻译教学所编写的实用教材,它遵循《高职高专教育英语课程教学基本要求》,本着"实用为主,够用为度"的指导思想,着重培养学习者常用商务文本的英汉互译能力。

本书全面系统地讲解了商务英语翻译方面的相关内容,合理地将翻译知识与日常商务知识及商务翻译技能融为一体,旨在帮助学生熟练掌握各种常用商务翻译术语、翻译原则和技巧,从而提高涉外商务翻译的能力。

本书可供高职高专及以上水平的商务英语专业教学使用,也可作为外贸从业人员的培训教材,还可作为英语爱好者的阅读资料。

本书封面贴有清华大学出版社防伪标签,无标签者不得销售。
版权所有,侵权必究。举报:010-62782989,beiqinquan@tup.tsinghua.edu.cn。

图书在版编目(CIP)数据

商务英语翻译教程/房玉靖,刘海燕主编. —2版. —北京:清华大学出版社,2019(2025.2重印)
(全国高职高专专业英语规划教材)
ISBN 978-7-302-52402-1

Ⅰ. ①商… Ⅱ. ①房… ②刘… Ⅲ. ①商务—英语—翻译—高等职业教育—教材 Ⅳ. ①F7

中国版本图书馆 CIP 数据核字(2019)第 042127 号

责任编辑:陈立静
装帧设计:杨玉兰
责任校对:李玉茹
责任印制:宋 林

出版发行:清华大学出版社
  网　　址:https://www.tup.com.cn,https://www.wqxuetang.com
  地　　址:北京清华大学学研大厦A座　　邮　编:100084
  社 总 机:010-83470000　　邮　购:010-62786544
  投稿与读者服务:010-62776969,c-service@tup.tsinghua.edu.cn
  质量反馈:010-62772015,zhiliang@tup.tsinghua.edu.cn
  课件下载:https://www.tup.com.cn,010-62791865
印 装 者:三河市君旺印务有限公司
经　　销:全国新华书店
开　　本:185mm×260mm　　印　张:13.75　　字　数:291千字
版　　次:2011年12月第1版　2019年8月第2版　印　次:2025年2月第9次印刷
定　　价:39.90元

产品编号:072129-01

前　言

　　《商务英语翻译教程（第2版）》是专为高职高专英语翻译教学所编写的实用教材。本教材遵循《高职高专教育英语课程教学基本要求》，本着"实用为主，够用为度"的指导思想，着重培养学习者常用商务文本的英汉互译能力。

　　本教材以外经贸工作的实际需求为出发点，以就业为导向，以职业能力为核心，针对典型工作任务所需的理论知识和实践技能要求，将各种工作任务分为四大模块，内容涉及各种公司业务常用的商务文本，力图通过模块化训练，使学生能够结合语言技能和商务知识，较为全面地掌握实用商务英语翻译技能，从而能基本胜任涉外行业的翻译工作。同时，也可进一步培养职业能力。

　　本教材有如下特点。

1. "教""学""做"三者有机结合

　　编写本教材时，我们充分考虑到高职高专学生的学习特点，针对每个模块设计了六项活动。

　　Warm-up（热身练习）旨在使学生对即将进行的翻译任务产生兴趣或有一个初步的认识；

　　Background（背景知识）旨在使学生了解完成相关翻译任务必备的一些背景知识；

　　Discussion（讨论）旨在使学生在教师的引导下讨论如何圆满完成相关翻译任务，

从而掌握相关翻译任务所需的基本翻译技能；

Follow-up（课堂练习）旨在趁热打铁，使学生巩固所学翻译技能；

Homework（家庭作业）旨在使学生能举一反三，更好地完成新的同类型的翻译任务；

Extend Your Eyes（拓展视野）旨在通过提供大量相关翻译任务常用表达，使学有余力的学生能掌握更多的相关词汇与句型，从而能完成更多同类型的翻译任务。

2. 模块教学，客观全面

全书内容根据实际工作情境，分为四大模块：招商引资、外贸业务、日常办公和企业宣传，有利于学习者全方位地了解涉外工作中的翻译业务。

3. 英译汉与汉译英相辅相成，强调双向翻译

实际工作情况中，不同商务文本的英译汉或汉译英比例不同，某些商务文本常需进行英译汉，某些商务文本则常需进行汉译英。例如，商务合同在实际工作中以英译汉居多，而产品说明书在实际工作中英译汉和汉译英均有。因此，本书根据实际工作情形，英译汉与汉译英兼顾，考虑到课堂实际操作，Warm-up（热身练习）和Follow-up（课堂练习）多数以英译汉为主，长度较短，Homework（家庭作业）则英汉翻译和汉英翻译兼顾。

4. 将翻译技巧有机融入翻译解析

在翻译实践中，每一种文本的翻译都需要综合运用多种翻译技巧，考虑到高职高专学生的具体情况，本教材将常用翻译技巧融入各种文本的翻译讲解之中，提供大量范例，针对各种文本的语言特点对其翻译技巧进行一些规律性的总结。

5. 第二版改动说明

根据近几年读者对本教材的使用反馈，第二版做了如下改动。

模块设计更为合理，保留第一版的四大模块，但第三模块重命名为"日常办公"，第四模块重命名为"企业宣传"，并将各模块的任务重新组合。

模块一"招商引资"由三个任务（Task 1~3）组成：保留一版的"名片"任务，新增"商务会展"和"招标文件"，一版中原属第一模块的"企业形象"和"商业广告"两项任务重新组合至模块四"企业宣传"中。

模块二"外贸业务"保留一版的体例结构，包括四个任务（Task 4~7）。

模块三"日常办公"将一版的"日常办公文本"任务缩编为"会议记录"任务（Task 8）；"商务旅游"任务重命名为"商务旅行"（Task 10）；"商务庆典与新闻发布"任务缩编为"新闻发布"并重新组合至模块四"企业宣传"中；"市场调研"任务扩编为"商务报告"（Task 11）；另将一版中原属模块四的"出国文书"任务（Task 9）重新组合至本模块中。

模块四"企业宣传"删除了一版中的"办公标识语"和"企业并购"两项任务，二版由"企业形象""商业广告"和"新闻发布"三项任务（Task 12~14）组成。

6. 练习和作业设计更为科学

部分使用一版教材的教师和学生反映，一版中的一些练习和作业或篇幅较长，或难度偏高，不太适合高职院校的教学特点，因此在二版中，编者对大部分任务的练习和作业都做了相应改动，使其更适合高职学生掌握。

本教材适用于高职高专院校商务英语专业的学生，也可供从事翻译、外事、外经贸、涉外旅游等行业的涉外工作者和有较好基础的英语自学者使用。

本教材由房玉靖和刘海燕担任主编，叶惠玲和樊文霞担任副主编，王薇参编。

本教材在编写过程中，得到多方教学同仁及业内人士的大力支持与指导，在此一并致谢。因多方面原因，书中难免存在错误和疏漏之处，恳请广大读者不吝赐教。

编　者

目 录

Task 1　Name Card ……………………………………………………………… 1

Task 2　Business Exhibition …………………………………………………… 16

Task 3　Bidding Documents …………………………………………………… 28

Task 4　Business Correspondence …………………………………………… 40

Task 5　Instruction Manual …………………………………………………… 55

Task 6　Business Documents ………………………………………………… 67

Task 7　Business Contract …………………………………………………… 81

Task 8　Meeting Minutes ……………………………………………………… 105

Task 9　Application Documents for Going Abroad ………………………… 116

Task 10　Business Travel ……………………………………………………… 126

Task 11　Business Report ……………………………………………………… 142

Task 12　Corporate Profile …………………………………………………… 154

Task 13　Commercial Advertisement ………………………………………… 165

Task 14　Press Release ………………………………………………………… 175

Reference Version ……………………………………………………………… 183

Bibliography …………………………………………………………………… 213

Name Card

Warm-up: Have a Try

1. Put the following Chinese into English

```
         ** (中国) 环保有限公司
                 王 **
                 总经理
    手机：136*******
    电子邮件：***********@126.com
    地址：芜湖市中山路 ***********
    邮政编码：241000
```

2. Put the following English into Chinese

> **The College of New Jersey**
> Donald Vandegrift, PhD
> Professor of Economics
> School of Business
> Add: PO Box 7718, Ewing, NJ
> Tel: 609-771-2294
> Email: vandedon@tcnj.edu

Background: Learn Something About Name Card

在商务活动中，交换名片是一种流行趋势，也是一种必要活动，特别是随着我国对外经济和文化交流的逐步增多，在对外交流中，将自己的名片印上英文是很有必要的。名片上通常印有姓名、工作单位、职务、职称、地址、电话、传真以及电子邮件地址等。

名片在英语中可称为 business card, visiting card, calling card 或 card。英文名片在语言上要求用词得体、语法规范、表达准确，它有以下两大显著特点。

首先，因名片的语言大部分为专有名词，因此首字母必须大写。其他一些非专有名词也应大写或首字母大写，因为在英语中大写代表着正式、庄重，而小写代表着随意、贴切。

其次，一张小小的名片，空间非常狭小，因此采用缩略语可以很好地传递更多的信息。如单词的缩略 (university 缩略为 uni.)、组合词的缩略 (Bank of China 缩略为 BOC) 等。

Discussion: Talk About How to Do the Task Well

1. 英语姓名结构和英文姓名的翻译

递交名片后，对方最先关注、最易记住的常常是上面的姓名，所以姓名的准确翻译十分关键。英语姓名的一般结构为：教名 + 自取名（中名）+姓。如 George Walker Bush（乔治·沃克·布什）。George 是教名 (Given Name)，Walker 是中名 (Middle Name)，即本人后取的另一个名字，排在教名后，在很多场合往往缩写，如 Walker 缩成首字母 W., 或者干脆略去不写。例如，为了与其父亲、美国第 41 任总统老布什的姓名区别开来，一般情况下，美国前总统小布什的名字经常会写成 George W. Bush。

Bush 是姓 (Family Name)，说明其家族渊源，这跟中国相似。

英语中的教名和中间名又称个人名，一般采用圣经、希腊罗马神话、古代名人或文学名著中的人名，以及祖先的籍贯、山川河流、鸟兽鱼虫、花卉树木等的名称。常用的男子名有 James、John、David、Daniel 和 Michael 等，常见的女子名有 Jane、Mary、Elizabeth、Ann、Sarah 和 Catherine 等。

在英语人名翻译中，我们一般采用音译法，应尽量采用褒义的或中性的字词，选择的汉字应具有"易识、易读、易写、易记"的特点。

因为文化差异的问题，我们在英汉人名采用音译的方式时，很难兼顾语义上的对等，这一点在英语人名汉译中普遍存在。例如，当我们把 Margaret 和 Charles 分别翻译为"玛格丽特"和"查尔斯"时，就把"明亮的""珍珠的"和"男子汉"这些原意忽略了。

汉语的人名通常可以反映出人的性别。例如"娜""丽""梅""玲"等字常出现在女性的名字中，而"伟""强""力"等字一般是男性人名的一部分。在英语人名汉译时，为了表现性别，可以尽量采用一些在汉语中带有性别色彩的字眼。例如，将 Mary 译为玛丽，Diana 译为戴安娜。

当有些英语人名中包括缩写时，我们一般采用部分翻译的方法，即将其字母缩写部分保留原样，其他部分仍然采用音译的方法。例如：J. C. Smith 翻译为 J. C. 史密斯。

2. 中文姓名的翻译

1) 常规姓名的翻译

姓名的翻译有很多种方法，但一般我们都按照最常规的方法来翻译。例如：把张艺广译为 Zhang Yiguang，我们就可以直接按照名片持有人的姓氏加名字来翻译，这样对接收名片的人来说通俗易懂，也容易记住。

2) 复姓的翻译

汉语姓名姓在前，名在后，而且通常是单姓，如赵、陈、钱、孙等。不过也有复姓的，如诸葛、司马、欧阳等。一旦遇到复姓就应该特别小心，以免译错。复姓的拼音应该连在一起。例如诸葛亮应译为 Zhuge Liang，欧阳中石译为 Ouyang Zhongshi。

3) 单姓的特殊翻译

众所周知，中国人的姓名和西方国家的排列顺序是不一样的，中国人是姓在前名在后，而西方国家则刚好相反。一般我们将英文姓名翻译成中文，会照顾外国的习惯，把他们的姓放在后名放在前，如美国前总统比尔·克林顿 (Bill Clinton)，其中 Bill 是名，Clinton 是姓。但中国人将自己的名字翻译成英文就五花八门了。有的按照中国的习惯把姓放在前面，例如：姚明 (Yao Ming)，就是把姓"姚"放在前，名"明"放在后。但有些人把自己的姓名翻译成英文时，将自己的姓放在后面，名放在前面，如果这样，"姚明"就变成了 Ming Yao 了。按照英美习惯，采用名在前，姓在后的次序拼写时，为了避免"姓"与"名"的混淆,通常在姓的前面可加上逗号,与名字分开,也可以采用缩写。例如:王建军可以翻译成 Jianjun, Wang 或 J. J., Wang。

另外,还可将人名中的姓采用全部大写的方法来翻译,即人名中的"姓"采用全部大写的方法,以起到突出醒目的作用,同时也表明是姓名中的"姓",以免外国人将"姓"与"名"搞错。例如,李逵可以翻译成 LI Kui。

4) 中英文名字混合翻译

当某人除了中文名字之外还给自己起了英文名字时,也可以把中英文名字结合在一起来翻译。也就是把中文"名"的部分翻译成英文名,而非原来的中文名,例如:张亚南,翻译为 Zhang Yanan,这样当然绝对没有错误。但她还有一个英文名字是 Carol。这样一来,在对她的名字进行英译时,就可以翻译为 Carol Zhang。在对外交流中,中西结合的名字更容易被外国人接受和记住。

3. 工作单位的翻译

单位部门名称在英语中属于专有名词范畴,要求专词专用,所以一个单位只能使用一种译名(词语排列及组合、缩写形式都应该统一不变),如中国银行,英译为 Bank of China,缩写为 BOC,不能作任何更改,按字面译为 the Chinese Bank 或 the China Bank,都是不妥当的。

按此原则,在翻译单位名称时,应首先查阅有关资料,确定是否有普遍接受的定译,尤其是政府机构的译名,更应采用中央有关部门对外正式名称,绝不能按字面即兴翻译,以致出现一个机构多个译名的混乱状况。

按照英语语法,专有名词的词首字母应大写,但是像 of、the、and 等虚词一般小写,如天津市政府,英译为 the Municipal Government of Tianjin。

单位名称中包含地名或人名的,应用汉语拼音,如天津,应音译为 Tianjin,而不能采用意译。单位名称中包含的企业名号,使用汉语拼音是最简便、也是最保险的方法,但绝不是最佳方法,最好是能音意兼顾。比如,天津"狗不理"包子这一老字号企业的"狗不理"名号译为 Go-Believe,该翻译音似汉语"狗不理",而其意为"诚信",能给消费者留下美好形象。

4. 公司名称的译法

(1) company,一般指已登记注册、具有法人资格的公司,不管其规模大小。表示公司的词中,似乎 company 使用最多。用于公司名称时,company 通常缩略成 Co.,如 Caterpillar Tractor Co.(美国履带拖拉机公司)。公司名称中的 company 一词也经常省略,如 Allied House(联合豪斯公司)。

company 为公司通称,可指多种公司,比如下面列出的示例。

affiliated company   附属公司;分公司、联营公司(也可用 affiliate)
associated company   联营公司、联号(有 20% 至 51% 的股份为另一家公司所有)

export and import company	进出口公司
holding company	控股公司
insurance company	保险公司
investment company	投资公司
joint-stock company	股份公司，合股公司
liability company	责任有限公司
limited company	股份有限公司
parent company	母公司
subsidiary (company)	子公司
public limited company	（英）股份有限公司
share company	（美）股份有限公司

美国常用 Co. Inc 取代 Co. Ltd，但也有美国公司用 Co. Ltd 的。如 International Engineering Co. Ltd. 国际工程公司（美）。

相反，也有英国公司用 Co. Inc. 的，但一般都省略了 Co.，只用 Inc。有时 Co. Ltd 也省略 Co.，只用 Ltd.。例如 Dun & Bradstreet Inc. 邓恩 - 布拉德斯特里特公司（英）。

(2) corporation，作为"公司"用，可缩略成 Corp.，美国英语一般认为 corporation 比 company 要大，为股份有限公司，相当于英国的 limited company，而美国有限公司的名称中常用 Inc.（由 incorporation 缩略而成），例如 Morton International Inc. 莫顿国际公司（美国）。

还有人认为，corporation 在美国英语中指具有独立法人资格的大公司，但也有例外。如果我们多加注意便可发现，凡公司名有 corporation 的一般都是美国公司。如：Lockheed Corporation 洛克希德公司。就是说，英国的公司很少用 corporation，澳大利亚、日本等国的公司少数时候也用 corporation。

(3) 其他表示公司含义的词语。

incorporation，一般指股份公司，较少用。例如 American Airlines Incorporation 美国航空公司。

firm，有"商号、公司"之意，多指两人或两人以上合办的企业，firm 直接用于公司名称少有。例如 The firm of Smith & Jones 史密斯与琼斯公司（非正式用语，firm 这里代替 company）。

agency 本意为代理、代理权等，作为"公司"，则是类似中间商的代理性质的公司。

airline (s), airways, air, avia, aviation 表示航空公司。

line (s)，单独使用或作为词缀用在轮船等公司的名称中，如：American President Lines 美国总统轮船公司，Eastern Shipping Line Inc. 东方轮船公司（菲）。

industries, industry, industrial 常用在公司名称中，通常表示"实业""工业"等意。例如 Farmland Industries 农场工业公司（美），Australian National Industries Ltd. 澳大利

亚国家工业公司。

product，一般译为"产品公司"（有时后面要加 corporation 等表示"公司"的词）。例如 American Home Product Corporation 美国家庭用品公司。

enterprise(s)，"企业公司""实业公司"，例如 Coca-Cola Enterprises 可口可乐企业公司（美）。

stores，除表示"商店"外，还有"百货公司"之意。例如 Great Universal Stores 大百货公司（英）。

service(s)，多指服务性质的公司。例如 Japan Postal Service 日本邮务局。

system，指由各相对独立机构组成的系统组织，例如 Columbia Broadcasting System 哥伦比亚广播公司。

group，"集团""集团公司"，例如 Citigroup 花旗集团公司（美），LG Group LG 集团（韩）。

holding，"控股公司"，例如 HSBC Holdings 汇丰控股公司（英）。

assurance, insurance，"保险公司"，例如 Sun Life Assurance of Canada 加拿大太阳人寿保险公司、Samsung Life Insurance 三星人寿保险公司（韩）。

laboratories，"制药公司"，例如 Abbott Laboratories 雅培制药公司（美）。

office，较少用于表示公司名称，常用来表示"分公司""办事处"等，例如 head office 总公司，life office 人寿保险公司，home office 国内总公司，fire office 火灾保险公司，Frankfurt Tourist Office 法兰克福旅游公司（德）。

proprietary，"控股公司"，常缩写成 Pty，多用于澳大利亚和南非。例如 Broken Hill Proprietary 布鲁肯希尔控股公司（澳大利亚），South African Industrial Cellulose Corporation (Pty.) Ltd. 南非工业纤维公司。

associates，"联号""联营公司"，常用复数形式，例如 Sanders Associates 桑德斯联合公司。

association，"联合公司"，例如 Reader's Digest Association, Inc. 读者文摘联合公司（美）。

alliance，"联盟"，例如 Sodexho Alliance 索迪斯联合公司（法）。

incorporated，"公司"，例如 Pacific Semiconductor Incorporated 太平洋半导体公司（美）。

son, brothers，也常放在公司名称里，一般要译出。例如 Lehman Brothers Holdings 莱曼兄弟控股公司（美），R. R. Donnelley & Sons Company 唐纳利父子公司（美）。

Messrs，有些公司名称由 Messrs (Mr. 的复数形式) 加老板的姓氏构成，Messrs 不必译出。例如 Messrs T. Brown & Co. 布朗公司。

trust，信托公司。energy，能源公司。electric，电气、电子公司。motors，汽车公司。

5. 部门、职务职称的翻译

在制作名片时，中国人习惯罗列头衔，把学衔、职称、职务及所有社会兼职甚至临时兼职等都放上去，但英语名片通常只放上一两个有实质性的职务。下面是一些部门名称的英文及其译法。

Head Office	总公司	Marketing Dept.	营销部
Headquarter	总部	Import & Export Dept.	进出口部
Board of Directors	董事会	After-sales Dept.	售后服务部
General Manager Office	总经理办公室	Accounting Dept.	财务部
General Office	总办事处	Public Relations Dept.	公关部
Production Dept.	生产部门	Technology Dept.	技术部
Product Dept.	产品部门	Training Dept.	培训部
Q & C Dept.	质量控制部门	Dispatch Dept.	发货部
Project Dept.	项目部	Purchasing Dept.	采购部
Engineering Dept.	工程部	Material Dept.	材料部
Industrial Dept.	工业部	Logistics Dept.	物流部
Branch	分公司	Advertising Department	广告部
Administration Dept.	行政部门	Planning Department	企划部
General Affairs Department	总务部	Information Office	问询处
Sales Department	销售部	Reception Desk/Center	前台/接待处
Sales Promotion Department	促销部	Customer Service Department	客服部
International Department	国际部	Call Center	电话中心
Business Office/Branch Office	营业部		
Product Development Department	产品开发部		
Personnel Department	人事部		
Research and Development Department (R&D)	研发部		
Human Resources Department	人力资源部		
Secretarial Pool	秘书室		

部分常用的职位、头衔中英文对照如下所示。

chief executive，CEO	公司总裁
president；general manager	总经理
chairman；president of the board；board chairman	董事长
senior advisor	高级顾问

vice/deputy president; vice/deputy general manager	副总经理
assistant president; assistant general manager	助理总经理
assistant to the president/general manager	总经理助理
executive vice manager	执行副经理
vice-manager-technology; technical manager	技术副经理
vice-manager-material	供应副经理
vice-manager-manufacturing	生产副经理
vice-manager-planning	计划副经理
vice-manager-personnel	人事副经理
editor-in-chief	总编辑
associate (deputy) editor (-in-chief)	副主编
executive editor; commissioning editor	责任主编
head director; chief	主任
deputy head; director; chief	副主任
chief engineer	总工程师
chief designer	总设计师
senior engineer	高级工程师
senior economist	高级经济师
assistant engineer	助理工程师
economist; economic administrator	经济师
accountant	会计师
agronomist	农艺师
designer	设计师
architect	建筑师
technician	技师
research fellow	研究员
chairman	主任委员
secretary general	秘书长
executive director	执行理事长
standing director	常任理事

6. 中英文地址的翻译

1) 英文地址的翻译

英文地址的表达顺序是由小到大，即按照：门牌号码、街名、区名、省市名、邮编、国名的顺序排列，与汉语的规则恰好相反。在翻译英文地址时，常用的翻译方法如下。

(1) 音译法。

例如：New York 纽约，Wall Street 华尔街。

(2) 意译法。

例如：Iceland 冰岛，Pearl Harbor 珍珠港，Buffalo 水牛城。

(3) 音译混译。

例如：New England 新英格兰，Port Victoria 维多利亚港，Cape Lopes 洛佩斯角，San Francisco 三藩市/旧金山，Surabaya 泗水/苏腊巴亚(印尼)，Vladivostok 海参崴/符拉迪沃斯托克(俄罗斯)，Zamboanga 三宝颜/桑博安加(菲律宾)，Wakayama 和歌山/若山(日本)。

翻译英文地址时应注意以下三点。

(1) 相同地名不同译法。

例如：Cambridge 剑桥(英国)/坎布里奇(美国)

San Francisco 旧金山(美国)/圣·佛兰西斯科(阿根廷)

Florence 佛罗伦萨(意大利)/佛洛伦斯(美国)

Montreal 蒙特利尔(加拿大)/蒙雷阿勒(法国)

Sabang 沙璜(印度)/萨邦(菲律宾)

Tanga 丹卡(缅甸)/坦噶(坦桑尼亚)/坦加(刚果)

A Den 阿殿(越南)/Aden 亚丁(也门)

长滩 Long Beach(美国)/长滩 Longbeach(新西兰)

法兰克福 Frankfurt(德国)/Frankfort(美国)

萨凡纳 Savannab(美国)/Savanna(美国)

维多利亚 Victoria(加拿大)/Vitoria(巴西)

(2) 有的地名不止一个国家有，而且中文译文相同，翻译的时候要在地名后面注明国家。例如 Vancouver(温哥华)要注明是美国还是加拿大。又如 Hamilton(哈密尔顿)、Kingston(金斯敦)、Newcastle(纽卡斯尔)等。

(3) 有的国家几个地方用相同的地名，翻译的时候要在地名后面注明其所在地区。例如，在美国有三个州都有 Amsterdam(阿姆斯特丹)，分别位于蒙大拿州、俄亥俄州和纽约州。

2) 中文地址的翻译

中文地址的排列顺序是由大到小：×国×市×区×路×号。在英译时，地名专名部分(如"黄岩区"的"黄岩"部分)应使用汉语拼音，且需连写，如 Huangyan 不宜写成 Huang Yan。各地址单元间要加逗号隔开，将邮编插入到行政区划与国名之间。例如"中国浙江省台州市黄椒路 102 号，邮编：318020"可译为 102 Huangjiao Road, Taizhou, Zhejiang 318020, China。

在名片上,地址应该保持一定的完整性,门牌号与街道名不可分开写,必须在同一行,不可断行,但各种名称可以断开。例如:

Room***No.***Road/Street,***City

Province(Post/Zip Code)

***(Country)

完整的地址由行政区划+街区名+楼房号三部分组成。

行政区划是地址中最高一级单位,我国幅员辽阔,行政区划较复杂,总体上可分成五级(括号内所注为当前国内通用译名)。

- 国家 (State):中华人民共和国 (the People's Republic of China;P. R. China;P. R. C;China)
- 省级 (Provincial Level):省 (Province)、自治区 (Autonomous Region)、直辖市 (Municipality directly under the Central Government,简称 Municipality);特别行政区 (Special Administration Region,SAR)
- 地级 (Prefectural Level):地区 (Prefecture)、自治州 (Autonomous Prefecture)、市 (Municipality;City);盟 (Prefecture)
- 县级 (County Level):县 (County)、自治县 (Autonomous County)、市 (City)、市辖区 (District)、旗 (County)
- 乡级 (Township Level):乡 (Township)、民族乡 (Ethnic Township)、镇 (Town)、街道办事处 (Sub-district)

中文地址翻译示例:

- 上海市崇明县中兴镇 Zhongxing Town, Chongming County, Shanghai (Municipality)
- 内蒙古自治区呼伦贝尔市 Hulunbeir City, Inner Mongolia Autonomous Region
- 浙江省台州市玉环县龙溪乡 Longxi Township, Yuhuan County, Taizhou City Zhejiang Province
- 苏州市金阊区金门街道 Jinmen Sub-district, Jinchang District, Suzhou City

居于地址体系的中间位置的是一些传统的村居街道及新兴的各种小区、新村、工业区等,街区名的常用译法如下。

- "路"可译为"Road"或缩写为"Rd."
- "街、道"可译为"Street"和"Avenue"
- "里、弄、巷"可译为"Lane"
- "胡同"可译为"Alley"
- "新村、小区"可译为"Village"或"Residential Quarter/Area"

楼房号的翻译,这是地址的最低一级,涉及对具体场所的命名及房号的标注。例如:5幢302室、3号楼2单元102室。这里的"幢""×××号楼"实际上是同一回事,一般均以 Building 来表示;"室"一般译作 Room 或 Suite。上述两例可分别译成：Suite 302, Building 5；Room 102, Unit 2, Building 3。Suite 往往由多个 room 组成，如 a three-room suite。目前我们普遍使用的几号室（房），往往都是套房，故我们在翻译房号时，不能受其后缀"房"或"室"影响，应尽量根据实际情况选择 Suite 或 Room。

此外，在这一级地址中还经常出现诸如"单元""大厦""层"等术语。例如，"东一办公楼五层 1—3 室"可译为 "Rm. 1-3, 5/F, Office Building E1"。

此外，名片由于空间有限，常将英文地址中的某些单词换成缩略语。常用的缩略语如下。

- 区：District—Dist.
- 工业的：Industrial—Ind.
- 街：Street—St.
- 路：Road—Rd.
- 道：Avenue—Ave.
- 大道：Boulevard—Blv.
- 楼层：Floor—"/F"或 Fl.
- 大楼/大厦：Building—Bldg.
- 公寓：Apartment—Apt.
- 房间：Room—Rm.

Follow-up: Do It Yourself

1. Translate the following English into Chinese

(1) Associate Engineer

(2) Training Supervisor

(3) Sales Representative

(4) Planning Department

(5) SUITE 304,145-157 ST JOHN STREET, LONDON, EC1V 4PY

(6) 770, 54th st, Brooklyn, NY 11220

2. Translate the following Chinese into English

(1) 采购部

(2) 营销部

(3) 高级文员

(4) 秘书

(5) 北京市海淀区西三环北路 2 号　邮编：100089

(6) 福建省厦门市莲花五村龙昌里 34 号 601 室

Homework: Practice Makes Perfect

1. Put the following name card into Chinese

Filmon Hardware, Inc.

John Taylor

Sales Manager

FHI Building, 725 Oak Park Avenue , San Diego, CA 91023

Tel: 2976 3322　　Fax: 2976 3366

E-mail: johntaylor@fhi.com

2. Design a name card according to the following information and then translate it into English

姓名：张大成

工作单位：内蒙古蒙牛乳业（集团）股份有限公司

工作部门：品牌管理中心

职务：品牌总监

工作地址：北京通州区食品工业园区一区 1 号

邮编：101107

电话：133********

传真：010 61526245

电子邮件：luan4u@126.com

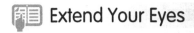
Extend Your Eyes

常见公司、企业集团名称

Household Electrical Appliance Co., Ltd.	家用电器有限公司
Technology and Trade Co., Ltd.	科技贸易公司
Iron and Steel Company	钢铁公司
Knitting Company Ltd.	针织有限公司
Industrial Group Corporation	实业集团公司
Electronic Technology Development Co.	电子技术开发公司
Woolen Textile Co., Ltd.	毛纺织有限公司
Fashion Company Ltd.	时装有限公司
Advertising Company	广告公司
Aquatic Product Company Ltd.	水产品有限公司
Travel Corporation	旅游公司
Garment Company Ltd.	服装公司
Electronic Equipment & Materials Corporation	电子器材公司
Textile Enterprise Group	纺织企业集团
Foreign Trade Company	对外贸易公司
Trading Company Ltd.	贸易有限公司
International Investment Company	国际投资有限公司
Plastic Products Co., Ltd.	塑料制品有限公司
International Economic Cooperation Corporation	国际经济合作公司
Garments Industrial Company	制衣实业公司
Computer Technology Service Corporation	计算机技术服务公司
Project Contracting Co., Ltd.	工程承包有限公司
Beverage Company Limited	饮料有限公司
Construction Engineering Co.	建筑工程公司
Porcelain Industry Complex	陶瓷企业集团

常见职位名称

Accounting Assistant	会计助理
Accounting Manager	会计部经理
Accounting Supervisor	会计主管
Administration Manager	行政经理

Administrative Assistant	行政助理
Advertising Staff	广告工作人员
Application Engineer	应用工程师
Bond Analyst	证券分析员
Bond Trader	证券交易员
Business Controller	业务主任
Business Manager	业务经理
Chemical Engineer	化学工程师
Civil Engineer	土木工程师
Clerk/Receptionist	职员/接待员
Clerk Typist & Secretary	文书打字兼秘书
Computer Engineer	计算机工程师
Economic Research Assistant	经济研究助理
Electrical Engineer	电气工程师
Engineering Technician	工程技术员
Export Sales Manager	外销部经理
Export Sales Staff	外销部职员
Financial Controller	财务主任
Financial Reporter	财务报告人
F.X. Settlement Clerk	外汇部核算员
Fund Manager	财务经理
General Auditor	审计长
General Manager's Secretary	总经理秘书
Hardware Engineer	(计算机)硬件工程师
Import Manager	进口部经理
Insurance Actuary	保险公司理赔员
Interpreter	口语翻译
Line Supervisor	生产线主管
Maintenance Engineer	维修工程师
Management Consultant	管理顾问
Manager for Public Relations	公关部经理
Manufacturing Engineer	制造工程师
Market Analyst	市场分析员
Market Development Manager	市场开发部经理
Marketing Manager	市场销售部经理

Marketing Executive	销售主管
Mechanical Engineer	机械工程师
Office Assistant	办公室助理
Operational Manager	业务经理
Personnel Manager	人事部经理
Product Manager	产品经理
Production Engineer	产品工程师
Programmer	程序员
Purchasing Agent	采购（进货）员
Quality Control Engineer	质量管理工程师
Real Estate Staff	房地产职员
Regional Manager	地区经理
Research & Development Engineer	研发工程师
Sales Assistant	销售助理
Sales Manager	销售部经理
Security Officer	安全人员
Service Manager	服务部经理
Software Engineer	（计算机）软件工程师
Systems Engineer	系统工程师
Tourist Guide	导游
Trade Finance Executive	贸易财务主管
Translator	翻译员
Typist	打字员

Business Exhibition

CHINA NATIONAL CONVENTION CENTER

 Warm-up: Have a Try

1. Put the following passage into Chinese

The World Expo is a large-scale, global, non-commercial exposition. Participants are mainly governments of various countries and international organizations. The World Expo constitutes an arena for the participating countries to display the achievements and prospects in their social, economic, cultural and technological sectors and is a grand event where people from various countries gather together to exchange experience, learn from one another and develop cooperation. It has been reputed as the equivalent of Olympic Games in the fields of economy, technology and culture.

2. Put the following passage into English

2010 上海世博会是第一次在发展中国家举办的注册类世博会。这是中国的机遇，也是世界的机遇。未来 6 个月，世界各国各地区将以世博会为平台，围绕"城市，让生活更美好"的主题，充分展示城市文明成果、交流城市发展经验、传播先进城市理念、相互学习、取长补短，为新世纪人类的生活、工作探索崭新的模式。

Background: Learn Something About MICE

商务展览是会展的一个组成部分，会展意即会议与展览，在英语中一般用 MICE 表达，即 Meetings（会议）、Incentives（奖励旅游）、Conferences / Conventions（大型企业会议）、Exhibitions / Exposition（活动展览）和 Event（节事活动）的第一个字母大写组成，是会展的英文缩写，是继 M&E (Meeting&Exhibition) 后对会展更全面的一种解释。维基百科对 MICE 这一缩略语的解释如下。

Meetings, incentives, conferences and exhibitions, or Meetings, Incentives, Conferences, and Events (MICE) is a type of tourism in which large groups, usually planned well in advance, are brought together for a particular purpose. Recently, there has been an industry trend towards using the term "meetings industry" to avoid confusion from the acronym. Other industry educators are recommending the use of "events industry" to be an umbrella term for the vast scope of the meeting and events profession.

世界会展业在过去 20 年里已经成为很多活动的聚焦点，从 20 世纪 90 年代中期开始，中国会展业在不长的时间内取得了突飞猛进的发展，也带动了很多相关行业的发展，特别是外贸行业。2010 年上海世博会之后，我国会展业进入了更加繁荣的发展时期。

MICE Tour（会展旅游）是从会展业发展出来的一个分支行业，指利用举行各种会议、大会和展览活动的机会所开展的特殊旅游活动； Incentives（奖励旅游）则是公司为了激励成绩优秀的员工、经销商或代理商而专门组织的旅游活动。

Discussion: Talk About How to Do the Task Well

会展文本属于商务文体，具有传递信息及宣传劝导两个功能，在语言表达上要设法把参展的好处介绍出来，以吸引国内外企业前来参展或赞助。要做好会展相关文本的英汉互译，首先需要了解会展英语独特的语言特点。

1. 专业词汇丰富，涉及面广

每年在全世界举办的会展不计其数，涉及轻工、化工、机械、纺织、食品、科技等诸多行业,会展相关业务涉及展位介绍、展品运输、展台接待、展后联络、商务洽谈、签订合同、投诉处理等诸多领域。因此,会展相关文本所使用的词汇非常丰富。以"会议"一词为例,根据不同的会议类型,就有相应不同的表达词汇。

例1. assembly　　　　　　集合;集会
     colloquium　　　　　　专题座谈会;学术讨论会
     conference　　　　　　专门会议;大型会议;协商会
     congress　　　　　　　代表大会
     debate　　　　　　　　辩论会
     forum　　　　　　　　论坛
     convention　　　　　　(正式)会议;(定期)大会;年会
     exhibition　　　　　　展览展示会
     general session　　　　全体大会
     meeting　　　　　　　(一般)会议
     panel　　　　　　　　小组讨论会
     reception　　　　　　招待会
     seminar　　　　　　　研讨会;讲座
     session　　　　　　　分会
     symposium　　　　　　专题讨论会(或报告会);座谈会
     trade show　　　　　　贸易展示会;展销会
     Webcasting　　　　　　网络会议
     workshop　　　　　　　现场讨论会;进修会

2. 普通词汇具有特殊含义

业内曾经有专家统计,一个展览会由大大小小的3600多项事件构成,因而会展词汇涵盖范围之广、层次之细,十分繁杂,许多日常用词在会展英语中具有特殊的意义,如"stand"在一般英语中用作动词,指"站,立,站起",而在会展英语中通常作名词,指"展位"的意思;"floor manager"一般译为"展区管理人",如果译为"地面管理人"则会让人产生误解;"正牌货"常译为"standard brand of goods",若译为"real goods"便不达意;"pavilion"在一般英语中指"大帐篷",而在会展英语中指"展馆"。

3. 多使用被动语态

会展材料旨在向参会者提供必要信息,帮助参展商顺利完成工作,为观众提供便利,因此会展英语在语言表达上无须强调句子动作的发生者,用被动句更能传达客观、礼貌的语气。

例 2. A comprehensive convention center is designed to host meetings and exhibits under one roof.

参考译文：综合性会展中心可以在同一大厅内举办会议和展览会。

例 3. The New York IAS is actually described as a premiere annual automotive event that is well recognized both nationally and internationally.

参考译文：纽约国际车展被认为是一项极为重要的汽车展会，每年举办一次，在国内外享有盛誉。

4. 经常使用一般现在时和现在进行时态

英语中的现在时态能让读者产生现时感，让所表达的内容更具可靠性和客观性。

例 4. A convention center has air walls to divide the space to fit the need of the meeting or the exhibit.

参考译文：会展中心有活动隔断，可以根据会议或展览会的需要来分隔场地。

例 5. The client company should be open to suggestions regarding the style and location of the event and the type of event program.

参考译文：关于展会风格、展会地点及展会议程类型，客户公司应该广泛听取意见。

针对会展文本的这些语言特征，翻译时需要注意以下几方面。

1) 会展名称的翻译要简洁、专业

中文会展名称往往含有多个地名，第一个地名是国家，第二个地名是举办城市（通常含在括号内）。

例 6. 中国（深圳）国际文化产业博览交易会　China (Shenzhen) International Cultural Industries Fair

相比之下，英语会展名称中常常不含地名，如果需要说明会展是在何处召开的，可在名称之后注上地名，一般也不会同时出现两个以上地名。

例 7. New York International Gift Fair　纽约国际礼品展

例 8. International Restaurant & Food Service Show of New York　纽约国际餐馆与服务展

例 9. Canadian Mining and Industrial Expo, Sudbury, Ontario（在安大略省萨德布利市举行的）加拿大采矿工业博览会

通过中外会展名称的比较，可以清楚地看到两者的区别主要在于书写格式上。由于英文词汇是多音节的，中文会展名称英译时如果原封不动地移植中文格式，只追求与中文名称字对字的对应，容易造成多重地名和名称偏长的问题，不符合英文会展名称的表达习惯。因此，翻译时需要进行格式上的变换，将地名（或部分地名）从会展名称中移除。

例 10. 中国义乌文化产品交易博览会已经成功地连续举办了三届。

原译：China Yiwu Cultural Products Trade Fair has been successfully held for 3 sessions continuously.

改译：Yiwu Cultural Products Trade Fair has been successfully held for 3 consecutive sessions in Yiwu of Zhejiang Province, China.

例 11. 第七届中国(深圳)国际品牌服装服饰交易会
The 7th China (Shenzhen) Int'l Brand Clothing & Accessories Fair

例 12. 第十五届中国国际科学仪器及实验室装备展览会将于 2017 年 4 月 6—8 日在北京国家会议中心举行。

参考译文：The 15th CISILE(CISILE 2017) will be held on April 6-8, 2017 at the China National Convention Center in Beijing, the capital of China.

CISILE 是 China International Scientific Instrument and Laboratory Equipment Exhibition 的缩写。

建议在英译时，尽量使用节略词(Clipped Words)，可使会展名称既言简又意明，且符合英文的行文特点。找不到节略词时，缩写(Abbreviation) 也是一个选择，但节略词显然更清楚。

例 13. The International BeerFest　国际啤酒节
BeerFest 是 Beer Festival 的节略词。

例 14. BOOKEXPO AMERICA　美国图书博览会
如果按汉语的思维习惯，可以译为 American Book Exposition，但英语中使用了组合式节略词 BOOKEXPO，并将 AMERICAN 后置为 AMERICA，更简练一些。

例 15. 第五届中国(广州)国际汽车展览会
原译：The 5th China(Guangzhou) International Automobile Exhibition
改译：The 5th Int'l Autoshow, Guangzhou, China

2) 将英语被动句直接翻译成汉语主动句
有些英语的被动句或结构可以根据句意和汉语的表达习惯直接翻译成主动句。

例 16. Create a database of people you've invited to the meeting or exhibition. This database can then be manipulated, categorized, and used to target certain groups of invites.

原译：您已发出会议或展览邀请的人员创立一个数据库。而后该数据库随后可进行管理、分类、应用于查觅参会人员。

改译：为您已发出会议或展览邀请的人员创立一个数据库。而后，您可以对该数据库进行管理、分类并利用该数据库查觅参会人员。

例 17. It is universally acknowledged that advance shipping enables exhibitors to confirm the arrival of their freight at the show. Additionally, freight arriving at the warehouse in a timely manner will usually be delivered to the booth during the contractor's move-in period at straight-time drayage rates.

原译：提早运输可以使参展商确认展品到达展览地。此外，及时运抵仓库的货物可以在承包商划定的入展期内以一般运价运到展台。

改译：人们普遍觉得，提早运输可以使参展商确认展品到达展览地。此外，及时运抵仓库的货物可以在承包商划定的入展期内以一般运价运到展台。

为达到较好的宣传效果，有的会展宣传资料篇幅较长，行文正式，句式严谨，翻译时需要综合使用各种翻译方法，以期准确而有效地传达原文信息。在此介绍一下增益法、分译法、顺译法和拆译法四种常用的翻译方法。

1) 增益法

在英汉翻译过程中，增益法是最常见的方法之一，主要是为了保持行文的流畅，使短语与短语之间、句子内容之间或句子与句子之间的衔接更加自然，或者使语意之间的逻辑关系更加明确等。

例18. Where a large number of under-age patrons are expected, the concept of a "Parent's Oasis" is used. The efforts in providing such a facility are more than offset by the reduction in effort needed to deal with the young audience at the conclusion of the event.

参考译文：在有很多未成年顾客的展会地点，应使用专供父母与孩子会面之用的"父母绿地"计划。提供这样的便利设施可谓事半功倍，展会结束时基本不用费神去处理小观众的问题。

在译文中采用解释性增益手段，增加了"可谓事半功倍"解释性表达作铺垫，起到了解释语意、概括语意和画龙点睛的作用，使译文准确而饱满，再现原文的风格。

2) 分译法

句前分译指把英语原句中某些词汇或短语抽出来放到句前翻译，一般来说，副词、介词短语、从句的句前分译比较常见。

例19. The unique "complex of show excitement" among exhibitors and attendees will make its debut in "New York Healthcare & Beauty Exposition", which, as a result, will make a special contribution to a sensational program involving the World's leading healthcare and beauty media to jointly promote the professional healthcare and beauty industry on both the consumer and industry trade levels.

参考译文：本届"纽约美容保健品展会"将在参展商和参观者中间首次出现独特的"煽情展会情节"。因此，本届展会将倾情奉献一台赏心悦目的特别节目，即与世界顶尖美容保健媒体联袂，在消费者层面和行业贸易层面上共同推动专业美容保健事业的发展。

英语原句中后面三行的内容被分成三个部分进行翻译，改译中分别译成三个独立的部分，但没有改变它们在原句中的位置或顺序，即 (1) make a special contribution to a sensational program 倾情奉献一台赏心悦目的特别节目； (2) involving the World's leading healthcare and beauty media 即与世界顶尖美容保健媒体联袂； (3) to jointly promote the professional healthcare and beauty and industry on both the consumer and industry trade levels 在消费者层面和行业贸易层面上共同推动专业美容保健事业的发展。另外，为了保证可读性，避免因修饰语过长而引起的语流堵塞，译文在分译点处重复 jointly 的意思，一处翻译为"联袂"，另一处翻译为"共同（推动）"，起到了有效连接的"纽带"作用。

3) 顺译法

顺译法指的是在保证意思准确、行文通顺的前提下，按照原句的结构顺序翻译成汉语的方法，最大限度地再现原文的风格。顺译法的成功翻译体现了英汉句子在句子结构和表达习惯方面存在的共核部分，最大限度地体现了英汉之间的"可译性"。

例 20. 滨海国际会展中心坐落于天津滨海新区核心区，交通运输网络方便快捷。建筑面积 120,000 平方米，拥有 40,000 平方米室内展厅及总面积达 7,500 平方米的会议设施，既可以举行各类博览会，又具备举办会议及各种大型活动的功能。自 2003 年投入运营以来，已举办各类展览、会议 126 次，并曾成功承办 2008 天津夏季达沃斯论坛（世界经济论坛）。

参考译文：Binhai International Convention & Exhibition Centre is located in the core area of Tianjin Binhai New Area. It has access to a convenient network of transportation. Its total construction area is 120,000 m^2, including indoor exhibition area 40,000 m^2, and convention facilities 7,500 m^2. The centre can host exhibitions, conferences and large-scale events. Since it was put in operation in Dec. 2003, it has hosted 126 conferences or exhibitions, including the Summer Davos Forum (World Economic Forum) in 2008.

4) 拆译法

在英汉翻译中，经常会遇到英语句式长、内在结构和成分复杂的句子，由于汉语多流水句，句子短，翻译时需要将英语长句的各种复杂成分从主干结构中抽离出来，译成外位成分，或是外形上相对独立却与原搭配成分保持"藕断丝连"关系的语言单位（常为句子），以保证信息传递的准确性和完整性，同时保证译文的可读性。这种翻译方法叫"拆译法"。

例 21. The "New York Healthcare & Beauty Exposition" consists of both domestic experts and consultants in healthcare and beauty industry, whose experience and expertise combined guarantee the credibility of this significant event as well as the orientation of the training and education programs, and international professionals from accredited training providers, whose professional qualifications and well-tailored concepts along with their admirable corporate training experience become the driving force as well as the spotlight of "New York Healthcare & Beauty Exposition".

参考译文："纽约美容保健品展会"由国内美容保健专家和顾问以及国外资质培训单位专家组成。国内专家和顾问的知识水准和培训经验保证了该重要展会的信誉，也保证了培训教育项目的导向；国外专家皆具有非凡的公司培训经验，他们的专业资质和先进的培训理念是"纽约美容保健品展会"培训项目的驱动力和风景线。

本句将两个由 whose 引导的非限制性定语从句分别抽出来单独翻译，很好地体现了原句的结构美和节奏美，原文一个长句(含两个长长的定语从句)转变为汉语的五个短句，更易被中文读者接受。

 Follow-up: Do It Yourself

1. Translate the following passage into Chinese

The domestic experts and the international professionals would never come to such an event with "doubtful feet and wavering resolution", thus ensuring the quality and success and simultaneously, leading a charm and romance to "New York Healthcare & Beauty Exposition".

2. Translate the following passage into English

广交会是一个重大的创举，通过广交会，新中国探索不同的方法来扩大对外贸易，加大对外开放程度。广交会已经成为中国企业和全球市场之间的桥梁和让世界了解中国的窗口，也已经成为国际合作的平台。广交会以中国外贸的"风向标"而闻名，它在中国外贸中发挥了不可替代的作用，被誉为国际商务领域的"友谊之路、贸易之桥"。

 Homework: Practice Makes Perfect

1. Try to find the English versions of the following MICE names on the Internet

(1) 2016 中国天津投资贸易洽谈会暨 PECC 国际贸易投资博览会

(2) 2016 天津·世界侨商名品博览会

(3) 第 12 届中国西部国际博览会

(4) 2016 南非食品与饮料技术博览会

(5) 2016 夏季中国(北京)婚博会

(6) 北京体育用品及运动时装贸易博览会

(7) 2016 第八届中国国际低碳产业博览会

(8) 第十四届中国国际科学仪器及实验室装备展览会

(9) 中国国际安全生产及职业健康展览会

(10) 中国国际养老服务业博览会

2. Translate the following passage into Chinese

Some organizations send brochures, more detailed descriptions of seminars biographies of speakers, entertainers, or presenters, map and direction for the site, and menus. Brochures for exhibitors and vendors must include a map of the exhibit space, booth dimensions, exhibit hours, setup and breakdown hours, and advance shipping information.

3. Translate the following passage into English

天津梅江会展中心 (MJCEC) 坐落于天津市宜居生态地区，濒临梅江风景区，环境优美，交通便利，总用地面积35.62万平方米，建筑面积10万平方米，拥有5万平方米的室内展览面积和3万平方米的室外展览区域，7000平方米的会议面积，可容纳2000人的高级宴会厅。

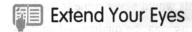

Extend Your Eyes

会展常用词组

1. accessible location	出入通道
2. advance set-up	提前布置
3. airport/strip shuttle service	机场接送服务
4. attendance	展览会人数（包括参展商和参观商等展览会上的各种类别的人）
5. attendee	展览会的参加者（一般指展览会或会议的代表、参观商和观众，但不包括参展商）
6. auditorium style	礼堂式布局
7. booth size	展位尺寸
8. complimentary arrangement	免费项目安排
9. controlled admission	限制入场
10. deposit reservation	押金预订
11. display case	展示柜
12. double-decker	双层展位（摊位）
13. double-faced panel	双面展板
14. exhibit designer/producer	展台设计/搭建商
15. exhibitor manual	参展商手册
16. facility	指展览馆或展览设施
17. FHC	展馆内用于标明灭火器箱位置的符号
18. floor plan	展馆平面图
19. focal point	焦点，中心
20. give-away	赠品
21. hall	对展览馆的泛称，也可指一个展馆中的一个具体的展厅

22.	host country	东道国
23.	labor cost	人工费用
24.	late tear-down	拖后撤台
25.	layout of the stand	展台布局
26.	magnetic board	磁力板
27.	move-in	展台搭建、布展期
28.	move-out	撤出，撤展
29.	multiple-story exhibit	多层展台
30.	new product introduction	新产品发布会
31.	off-site event	会外活动，会后活动
32.	on-site registration	现场报到/注册
33.	overflow arrangement	人流疏导方案
34.	padded chair	有坐垫的椅子
35.	permanent stage	固定舞台
36.	physical requirement	硬件方面的需求
37.	portable wall	活动墙，分隔墙
38.	press room/ press center	（博览会）新闻中心
39.	product/machine demonstration	产品/机器展示
40.	sample fairs	样品展
41.	scaled drawing	比例图
42.	service desk	设在展览会现场、供参展商订购各种服务的服务供应处
43.	set up	展台搭建；展览会开幕前的布展
44.	show break	展览会结束和开始撤展的时间
45.	space rate	摊位租金（以每平方米计算）
46.	square feet	平方英尺
47.	stacking armchair	可摞式扶手椅
48.	teardown	撤展（与"dismantle"意义相同）
49.	valet parking	代客泊车服务
50.	UFI (=Union of International Fair)	国际展览联盟

会展常用句型

1. The registration process, like any other step in putting together a meeting and convention, is very important.

同会议的其他环节一样，报到注册过程非常重要。

2. Careful planning and skilled organization are required to prevent advance registration from creating more problems than it solves.

为了防止提前注册产生的问题比解决的问题还要多，（组办者）需要进行细致的计划和有技巧的组织。

3. ...the primary incentives to register early are the avoidance of standing in line for on-site registration and the guarantee of reserved tickets for events that might become sold out.

提前注册的主要好处是可以避免现场注册时的排队等候以及保证有某些活动的预留票，否则，这些票很可能已经售完。

4. If you can budget better for your food functions, you can save quite a bit from your budget.

如果餐饮方面的预算比较详细，那你将会节省很大一笔开支。

5. ...you may also want to use color coded forms with one color for staff, one for exhibitors, one for presenter, one for full registration,one color each for the one-day registration so they can all be spotted and tallied easier.

你还可以设计不同颜色的报到表用以区分职员、展商、全程与会者和单日与会者。由于颜色的差别，工作人员可以立刻把不同的与会者区分开来。

6. Therefore, airlines stationed personnel right at the terminal for assistance, which will offer peace of mind for your attendees who use credit cards.

因此，（为解决这个问题）航空公司在那些终端机器前安排了一些工作人员提供帮助。这让与会者在使用信用卡时高枕无忧。

7. ...the benefits of online registration really outweigh the disadvantages.

……网上报到的利远大于弊。

8. The process of site selection goes from broad to narrow. Cost and convenience rank well before the other factors in the eyes of the meeting and exhibition managers.

会址的选择过程是一个从大到小不断缩小范围的过程。对会议和展览会策划人员来说，价格和便利的重要性远大于其他因素。

9. ...be away from the traffic, from the hustle and bustle. ...in close proximity to hotels or other housing facilities, thus providing easy access to sleeping rooms for attendees.

……远离交通和喧闹，……临近酒店或其他住宿设施，给与会者提供方便的住宿服务。

10. If you send us your registration form and registration fees within two weeks, it is still possible for you to get one booth.

如果您递交注册表并在两周内缴纳注册费，还是有可能租到一个摊位的。

11. It's a good idea to offer them something substantial to eat rather than leaving them

on their own for dinner.

明智之举是为他们提供一些实实在在的饭菜，而不是不管不问，让他独自解决吃饭问题。

12. Choosing a suitable venue is the common wish of the organizer, undertaker and participants.

选择一个适合的场馆是组织者、承办者和参与者的共同愿望。

13. Where would be a nice location for our household electric appliance?

我们要举办的家用电器展览选址在哪里比较合适？

14. It would be an easy, convenient access for show attendees, exhibitors and freight delivery.

对于参展人员、参展商和运货来说，这个位置非常的便利。

15. There are about 15000 products on display. The exhibits are mainly new products which have been produced by various factories.

本展会共展出 15000 种产品，参展品主要是各个厂家的新产品。

16. Cancellation will only be accepted in writing before the stipulated deadline. All canceled orders will be subject to a 30% cancellation charge.

取消展位必须于截止日期前以书面形式提出，所取消的申请需缴付 30% 作取消手续费用。

17. The nine-square-meter booth costs at least RMB23,000 yuan per unit while the six-square-meter booth is at least 17,000 per unit.

标准摊位是 9 平方米的，每个起价是 2.3 万元人民币；（非标准摊位是）6 平方米的每个起价是 1.7 万元人民币。

18. The client company should be open to suggestions regarding the style and location of the event and the type of event program.

关于展会风格、展会地点及展会议程类型，客户公司应该广泛听取意见。

19. The common complaints of exhibitors are that closing hours of the exhibit hall are unscheduled and that they are assigned in another hotel than the delegates'.

参展商普遍抱怨展厅的时间安排缺乏时限性，还抱怨把他们安排在与会议代表不同的宾馆住宿。

20. The Internet will continue to drive the development of the global event management industry. Meeting organizers must use this dynamic technology quickly and accurately to ensure that their event remains competitive throughout the twenty-first century.

互联网将继续推动全球会展管理业的发展。会展策划人必须迅速而准确地利用这一不断更新的技术，以保证在 21 世纪的会展竞争中永远立于不败之地。

Bidding Documents

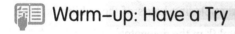

Warm-up: Have a Try

Try to translate the following document into Chinese

INVITATION TO TENDER

Date:

Tender No.

1. The People's Republic of China has applied for a loan and credit from the World Bank towards the cost of_____Project.It is intended that part of the proceeds of this loan and credit will be applied to eligible payment under various contracts for_____

_____, _____, _____.Tendering is open to all tenderers from eligible source countries as defined under the "Guidelines for procurement" of the World Bank.

2. _____Company now invites sealed tenders from pre-qualified tenderers for provision of the necessary labor, materials, equipment and services for the construction and completion of the project.

3. Pre-qualified tenderers may obtain further information from_____, and inspect the tender documents at the office of_____.

4. A complete set of tender documents may be obtained by any pre-qualified tenderer for the cost of RMB_____or US$_____on the submission of a written application to the above.

5. All tenders must be accompanied by a Tender Security in an acceptable form and must be delivered to_____Company at the above-mentioned address (refer to Item 3) on or before_____.

6. Tenders will be opened in the presence of those tenderers' representatives who choose to attend at_____(time).

7. If a pre-qualified foreign tenderer wishes to form joint venture with a domestic contractor, such a request will be considered if received within_____days before the closing date for submission of tenders. The selected local contractor shall be subject to approval by the Employer.

8. The Pre-Tender Meeting will be held on_____at the following address:_____.

Background: Learn Something About Bidding Documents

招投标是一种传统的贸易方式，经常用于国际工程承包和大宗物资的采购业务。随着国际经济和地区经济一体化进程的加快，国际招投标作为一种重要的国际经济合作的形式在世界经济活动中的地位越来越重要。国际招投标文件的语言主要是英语，因此招标文件的翻译就显得尤为重要。

1. 招标方式

在不同的法规体系下，对招标方式 (type of tendering) 的规定不尽相同。

(1)《世界银行采购指南》定义了以下招标/采购方式。

• 国际竞争性招标 (international competitive bidding)

• 有限国际招标 (limited international bidding)

• 国内竞争性招标 (domestic competitive bidding)

• 询价采购 (shopping)

- 直接签订合同 (direct contracting)

(2)《中华人民共和国招投标法》定义了两类招标方式。
- 公开招标 (open tendering)
- 邀请招标 (selective tendering)

2. 招标文件相关要素

虽然根据不同招标方式，招标文件具体细节也不尽相同，但一般说来，招标文件应包括招标通告、投标者须知、投标文件、格式、合同格式、工程合同条款、技术规格、货物清单或工程量清单和图纸，以及必要的附件，如各种担保的格式等。以国际竞争性招标文件为例如下。

国际竞争性招标文件
The Bidding Documents For *****（缩简形式）

目 录
Table of Contents

第一章 投标人须知	Section 1 Instructions to Bidders
1 说明	1. Explanation
2 招标文件	2. The Bidding Documents
3 投标文件的编制	3. Preparation of Tender Documents
4 投标文件的递交	4. Submission of Bids
5 开标与评标	5. Opening and Evaluation of Bids
6 授予合同	6. Award of Contract
第二章 合同通用条款	Section 2 General Conditions of Contract
第三章 合同格式	Section 3 Contract Form
第四章 投标文件格式	Section 4 Formats of Bids
第五章 投标邀请	Section 5 Invitation for Bids
第六章 投标资料表	Section 6 Bid Data Sheet
第七章 合同资料表	Section 7 Contract Data Sheet
第八章 货物需求一览表及技术规格	Section 8 Schedule of Requirements and Technical Specifications

3. 了解国际招标基本流程

根据不同招标方式，具体流程以个例要求为准，例如（缩略版）：
第一步：编制招标文件 prepare the bidding documents
第二步：报送相关文件 submit the doc. to relevant department
第三步：相关部门批复 relevant department reply

第四步：发布招标公告 issue the bid information
第五步：开标 date of bid opening
第六步：评标 date of bid evaluation
第七步：公示 evaluation result's notification
第八步：发中标通知书 deliver Notification of Award
第九步：签订合同 sign the contract

Discussion: Talk About How to Do the Task Well

1. 招标文件词汇使用特点

由于招标文件具有法律效力，因此在进行翻译时具有以下特点。

1) 大量使用专业术语

招标文件中许多名称有固定的译法，不如其他类型文本翻译那样可以由其他词代替，如果不熟悉招标专用术语，翻译起来往往不得要领。

例如：pre-qualify 在招标文件中意为"对投标人进行投标资格预审"，与此对应，post-qualify tenderers 则指在没有进行投标人资格预审的情况下，在开标后对投标人进行的资格审查，可以译为"对投标人进行资格后审"。再如 pre-qualification of tenderers 应译成"投标人资格预审"。

2) 招标专用词汇使用一致性

根据不同版本国际性文件，如《世界银行采购指南》《世贸组织政府采购协议 (WTO GPA)》，一些专业词汇翻译不尽相同，因此在进行招标文件翻译时一定要注意一致性问题。以下词汇在翻译时可有不同方式。

- 投标邀请 Invitation to Tender/Invitation for Bids
- 投标人须知 Instructions to Tenderers/Instructions to Bidders
- 合格的投标人 Eligible Tenderers/Eligible Bidders
- 招标文件 Tendering Documents/Bidding Documents
- 投标文件原件 Original Tender/Original Bid
- 投标文件副本 Copy of Tender/Copy of Bid
- 投标价格 Tender Prices/Bid Prices
- 投标保证金 Tender Security/Bid Security
- 开标 Tender Opening/Bid Opening

同时在不同法规体系的招投标书中，对于专业词汇的使用具有较大区别，甚至招标和投标用词完全颠倒的情况。例如：tenderer 一词，在不同的国际性文件中既可翻译成招标人，又可翻译成投标人，因此，在招投标项目文件翻译过程中，首先要对招标文件进行完整的分析，找出招标文件采用的是哪种文本规范或者招标文件需要按照哪种文本规范进行翻译。这样，就能准确把握其中的专业词汇，保持文本一致性，不至于产生误译。

3) 情态动词的选用

如同所有的法规性文件一样，招标文件在情态动词的选用上特别慎重。will, shall, should, may, must各司其职，不可混淆。由于国际招标文件具有法律效力，所以在翻译中大量使用了shall一词。在书面英语中，shall最好与第一人称合用，但在条约、规章、法令等文件中，常可用shall来表示义务或规定，一般用于第三人称，表示"应、必须"的含义。同样must、should在招标文件中也经常用来表达义务，而当需要弱化义务时，招标文件经常选取may。

例1. The bidder shall bear all costs associated with the preparation and submission of its bid.

参考译文：投标人须承担由于编制和提交其投标书而引起的一切费用。

Bidders should not be associated, directly or indirectly, with a firm or any of its affiliates which have engaged by the Tenderer to provide consulting services for the preparation of the design, specifications, and other documents to be used for the procurement of the goods to be purchased under this Invitation for Bids. (should表示义务)

参考译文：投标人不得直接或间接地与招标人为采购本次招标的货物进行设计、编制规范和其他文件所委托的咨询公司或其附属机构有任何关联。

例2. The Suppliers may participate in the bids only if they are legally and financially autonomous, if they operate under relevant law, and if they are not a dependent agency of the Tendering Agent and the Tenderer. (may体现弱化)

参考译文：只有在法律上和财务上独立、合法运作并独立于招标人和招标机构的供货人才能参加投标。

4) 书面用词的选用

由于标书是正规、严肃的法律文件，它不允许有俗语、方言或口语化的语言，因此标书中多用正式、规范、严谨的词语，具体体现如下。

(1) 多用繁复的介词短语代替简单介词，例如：in the nature of (like)；for the purpose of (for)；in case of (if)；in accordance with (by/under)；in favor of (for/to)；on the grounds that (since/because)；with reference to (about)；in the event of (if)

例3. 本款所述的"原产地"是指货物开采、生长或生产或提供有关服务的来源地。

参考译文：For purposes of this clause, "origin" means the place where the goods are mined, grown or produced, or the place from which the related services are supplied.

例4. In the event of any discrepancy between them, the Chinese shall prevail.

参考译文：两种文字具有同等效力；中文本与英文本如有差异，以中文本为准。

(2) 多用复杂动词代替简单动词，例如：procurement (buy)；jeopardize (harm)；

supplement (add); grant (give); acquire (get); commence (begin); inform (tell)。

(3) 用一些生僻词代替常用词，例如：prior to, before; expiry, end; certify, prove; solicit, seek 等。

5) 公文副词的选用

国际招投标文件中的许多文件属于法律性公文，所以有些词语要用公文语词语，特别是酌情使用英语惯用的一套公文语副词，就会起到使译文结构严谨、逻辑严密、言简意赅的作用。这种副词为数并不多，常用的这类词是由 here, there, where 加上 after, by, in, on, to, under, upon, with 等副词，构成一体化副词，示例如下。

从此以后，今后：hereafter

此后，以后：thereafter

其上：thereon/thereupon

在其下：thereunder

对于这个：thereto

对于那个：whereto

在上文：hereinabove; hereinbefore

在下文：hereinafter; hereinbelow

在上文中，在上一部分中：thereinbefore

在下文中，在下一部分中：thereinafter

例 5. Both the Purchasers and the Contractor shall be hereinafter collectively referred to as "the Parties" and individually as "the Party" and shall include their successors and permitted assigns.

参考译文：业主和承包商在下文中统称为"缔约方"，单独一方称为"一方"，双方必须包括其继承人和允许授予人。

6) 用名词结构替代动词结构

在招标文件中，有时为了强调行为而不是行为人，会用名词结构替代动词。

例 6. 投标人没有按照招标文件要求提交全部资料，或未能提交在各方面对招标文件做出实质性响应的投标书，其风险将由投标人承担，并可能导致其投标被拒绝。

参考译文：Failure to furnish all information required by the bidding documents or to submit a bid not substantially responsive to the bidding documents in every respect will be at the Bidder's risk and may result in the rejection of its bid.

在该句中用 failure to do 替代 any bidder who fails to do，体现了由于无法完成某条件而产生的后果，而不是针对行为主体。

2. 招标文件句式使用特点

与普通英语相比，英文招标文件的句子较长，结构较为复杂。由于招标文件涉及条件多，各方权利、义务多，因此使用长句可以用来排除被曲解、误解或出现歧义的可能性。招投标文件中大量使用状语（从句）和定语（从句）等，对主句意义进行解释、限制或补充，这样使招投标文件逻辑严谨、文风庄严，也可以对各方履行权利与义务的条件、方式、地点以及时间等进行限制，从而使招投标文件不留漏洞，避免今后可能发生的争端，以维护各方的利益。

例 7. The tenderer should be informed that, if he has delivered, posted or dispatched his tender prior to the formal submission date he has the right to modify or make corrections to it, provided that any such modifications or corrections are received by the employer/engineer in writing prior to the time specified for submission of tenders. The original tender thus modified or corrected would then be considered as the official tender.

参考译文：应通知投标人，如果他在正式的提交日之前递交、邮寄或发送了他的投标书，他有权对其做出修改或更正，但规定，关于任何此类修改或更正，投标人必须使雇主/工程师在规定的投标书提交日期之前收到书面文本。如此修改或更正后的投标书正本即被认为是正式的投标书。

该句使用条件状语从句，因为根据句意，虽然规定投标人有权修改他发出的标书，但是他的这一权利受到"如果他在正式的提交日之前递交、邮寄或发送了他的标书"和"但规定，关于任何此类修改或更正，投标人必须使雇主/工程师在规定的投标书提交日期之前收到书面文本"两个条件约束，因此通过使用条件状语从句（"if he has delivered, posted or dispatched his tender prior to the formal submission date." "provided that any such modifications or corrections are received by the employer/engineer in writing prior to the time specified for submission of tenders."），清楚表达限定，规避风险。

通过上面的例子可以看出招标文件使用长句所体现的优势，因此如何做好招标文件长句翻译就显得尤为重要。下面是招标文件长句翻译的一些技巧。

1) 被动语态的使用

在英文招标文件中经常可以看见简单被动句式的使用，凡是无须说明行为人、没有行为人或须弱化行为人的情况下，英语经常使用被动语态，在翻译成汉语时，虽有"把"和"被"字可以利用，但有时为了句意表达的连贯通顺，经常转换成主动句。

例 8. The goods required, bidding procedures and contract terms are prescribed in the bidding documents, which is compiled in both English and Chinese.

参考译文：要求提供的货物、招标过程和合同条件在招标文件中均有说明。招标文件以中、英文两种文字编写。

虽然在中英互译中主动语态和被动语态经常互换，但在强调由某些条件而产生的后果时或强调各方权利、义务时，被动则不宜译成主动。

例 9. 如果投标人不接受对其错误的更正，其投标将被拒绝。

参考译文：If the bidder does not accept the correction of the errors, its bid will be rejected.

例 10. 实质上没有响应招标文件要求的投标将被拒绝。投标人不得通过修正或撤销不合要求的偏离或保留从而使其投标成为实质上响应的投标。

参考译文：If a bid is not substantially responsive, it will be rejected and may not subsequently be made responsive by the Bidder having corrected or withdrawn the non-conforming deviation or reservation.

2) 平行结构在条件状语从句中的使用

招标文件由于经常涉及诸多条件限定，因此条件状语从句的使用也非常频繁，但由于有时某一行为的限定条件过多，因此在招标英语中经常使用条件状语的平行结构。

例 11. The Evaluation Committee will examine the bids to determine whether they are complete, whether the bids are generally in order, whether required securities have been furnished, whether the documents have been properly signed, and whether any computational errors have been made.

参考译文：评标委员会将审查投标文件是否完整、总体编排是否有序、投标人是否提交了投标保证金、文件签署是否合格、有无计算上的错误等。

例 12. The Suppliers may participate in the bids only if they are legally and financially autonomous, if they operate under relevant law, and if they are not a dependent agency of the Tendering Agent and the Tenderer.

参考译文：只有在法律上和财务上独立、合法运作并独立于招标人和招标机构的供货人才能参加投标。

3) 断句的使用

在处理招标文件长句时，在保证句意准确的前提下，有时可以在翻译过程中，在适当处断句，分解句子，化整为零。

例 13. The Tendering Agent may, at its discretion, extend this deadline for the submission of bids by amending the bidding documents in accordance with ITB Clause7, in which case all rights and obligations of the Tendering Agent/the Tenderer and Bidders previously subject to the deadline will thereafter be subject to the deadline as extended.

参考译文：招标机构可以按本须知第 7 条规定，通过修改招标文件自行决定酌情推迟投标截止期。在此情况下，招标机构、招标人和投标人受投标截止期制约的所有权利和义务均应延长至新的截止期。

将英文长句化整为零，译成中文短句，同时注意 tenderer and bidder 的使用。

例 14. If a bid deviates from the schedule and if such deviation is considered acceptable to the Tenderer, the bid will be evaluated by calculating interest earned for any earlier payments involved in the terms outlined in the bid as compared with those stipulated in this invitation, at a rate per annum as specified in the Bid Data Sheet.

参考译文：如果投标文件对此有偏离但又属招标人可以接受的，评标时将按投标资料表所述的利率计算提前支付所产生的利息，并将其计入其评标中。

Follow-up: Do It Yourself

Translate the following sentences

(1) Tenderers shall submit a tender bond that is no less than 2% of the total sum of the tender offer. It shall be part of the tender.

(2) The Contract shall be construed according to laws of the People's Republic of China.

(3) Goods and services to be provided by tenderers shall be quoted in the currency of US dollar.

(4) 所有标书须在截止日期当日或之前投递至以下地址。

(5) 投标方的标书要准备1份原件和6份复印件。

Homework: Practice Makes Perfect

Translate the following paragraph into English

投标者须知

一、工程概述（根据具体情况写）

二、资金来源

中华人民共和国向世界银行（以下简称 IFI）申请一笔贷款，用以支付_____工程。其中部分贷款将用于支付此合同工程。只有应中国政府的要求，根据贷款协议的条件，IFI 才会同意付款。除中国外，任何组织不能从贷款协议中获得权利或取得贷款。

三、资格要求

（一）所有根据世行的"采购指导原则"具有资格的国家均可投标。

（二）本合同项下的一切货物、服务均应来自上述具有资格的国家。本合同项下的一切开支仅限于支付这样的货物和服务。

（三）货物、服务来源地与投标者国籍含义不同。

（四）为说明自己有资格中标，投标者应向业主提供（一）所规定的证明，保证有效地执行合同。为此，业主和中国A公司在公布中标者前，可要求投标者更新其先前提供的资格证明材料。

（五）投标者可更新资格证明申请，在投标日亲手交出。

四、投标费用

投标者承担准备和提交其标书所需的全部费用。无论投标情况怎样，业主和其代

理人中国 A 公司都不负担这些费用。

五、现场参观

建议投标者去工程现场参观，以便获得足够的信息准备标书，撰写合同。现场参观费用由投标者自己承担。

Extend Your Eyes

招投标常用词汇

招标	Bidding
投标（投标文件）	Bid
投标人	Bidder
投标邀请	Invitation for Bids
投标人须知	Instructions to Bidders
合格的投标人	Eligible Bidders
招标文件	Bidding Documents
投标文件正本	Original Bid
投标文件副本	Copy of Bid
投标价格	Bid Prices
投标保证金	Bid Security
开标	Bid Opening
招标公司	Tendering Co.
联营体	joint venture
招标代理	bidding agency
采购公告	procurement notice
招标公告	notification of bidding
招标文件	bidding documents
招标号	bidding no.
招标资料	bidding data sheet
招标附录	appendix to tender
投标保证金	bid security; tender bond
履约保证金	performance security
投标书的提交	submission of bid
开标	bid opening
评标	bid evaluation

授予合同	award of contract
中标通知	notification of award
投标货币	Tender Currency
投标有效期	valid period of tender
政府采购协议	government procurement agreement
项目评估文件	Project Appraisal Document (PAD)
撤标	withdrawal of bid

招投标常用句型

1. 投标人提供的货物和服务用美元货币报价。

Goods and services to be provided by tenderers shall be quoted in the currency of US dollar.

2. 投标人应提交金额为不少于投标报价总价2%的投标保证金，并作为其投标的一部分。

Tenderers shall submit a tender bond that is no less than 2% of the total sum of the tender offer. It shall be part of the tender.

3. 投标保证金是为了保护招标机构和买方免遭因投标人的行为而蒙受损失。

Tender bond is designed to protect Tenderee and Buyer from losses because of any actions of tenderers.

4. 未中标的投标人的投标保证金，将尽快并不晚于按照本须知第16条规定的投标有效期满后三十(30)天原额退还投标人。

Tender bonds of tenderers who fail in the tender will be returned to tenderers in full amount as soon as possible and no later than thirty (30) days after the expiration of the valid period of the tender as provided in Clause 16 of the Notice.

5. 下列任何情况发生时，投标保证金将被没收。

Tender bond will be confiscated in case.

6. 投标人在招标文件中规定的投标有效期内撤回其投标。

Tenderers withdraw their tenders within the valid period of the tender as provided in the tender invitation documents.

7. 投标应在规定的开标日后的180天内保持有效。投标有效期不满足要求的投标将被视为非响应性投标而予以拒绝。

A tender remains valid within the 180 days after the prescribed tender opening date. Tenders with an ineligible valid period shall be rejected as non-responsive tenders.

8. 投标人应在投标报价汇总表和投标分项报价表上标明本合同拟提供货物的单价(如适用)和总价。

On the tender offer summary sheet and the item tender offer sheets, tenderers shall indicate clearly the unit price (if applicable) and the total price of the goods planned to be provided according to the Contract.

9. 投标人应在投标价格表中报出技术规范中所列的随机备品配件、专用工具及仪器的单价。

In the tender price sheet, tenderers shall include the unit prices of the attached parts and components, special tools and instrumentations that are listed in the Technical Specifications.

10. 我们同意遵守以上规定的投标条款。

We agree to abide by the conditions of Tender specified above.

11. 不适当的（如用电话）或不负责任的报价将被拒收。

An inadequate (e.g. by telephone) or irresponsible quotation may be reason for rejecting the quotation.

Task 4

Business Correspondence

Warm-up: Have a Try

Try to translate the following counter offer into Chinese

Dear Sirs,

Thank you for your letter dated April 23rd.

We are very sorry that on account of our oversight we made some mistakes in the establishment of the L/C. We have had the L/C amended accordingly and have instructed our bank to send the necessary amendment by telex and hope that everything now is in order. As the goods are badly needed, we hope you will expedite the shipment.

You can be assured that if the goods are found to our buyers' satisfaction upon arrival, they will most likely place repeat orders in large quantities.

Yours faithfully,

× × ×

Background: Learn Something About Business Correspondence

1. 商务信函的 12 种要素

信头 (letterhead)、案号 (reference)、日期 (date)、封内地址 (inside address)、注意项 (attention line)、称呼 (salutation)、事由栏 (subject)、信的正文 (body of letter)、信尾敬语 (complimentary close)、签名 (signature)、缩写名、附件及分送标志部分 (IEC: initials, enclosures and carbon copies block) 及附言 (postscript)。

Sample

TIANJIN CARPETS IMPORT & EXPORT CORPORATION

45 BAODING STREET, TIANJIN, CHINA

Telephone: 31022348   Fax: 26320767   Email: tjcar@public.tpt.tj.cn

Our Reference No. J/W-CO18

Your Reference No.

Date: 30th November, 2009

Messrs. Williams & Warner
36 Tower Street
Sydney, Australia

Attention: Mr. Arnold Simpson, Sales Department

Dear sirs,

Re: SHEEP WOOL

With reference to our Order TC303 of 30 September for 50M/T Sheep Wool, we shall be glad to know when we may expect delivery, as these are urgently required.

When we made the initial inquiry, your department assured us that delivery would only take two months, and we placed the order on that understanding as we wished to have the WOOL before the end of November. Your failure to deliver by the promised date has caused us great inconvenience.

Will you please inform us of the earliest possible date when you can deliver these goods? Should the delay be longer than two or three weeks, we shall regretfully have to cancel the order.

Yours faithfully,

Tianjin Carpets I/E Corporation

(Sig.) _____

(Manager)

其中，信头、日期、封内地址、称呼、信的正文、信尾敬语和签名属于标准要求，是正式商务信件中必不可少的，其他要素可根据具体情况选择使用。

2. 涉外商务信函语篇风格的特点

涉外商务信函的语言规范遵循 7C 原则，具体如下。

1) 完整原则 (Completeness)

为了将事件背景、计划与细节完整地展现出来，商务信函通常用层次复杂的从句和长句，翻译时务必将原文中的信息完整地传递给读者，不能因句式复杂而有疏漏。

例 1. The enclosed fee schedule quotes a fixed price for handling different types of tax returns as well as quarterly consultations billed on an hourly basis.

参考译文：随附的费用安排表是一份有关处理各种纳税申报表和以小时计算的季度咨询的规定报价。

译文修饰语成分的位置安排妥当，术语准确，信息完整、无遗漏。

例 2. The commission we allow to our agents in other areas at present is 5% on the value of shipment payable monthly, and we hope that if we offer you the same terms it will be satisfactory.

参考译文：我们目前给其他地区代理商装运货物总值 5% 的佣金，此佣金按月支付。如果我们给您相同的条件，希望您满意。

译文将 payable monthly 处理为小句，避免定语过长，而所表达的信息仍然完整。

2) 简洁原则 (Conciseness)

简洁就是用最简单的话语准确地表达自己的意思，好处是开门见山、直入主题，翻译的时候也要同样注意译出此特点。

例 3. We would like to know whether you would allow us to extend the time of shipment for twenty days. And if you would be so kind as to allow us to do so, kindly give us your reply by fax without delay.

参考译文：我们很想知道您是否允许我们将交货时间延期二十天，如果贵方友好地容许我方延期二十天交货，请速电复，请勿延误。

此句表达上的过分客气使得句子冗长而不清楚，为了更好地表达主要意思，这句可以压缩为：

例 4. Please reply by fax immediately if you will allow us to delay the shipment until April 21.

参考译文：如果同意我方将交货时间延期至四月二十一日，请速电复。

3) 具体原则 (Concreteness)

商务信函应力求具体、明确、形象，力避含糊、空泛、抽象。如在报盘、还盘、理赔时，需要使用具体的事实和数据。

例 5. This stove is absolutely the best on the market.

参考译文：这种炉子绝对是市场上最好的炉子。

这句话是用来介绍商品的，但没有具体介绍商品的性能，而是抽象地断定这种炉子是"市场上最好的"。这样介绍商品，不但不能达到推销的目的，反而使人对写信人有"卖狗皮膏药"的感觉。

最好改写为：

Our model A195 is designed on modern lines, without any increase in fuel consumption, 25% more heat than the older models. So you will agree that it is the outstanding stove for economy of fuel.

参考译文：我们的 A195 型炉子是按近代样式设计的，在不增加燃料消耗的情况下，比其他各种旧式炉子温度高 25%。所以，你会同意，这是优良的节约燃料的炉子。

4) 正确原则 (Correctness)

正确原则要求不仅语法和拼写要正确，语言要叙述恰当，商业专门术语的运用也要正确，否则可能引起严重的后果。翻译时要特别注意关于商业环节的细节和术语，务求准确无误。

例 6. We are pleased to inform you that your bankers have accepted our draft for US$5,800, payable within thirty days after sight and have successfully negotiated with all the relevant documents.

参考译文：很高兴告知贵方，贵方银行已经接受我方见票后 30 天付款的金额为 5800 美元的汇票，并已凭全部相关单据议付完毕。

此处的 draft, after sight, negotiate 等词汇均为国际贸易术语，分别译为"汇票、见票后、议付"等中文专业词汇，如果按字面意义理解则易发生翻译错误。

5) 清晰原则 (Clarity)

商务英语信函尤其注重在开篇部分清晰阐明写信目的。在内容上，特别注重数字、日期、事实细节和技术细节的清晰性。结构方面，要求逻辑性强，条理清晰。翻译时要将这些细节表达清楚，不能产生歧义。

例 7. Thank you for your letter dated August 2, 2009, enquiring about the title mentioned above. We are pleased to say that this title is in stock and we'll reserve a copy for you until August 31.

参考译文：您 2009 年 8 月 2 日询问上款书的信函已收到。谨此说明我们此书有现货，且可为您保留一本至 8 月 31 日。

6) 体谅原则 (Consideration)

体谅原则强调从对方的角度来考虑问题，体谅对方，在表达方式上多用"您为重"(you-attitude) 的视角来突出对读者情况的考虑等。在句式变换上，用疑问句或陈述句取代祈使句表示建议或请求。翻译时也要考虑读者的感受和心理，再现原文的体谅态度。

例 8. Your approval and instruction to the Maintenance Office to do the repairs will be highly appreciated.

参考译文：敬请惠准拨交维修部门进行修理。(以古雅用语来译，既正式又体现尊重。)

7) 礼貌原则 (Courtesy)

礼貌原则是商务信函最突出的特点，也是商务信函语言与表达方式的根本性原则。在礼貌原则的指导之下，商务信函大量使用程式化礼貌用语和表达方式；使用中性词汇，避免性别歧视；在表达要求、请求、不满和责备时，经常使用过去式、虚拟语气和被动语态，使语气委婉温和，避免唐突失礼。翻译时要使用汉语公文中的敬语体现出礼貌的语气。

例 9. I should be pleased to discuss the building with you in greater detail if you would suggest a time convenient to you.

参考译文：您若时间方便，我愿与您讨论该建筑的更多细节。

例 10. I would be glad if you would clear this balance as soon as possible.

参考译文：如您能尽快结清欠款，我将不胜感激。

Discussion: Talk About How to Do the Task Well

1. 专业术语与外来词

商务信函使用大量的专业术语、外来词、行话、套语，为了体现翻译的规范性和准确性，就要采用对应的汉语术语翻译原文中的商贸术语。

1) 专业术语类

trimming charges	平仓费	insurance policy	保险单
coverage	保险项目	establishment	开证
counter-suggestion	反还盘	surcharges	附加费
pro forma invoice	形式发票	premium	保险费
clearance sale	清仓削价销售	underwriter	保险人
L/C	信用证	CIF	到岸价格
FOB	离岸价格	bid	递盘
Cash Before Delivery	付款发货	counter-offer	还盘
irrevocable letter of credit	不可撤销信用证		

例 11. We shall cover TPND on your order.

参考译文：我们将为你方的货物投保盗窃和提货不着险。

例 12. We appreciate it if you would let us know by returning your lowest possible price for the following goods on FOB London.

参考译文：请报下列商品伦敦船上交货之最低价。

2) 外来词类

拉丁语的 status quo（现状），意大利语的 del credere（保付货价的），汉语中的 litchi（荔枝）、tungoil（桐油）、mango（杧果）等。

3) 行话

长期的函电交往使人们在使用术语上达成共识，本来意义差异很大的词汇在特定的语境中所表达的内涵和外延却非常相似。举例如下。

offer, quotation 表示"报价，发盘"

pamphlet, brochure, booklet, sales literature 表示商家用于宣传介绍自己公司或产品的"说明材料"

shipment 和 consignment 表示"所发出的货物"

financial standing/reputation/condition/position 用于表示公司的"资信财务情况"

fulfill/complete/execute an order 用于表示"执行订单"

a draft contract 或 a specimen contract 表示"合同样本"

4) 商务会话

英文函电中有许多商务套语，注意翻译成符合汉语商务语言规范的术语或套语。

例 13. The duplicate shipping documents including bill of lading, invoice, packing list and inspection certification were airmailed to you today.

参考译文：包括提单、发票、装箱单和检验证书在内的装运单证副本今日已航邮贵处。

例 14. Please be informed that, on account of the fluctuations of foreign exchanges, the quotation is subject to change without previous notice.

参考译文：兹告知贵方，由于外汇的波动，报价随时可能改变，不另行通知。

例 15. Full information as to prices, quality, quantity available and other relative particulars would be appreciated.

参考译文：请详告价格、质量、可供数量和其他有关情况。

例 16. We are looking forward to a favorable reply.

参考译文：静候贵方佳音。

例 17. Would you let us know your terms of payment?

参考译文：能否告知贵方付款条件？

例 18. We should be grateful if you would give us further details of Chinese leather shoes.

参考译文：如能告知中国皮鞋的详情，将不胜感激。

例 19. Please inform us how soon you can make delivery.

参考译文：请告知何时能交货。

2. 数字和日期

商务信函准确性主要体现在数量词的大量运用。商务信函中的时间、价格、数量、金额、规格等问题贯穿商贸活动始终，数字的表达应言之确凿，避免模棱两可。

例 20. The vender shall deliver the goods to the vendee by June 15.

参考译文：卖方须于 6 月 15 日或之前将货物交给买方。

例 21. The market here for this product is active, and the best price we can offer is US $150 or over per long ton.

参考译文：该产品在本地的销售看好，我方出价可达每长吨 150 美元或以上。

3. 文体对等

商务信函是一种公文性质的信函，其主要内容涉及公事，交流目的主要在于磋商公务，以朴素纪实、严谨规范、庄重典雅的特点而著称。具体在遣词造句上表现如下。

1) 用词规范正式

商务英语信函虽然有口语化的趋势，但毕竟还是一种正式的文体，所以正式词汇和中性词汇多于非正式词汇的应用，经常以意义相同或相近的书面词语代替基本词汇和口语词汇，如以 inform 或 advise 代替 tell，以 duplicate 代替 copy，以 dispatch 代替 send，以 otherwise 代替 or；以介词短语代替简单的介词，如以 as for, in respect to, in connection with 和 with regarding to 等代替 about 等。

例 22. We are pleased to advise you that your order NO. 105 has been dispatched in accordance with your instruction.

参考译文：我们很高兴地通知你们：第 105 号订单货物已遵照你方指示运出。

例 23. We will meet you half way by offering a discount of 5% in view of our long pleasant relations.

参考译文：鉴于我们之间长期愉快的业务关系，本公司将酌情考虑给予5%的折扣。

商务信函中还经常使用 here/there+ 介词构成的古体复合词，如 hereafter, hereby, hereunder, hereto, hereinafter, herewith, thereafter, therein, therefrom 等。

例 24. All offers and sales are subject to the terms and conditions printed on the reverse side hereof.

参考译文：所有报盘和销售均应遵守本报价单背面所印的条款。

例 25. In such a case, Seller is bound to reimburse Buyer for any loss or damage sustained therefrom.

参考译文：在此情况下，卖方负责偿还买方由此所遭受的损失。

2) 用语朴素，淡于修饰

商贸信函的主要功能是传递信息，使收发信函双方发生贸易往来，达成交易，因此除了必须使用专业术语等手段准确传达自己的信息意图外，还要求信函语言明白易懂，朴实平易。

例 26.

Dear Sirs,

Thank you for your interest in our fireworks.

In reply to your enquiry of November 15, we are really sorry to say that we cannot divulge any of our sales information. We hope this will not bring you too much inconvenience.

Yours truly,
× ×

参考译文：

敬启者：

承蒙贵方对我们的烟花感兴趣，十分感谢。

兹复贵方 11 月 15 日询价函，我们非常抱歉地奉告，我们不能泄露我方任何销售情况。我们希望这不会给贵方带来很多不便。

× ×

敬上

3) 商务信函主要使用陈述句、祈使句和疑问句，少用感叹句

例 27. We thank you for your promptness in delivering the coffee we ordered on 20th, July.

参考译文：收到我方 7 月 20 日订购的咖啡，并对你方迅速交货表示感谢。(陈述句)

例 28. Please look into the matter at once and let us have your definite reply by cable without any further delay.

参考译文：请立即介入此事，并尽快电告确切答复。(祈使句)

例 29. Would you please send us a copy of your catalogue?

参考译文：能否向我公司邮寄一份贵公司的产品目录？（疑问句）

4) 函电英语采用大量的并列句和复合句

例 30. The Credit could cover 85% of the local expenses if they are made under the responsibility of the British Contractor and within the limit of the down payments paid on the Contract, i.e., 15% as a maximum.

参考译文：此项贷款可支付当地费用的 85%。但此项费用必须是英国承包商直接负责支付的，并必须在合同付款的幅度以内，即最高不得超过合同金额的 15%。

5) 虚拟语气的运用

虚拟语气可表主观愿望和假想虚拟的情况，并可使语气委婉，谓语由 should, would, could, might 加动词原形构成。

例 31. We could suggest, therefore, that you cut your order to half and pay cash for it.

参考译文：因此我方建议贵方削减一半订单并以现金支付。

4. 商务英语信函翻译的注意事项

1) 商务信函以传递信息的功能为主，可按原句结构直译

由于较少运用修辞手段，商务信函一般不存在语言与文化的差异，在翻译时无须作太多变动。

例 32. I have pleasure in apprising you that, under the auspices of several highly respected and influential houses here, I have commenced business as a shipping and assurance broker and general agent.

参考译文：我十分高兴地通知您，在本地几家有名望、有影响力的公司的支持下，我做起了运输与保险经纪以及总代理的生意。

2) 商务英语信函重在纪实、简洁和准确

翻译时不求虚饰，但求简洁、严谨、准确，保留原文的简洁流畅与易懂性。同时须确保事实细节(如日期、数量、金额等)的准确翻译，不得疏漏。

例 33. We shall quote immediately our price for "Ever-lasting" Brand bicycles, CIF Marseilles, including 3% commission.

参考译文：我方即报"永久"牌自行车 CIF 马赛价，包括 3% 佣金。

例 34. If you can accept $275 and send us a pro forma invoice, we will open a letter of credit for 1,000 sets.

参考译文：如果贵方能够接受 275 美元的价格并寄送形式发票，我方即开立 1000 套的信用证。

3) 翻译时应注意保留原文的文体正式性和委婉礼貌性

对原文情态、礼貌程度、语气和态度应当仔细分析，整体把握，并在译文中充分再现。

4) 汉语商务信函用语和行文都讲究郑重，常用文言词语，套语亦多

常用的信函词语包括"收悉、承蒙、乞谅、见告、为盼、赐复"等，这些词现在都还可以使用。

Follow-up: Do It Yourself

1. Translate the following sentences into English

(1) 我方十分抱歉不能答应你方要求。

   We very much regret our inability to＿＿＿＿＿＿＿＿＿＿＿＿＿＿＿＿＿．

(2) 新调整的价格将于下月一日起生效。

   The newly adjusted prices will ＿＿＿＿＿＿＿＿＿＿＿＿＿＿＿ from the first of next month.

(3) 如果你方价格具有竞争性，且交货时间可以接受，我们打算向你方大量订购。

Should your price be found competitive and delivery date acceptable, we intend to _____.

(4) 我们对中国产品的质量有信心，如蒙寄样，不胜感激。

We _____ the quality of Chinese products. _____ if samples could be forwarded to us.

(5) 鉴于我们双方长期友好关系，我们对此次交易例外接受60天付款交单。

_____, we exceptionally accept 60 days D/P for this transaction.

2. Translate the following business letter into Chinese

Dear Sirs,

We acknowledge your letter of 16th August and have noted your proposal for payment by T/T.

We are pleased to say that we agree to your above proposal. However we consider it advisable to make it clear that for future transactions T/T payment will only be applicable if the amounts involved for each transaction is not up to USD10 000. Should the amount exceed that figure, payment by L/C would be required.

Yours faithfully,
Tom White

Homework: Practice Makes Perfect

1. Translate the following Chinese sentences into English

(1) 我们对各种中国自行车感兴趣，请将相关产品的价格表寄给我们。

(2) 你方价格过高，我们无法销售你方产品。

(3) 请告知你方是否要求我们进一步提供情况。

(4) 我们期待收到你方信中所提到的样品和价格表。

(5) 我们获悉贵公司是一家经营化工产品的国营公司。

(6) 然而，一旦供应情况好转，我方将重谈此事，并以电子邮件联系你方。

(7) 因为存货稀少且需求活跃，我方愿将订单增加到1000台。

(8) 对于任何装运的延误，我方将保留撤销该订单或拒收货物的权利。

(9) 我们不否认日本产品的质量比中国产品质量优良，但差价无论如何不能达到50%。

(10) 有迹象表明几批其他供货渠道的类似品质的货物正以比你方低大约 10% 的价格出售。

2. Translate the following business letter into Chinese

Dear Sirs,

We owe your name and address to the Commercial Counselor's Office of the Swedish Embassy in Beijing who have informed us that you are in the market for Bicycles made in China.

We avail ourselves of this opportunity to contact you for the establishment of trade relations with you.

We are a corporation, handling the export of Chinese Bicycles. In order to acquaint you with our business lines, we enclose a copy of our Export List covering the main items available at present.

Should any of the items be of interest to you, please let us know. We shall be glad to give you our lowest quotation upon receipt of your detailed requirements.

We look forward to receiving your enquiries soon.

Yours faithfully,
Tom White

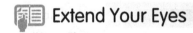
Extend Your Eyes

商务信函常用开首语

1. 我们高兴地收到贵方 2004 年 4 月 30 日来函。

   We have pleasure in acknowledging the receipt of your letter of 30th April, 2004.

2. 谢谢贵方 4 月 30 日的询盘,并已获得我们充分注意。

   We thank you for your enquiry of the 30th April, which has had our best attention.

3. 我们收到您 4 月 30 日第 M8301 号来函。

   We are in receipt of your letter Ref. M8301 dated the 30th April.

4. 我们收到贵方上月 1 日来函及附件。

   We acknowledge the receipt of your letter of the 1st ultimo with the enclosure.

5. 贵方上月 22 日来函及所附订单第 212 号一并收到。

   Your letter of 22nd ultimo, together with the order No.212 enclosed, has been received.

6. 我们收到贵方 5 月 3 日来函及所附的订单 356 号,谢谢。

   We acknowledge you of May 3 enclosing order No. 356, for which we thank you.

7. 收到贵方7月31日来函及所签回的售货确认书21850号一份。

We are in possession of your letter of the 31st July enclosing a counter-signed copy of our S/C No.21850.

8. 为复贵方2004年1月12日jG/HK号来函，兹告……

In response to your letter No. jG/HK dated 12th January, 2004, we wish to state that...

商务信函正文常用语

1. 我们愿与贵公司建立商务关系。

We are willing to establish trade relations with your company.

2. 我们希望与您建立业务往来。

Please allow us to express our hope of opening an account with you.

3. 我公司经营电子产品的进出口业务，希望与贵方建立商务关系。

This corporation is specialized in handling the import and export business in electronic products and wishes to enter into business relations with you.

4. 请允许我们自我介绍，我们是……首屈一指的贸易公司。

Let us introduce ourselves as a leading trading firm in...

5. 本公司经营这项业务已多年，并享有很高的国际信誉。

Our company has been in this line of business for many years and enjoys high international prestige.

6. 我们的产品质量一流，我们的客户一直把本公司视为最可信赖的公司。

Our products are of very good quality and our firm is always regarded by our customers as the most reliable one.

7. 我们从……获知贵公司的名称，不知贵公司对这一系列的产品是否有兴趣。

Your name has been given by... and we like to inquire whether you are interested in these lines.

8. 我们新研制的……已推出上市，特此奉告。

We are pleased to inform you that we have just marketed our newly-developed...

9. 我们盼望能成为贵公司的……供应商。

We are pleased to get in touch with you for the supply of...

10. 我们的新产品刚刚推出上市，相信您乐于知道。

You will be interested to hear that we have just marketed our new product.

11. 相信您对本公司新出品的……会感兴趣。

You will be interested in our new product...

12. 我们对贵方的新产品……甚感兴趣，希望能寄来贵公司的产品目录及价目表。

We are interested in your new product... and shall be pleased to have a catalog and price list.

13. 我们从纽约时报上看到贵公司的广告,但愿能收到产品的价目表及详细资料。

We have seen your advertisement in The New York Times and should be glad to have your price lists and details of your terms.

14. 获知贵公司有……上市,望能赐寄完整详细资料。

We hear that you have put...on the market and should be glad to have full details.

15. 如蒙赐寄贵公司新产品的详细资料,我们将深表感激。

We should appreciate full particulars of your newly developed product.

16. 如蒙赐寄有关……的样品和价目表,我们将甚为感激。

We should be obliged if you would send us patterns (or samples) and price lists of your...

17. 很高兴寄你一邮包,内装……

We are pleased to send you by parcel post a package containing...

18. 欣寄我方目录,提供我方各类产品的详细情况。

We have pleasures in sending you our catalogue, which gives full information about our various products.

19. 奉上我方产品样品,在贵方展厅展出。

We should be pleased to let you have samples to give a demonstration at your premises.

20. 为使贵方对我方各种款式的手工艺品有一初步了解,今航邮奉上我方目录和一些样品资料,供贵方参考。

In order to give you some idea of various qualities of handicrafts we carry, we have pleasure in forwarding you by airmail one catalogue and a few sample books for your perusal.

21. 随函附上本公司新出品的……样品,请查收。

You will find enclosed with this letter a sample of new...

22. 随函附上购货合同第××号两份,希查收,谅无误。请会签并退我方一份备案。

Enclosed please find two copies of Purchase Contract No..., which we trust will be found in order. Kindly sign and return one copy for our file.

23. 我们确认向贵方购买……,随函附上订单确认书供参照。

We confirm having purchased from you...A confirmation order is enclosed for your reference.

24. 我们深盼与英国公司接洽,希望成为其销售代理商之一。

We are anxious to contact some British firms with a view to acting as their selling agents.

25. 如蒙考虑担任销售你们……代理商，我们将十分高兴。

   We should be glad if you would consider our application to act as agents for the sale of your…

26. 兹函请提供……的报价。

   We are writing to invite quotations for the supply of...

27. 请将定期供应……之报价赐知。

   Please let us have a quotation for the regular supply for...

28. 请将下列货品的最低价格赐知。

   Kindly quote us your lowest prices for the goods listed below.

29. 随函寄上询价单一份。

   We are enclosing here with an inquiry sheet.

30. 如果贵方对……感兴趣，请告具体询价。

   If you are interested in our..., please let us know with a specific inquiry.

31. 一收到贵方具体询价单，我方马上航空邮上样品册并报价。

   Quotations and sample books will be airmailed to you upon receipt of your specific inquiry.

32. 我们发现你方报价比我们从其他地方收到的略微偏高，请你方降价，以适应竞争。

   We find your quotation slightly higher than those we have received from other sources, and ask you to reduce your price to meet the competition.

33. 我们很抱歉地通知你方价格无竞争力，若贵方能降低价格，使我方可接受的话，我们仍对交易感兴趣。

   We're sorry to inform you that your price has been found uncompetitive, but we're still interested in doing business if you can bring down your price to a level acceptable...

商务信函常用结尾语

1. 殷切地等待贵方早日答复。

   We are awaiting your early reply with interest.

2. 我们将感谢贵方的迅速答复。

   Your prompt reply will be appreciated.

3. 对于您在这方面的密切合作预致谢意。

   Thank you in advance for your close cooperation in this respect.

4. 我们将感谢贵方对上述各点迅速加以注意。

Your prompt attention to the said points will be appreciated.

5. 我们将乐于收到贵方来函，并保证给予充分注意。
   We shall be pleased to receive your letter and assure you of our best attention.

6. 贵方向我方提出的任何新的订单都将受到我们的充分注意。
   Any further orders that you may place with us will receive our best attention.

7. 请放心，我们将尽一切努力以满足贵方的要求。
   Please be assured that we shall spare no effort to satisfy your requirements.

8. 希望收到贵方关于进一步消息的回信。
   We hope to receive your further information by return of post.

Task 5

Instruction Manual

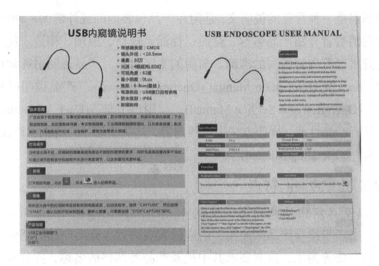

Warm-up: Have a Try

1. Put the following English into Chinese

Lacovo

Lacovo, scientifically prepared with choice ingredients including malt extract, milk, powder cocoa, fresh butter and eggs, is rich in vitamins A, B, D and organic phosphorous. It promotes health and aids convalescence and is especially good for neurasthenia and mental exhaustion. Take regularly, Lacovo helps build up body resistance against disease. A nourishing beverage for all ages. An excellent gift in all seasons.

For drinking hot: put two or three teaspoonfuls of Lacovo in a cup, then add hot water and stir until the grains are thoroughly dissolved. Add sugar and milk to taste.

For drinking cold: put two or three teaspoonfuls of Lacovo in a glass of cool-boiled water and stir until the grains are thoroughly dissolved. Then add fresh milk or condensed milk. It makes a delightful and wholesome drink in summer.

2. Put the following Chinese into English

为使本机发挥最佳性能，经久耐用，不出故障，请仔细阅读说明书。

工作时请注意不要把食物、饮料等放在键盘附近，以免不慎碰倒，引起短路。

如果遇到问题，在打电话给客服部之前，请先参考本疑难排解说明。

Background: Learn Something About Instruction Manual

产品说明书是一种常见的说明文，是附在产品包装内部或外部的一种宣传小册子，是生产厂商向消费者介绍产品名称、性质、性能、规格、原理、构造、使用方法、保养维护、注意事项等内容编写的准确、简明的文字材料。产品说明书通常可以翻译为 Instruction Manual 或 Description Manual (Operation Manual)。产品说明书也叫"操作与维修手册"(Operation and Service Manual)、"用户手册"(User's Manual) 等。有些产品说明书只有产品性能、操作方法说明等内容，这类说明书可称为"产品使用手册"或"操作手册"(Operating Manual)。

1. 产品说明书的词汇特点

1) 名词以及名词化结构的大量使用

产品说明书用于指导产品的使用，内容以客观描述、介绍产品的规格、性能、使用方法和维护方法等为主，这就要求其中提及产品各部件的名称，并且要在附图（结构图、电路图、原理图等）上说明各部分的名称并附上零件表，整个说明过程需要大量使用名词。

例 1. Ingredients: fresh beef of high quality, sugar, chilli oil, sesame oil, salt, condiments.

参考译文：配料：优质鲜牛肉、白砂糖、辣椒油、芝麻油、盐、调味料。

例 2. Simple construction, easy operation and maintenance, and comparatively high productivity.

参考译文：结构简单，操作容易，维修方便，生产率较高。

原文本使用 construction, operation, maintenance 和 productivity 四个名词，形式简单，结构紧凑。因此，对应的译文也使用名词结构，从形式上对应产品特征。

此外，还有非谓语动词的名词化，动词-ing 形式，以名词的形式表达了动词的含义。

例 3. When canceling a print job from the driver, the Power light blinks briefly.

参考译文：从驱动程序取消一个打印作业时，电源指示灯会暂时闪烁。

也可以综合使用 -ing, -ed 和不定式，以精练的结构表达复杂的含义。

例 4. Imbued with fresh juicy peach essence and enriched with tropical fruit extract, the refreshing and sweet softening lotion cleanses and hydrates your skin. It softens the skin's out layers, allowing nutrients to be more easily absorbed.

参考译文：柔肤液清新甜美，蕴含鲜美多汁的蜜桃精华和热带水果的萃取成分，再次洁净肌肤并为肌肤注入大量水分，同时软化角质，促进肌肤对后续保养品的吸收。

2) 术语的大量使用

为了向受众传达某些专业背景知识，方便顾客根据自身情况做出选择，说明书中通常包含术语。术语是指专业领域内的词或者词组，具有特定的概念。Composition（成分）、Indication（适应症）、Packing（包装）、Expiry Date（失效日期）、Manufacturing Date（出厂日期）等词汇，其翻译是固定的，需要查找行业术语词典或者咨询专业人士，以确保翻译的正确。

还有一些平时常见的普通名词，但在某个特定领域却有其独特的含义。例如 active capital 在金融产品的说明书中要译为"流动资本"，而不是首都或者大写字母；在机械类文本中 pig caster 要译为"生铁浇注机"，而不能是"猪浇注机"；drive motor 要译为"驱动电动机"，而不是"驾驶摩托"。翻译时不仅要查找字典，还要尽量查阅与所译说明书类似行业的平行文本，参考其中属于这一行业的翻译。

例 5. X band... most common for moving and stationary; can be used in "Instant-on" mode; this frequency is shared with burglar alarms and door openers.

band 一词本身是个多义词，生活中常用的意思有"乐队；人群，团伙；带子，颜色带"。某产品说明书中该词多次出现，并且前面伴随着大写字母 X, K, Ka 等，若不理解 band 在文中的意思，那几个词语便没法进行准确的翻译。仔细查阅资料可发现，band 一词在无线电波领域表示"a range of radio waves"，"X band"便是"X 波段"，是指工作频率在 10.500 至 10.550 千兆赫的频率。

参考译文：X 波段……移动式或固定式；可使用即开模式；此波段上使用的还有防盗报警器和自动门。

3) 缩略语的使用

不同类型的缩略语处理方式不同。

有些缩略语是国际单位，如 oz（盎司）、ft（英尺）、°F（华氏度），在翻译时可以直接译出，或者换算并注明其对应的中文常见单位 mL（毫升）、m（米）和℃（摄氏度）。

有些缩略语是常见单词的缩写，如 DV = digital video，LED=light-emitting diode，OEM=Original Equipment Manufacturer，CPU=central processing unit，这些缩略语已经广为人知并且不会产生误解，翻译时可以选择保留英文或者添加中文注解的方式。如 DV（数码摄录机），LED（发光二极管），OEM（原始设备制造商），

CPU（中央处理器）。

有些缩写的原始词汇有多种可能，如 DC 可能是哥伦比亚特区 (District of Columbia)，也可能是直流电 (Direct Current)，翻译时需要根据文本类型和行业背景进行选择。

例 6. Switch on and improve the influence of DC Drive on the LCD.

参考译文：打开开关，改善直流驱动对液晶显示器的影响。

例 7. The on-site maintenance is available among 28 states and Washington DC.

参考译文：28 个州和华盛顿特区内的用户俱可享受上门维修服务。

2. 产品说明书的句法特征

1) 多使用简单句或者并列句，少用从句

产品说明书讲究言简意赅、通俗易懂，避免繁杂冗长。因此产品说明书中句子大部分都是只有一个主谓结构的简单句。

例 8. After cleansing, dampen a cotton ball with toner and gently sweep over face and neck.

参考译文：洁面后，用爽肤水弄湿棉花球，轻捏拭抹面部及颈部。

产品说明书有时也使用 and 连接两个主谓结构形成并列句。

例 9. The wiring should be in good condition and core flex should not be exposed.

参考译文：这些配线必须完好无损，中心导体不得裸露。

例 10. It is reliable in usage, convenient in maintenance and able to work under very bad conditions.

参考译文：该机器操作时安全可靠，便于维修，能在恶劣条件下工作。

2) 多采取描述性句型，时态上多使用一般现在时

例 11. Exquisite foam whisks away impurities and excess oil. The skin becomes pure, fresh and vitality for the application persistently.

参考译文：泡沫细腻，洗去肌肤污垢和多余油脂。持续使用，营造肌肤清新蓬勃、清滢剔透、水感活力。

使用之后的效果，势必将来才可显示出来，但是说明书中使用一般现在时表示将来，反映了按照规律通常会出现的效果，展示了厂家对产品的信心，起到了良好的宣传作用。

3) 多使用陈述句和祈使句

产品说明书往往以一种客观冷静的语气与预期读者进行交流，很少使用过于委婉礼貌的语言，尤其是说明书的警告、注意事项和操作要点等项，目的在于引起使用者的特别注意。经常使用祈使句来表示指示、叮嘱、强调、命令、警告等语气。

例 12. For best results, use warm water.

参考译文：使用温水，效果更好。

例 13. Remove the batteries from the appliance if you are not going to use it for quite some time.

长时间不使用本设备，请取出电池。

例 14.

Important Safety Information

Do not disassemble this machine or attempt any procedures not described in this manual. Refer all servicing to qualified service personnel.

Do not install or use the machine near water, or when you are wet. Take care not to spill any liquids on the machine.

参考译文：

重要安全提示

请勿拆装本机或尝试执行说明书中未述及的程序。请将所有机器维修工作交由合格的维修人员处理。

请勿在靠近水源的地方或您浑身湿透时使用本机。请勿使任何液体溅到机器上。

4) 多使用省略句

产品说明书简洁明了的文体特征使大量省略句被使用，这大大缩短了篇幅，也增强了可读性。通常产品说明书反映的信息对象已经明确，即生产厂家对消费者提供购买和使用指导。针对一些操作程序类的信息，操作者便是消费者，文中无须再强调，所以往往主动句中会省略主语，如 you、the customer、the user 等词通常不会出现。

例 15. Contraindications: None known.

参考译文：禁忌症：尚未发现。

例 16. Feel clean and promote a fresh, radiant looking complexion. Clear away hinder for the subsequent skin care.

参考译文：肌肤清柔澄净，富有光彩。为后续的肌肤护理扫清障碍。

3. 产品说明书的文本结构特征

例 17. (见下图)

产品说明书文本通常包括三部分：标题、正文和落款。可以包含目录、标题格式、图片索引、字号、字体以及一些警示符号，信息全面，排版美观。

1) 标题 (Title)

产品说明书的标题通常出现在说明书的第一页第一行，视觉效果明显，通常是由产品名称或者是所说明的对象构成。如样例中的 iPad User Guide (iPad 用户指南)。

2) 正文 (Body)

正文是产品说明书的核心内容，介绍产品的特征、性能、使用方法和注意事项等。

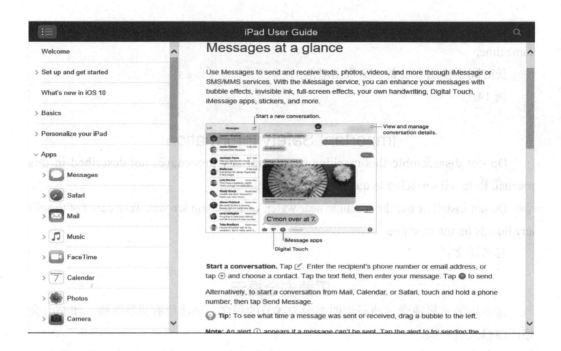

如果需要说明的内容较多，可以采用目录的形式只列明每部分的标题，如样例中所示：

What's new in iOS 10（iOS10 新性能）

Basics（基本性能）

Personalize your iPad（个性化设计）

Apps（应用程序）

根据内容需要还可以设置子目录或是多级子目录，如 Apps（应用程序）中就包括

Message（信息）

Safari（浏览器）

Mail（邮件）

Music（音乐）

FaceTime（视频通话）

Calendar（日历）

Photos（照片）

Camera（相机）

选择需要查询的子目录进入，即可查阅相关内容。

有些说明书中还会包括仪表盘、显示器等上的标记和符号。这些标记和符号往往是某一具体领域的标准化表达方式。例如 ⏻ 表示开关；🔊 表示音量大小；🎧 表示耳机。通过这些标记和符号，读者便能更快地掌握操作的步骤。

3) 落款 (Signature)

说明书的落款出现在封面的标题之下或者文本的末尾，包括产品商标、厂家名称、地址、电话、注册证号或是批准文号等。

© Copyright 版权所有

®Registered Trademark 注册商标

TM Trademark 美国的商标通常加注 TM，并不一定是指已注册商标。

Discussion: Talk About How to Do the Task Well

翻译商品说明书的注意事项如下。

1. 词汇专业简洁

在词汇层面，汉语电子产品说明书通常保留专业术语的英文表达。这些英文表达的保留一方面可以使句式简洁化，另一方面对于中国的使用者来说，更加熟悉这些专业术语的英文表达形式。例如，微软的办公软件系列的 Word、Excel 就不需要翻译为"微软文字处理器应用程序"和"微软办公表格处理应用程序"。

2. 句子简短准确

在句法层面，汉语电子产品说明书同样倾向于使用祈使句和省略句。与英文电子产品说明书中经常出现的"Never""Don't""No"等表示祈使意义的词不同，汉语中常使用"请您不要""请勿""请务必"等委婉的祈使表达。这样更拉近了读者与产品之间的距离，给读者以亲切感。

例 18. Do not spray over food or tableware. Do not use or store near fire. Do not strike. It should be kept in cool place and kept away from the children.

参考译文：请勿向食物和餐具喷洒。请勿在近火源处存放或使用。请勿敲撬。宜放在阴凉、儿童不易碰到的地方。

3. 保留文本特征和标识符号

例 19.

SONY®   LCD — Protector
                                                         PCK- L30WCSB

Please make sure this product is compatible with your camera before purchase.

WIDE LCD

Easy to attach with 3 layered structure.

Allows for touch panel function.

Include Items: LCD Protector (1)

Dimensions: Approx. 2 3/4 ×1 9/16 in. (w/h) (67.4mm × 38.5mm)

Sony Corporation

Made in Japan

http:// www.sony.net

翻译时需要注意原文不同位置的字体字号,如商标以及落款信息等文本特征和标识符号。

参考译文:

SONY®　　　　　　　　　　　　　　　　　　　　　　液晶屏保护膜

PCK- L30WCSB

请在购买时确认是否与您持有的商品相对应。

宽屏

采用易于粘贴的 3 层结构。

供触摸面板功能使用。

所含物品:液晶屏保护膜 (1)

尺寸:约 67.4mm × 38.5mm (宽 / 高)

索尼株式会社

日本制造

网址:http:// www.sony.net

 Follow-up: Do It Yourself

1. Put the following English into Chinese

(1) When frying, take particular care to prevent oil and grease from catching fire.

(2) Regular use of the cream results in the increase of skin cell vitality and improvement of metabolism to restore youthful fairness of the skin.

(3) In addition, you can connect it to any telephone line so that you can send and receive emails and faxes and get on the Internet.

(4) Connect the blue connector of the video cable to the blue video connector on the back of your computer.

(5) Store in a dry place at room temperature. Protect from light and in airtight container.

2. Put the following Chinese into English

(1) 该面膜富含高效美白滋养精华，淡化斑点，使皮肤再现净透与白皙。

(2) 本品为黄色糖衣片，除去糖衣后显棕褐色；味苦。

(3) 接电源时，必须先检查插座是否带有地线插孔，电源电压是否与该电器内部参数标牌上所标电压相匹配。

(4) 切勿将插座、插头浸水或溅湿，防止漏电，严禁将壶体浸入水中。

(5) 建议饮法：取3~5朵菊花用沸水直接冲泡，可根据自己的喜好添加其他辅料。

Homework: Practice Makes Perfect

1. Translate the following product instruction into Chinese

ANTI-TARNISH SILVER POLISHING CLOTH

This silver polishing cloth is made of high quality cotton impregnated with a silver cleaner and anti-tarnish agent.

Use as an ordinary cloth on lightly tarnished silver and silver plate to obtain a brilliant with a long lasting protection against tarnish. The cloth remains effective as long as it is not washed.

FROM GERMANY

2. Translate the following product instruction manual into Chinese

Read these instructions for use carefully before using the appliance and save them for future reference.

- Check if the voltage indicated on the appliance corresponds to the local main voltage before you connect the appliance.
- Check the condition of the mains cord regularly. Do not use the appliance if the plug, the cord or the appliance itself is damaged.
- If the mains cord is damaged, it must be replaced by Philips, a service centre authorized by Philips or similarly qualified persons in order to avoid a hazard.
- Keep this appliance away from water! Do not use this product near or over water contained in baths, washbasins, sinks etc.
- When used in a bathroom, unplug the appliance after use since the proximity of water presents a risk, even when the hairdryer is switched off.
- For additional protection we advise you to install a residual current device (RCD) with a rated residual operating current not exceeding 30mA in the electrical circuit supplying the bathroom. Ask your installer for advice.

- Keep the appliance out of the reach of children.
- Never block the air grilles.
- If the appliance overheats, it will switch off automatically. Unplug the appliance and let it cool down for a few minutes. Before you switch the appliance on again, check the grilles to make sure they are not blocked by fluff, hair, etc.
- Always switch the appliance off before putting it down, even if it is only for a moment.
- Always unplug the appliance after use.
- Do not wind the mains cord round the appliance.

Extend Your Eyes

产品说明书常用词汇

1. 机电产品类

steamroller	压路机
gear	齿轮
bulldozer	推土机
processing range	加工范围
mechanical digger, excavator	挖掘机
output	输出，产量
weeding machine	除草机
power	功率
tractor	拖拉机
overall dimensions	外形尺寸
seeder, broadcaster	播种机
wire drawing machine	拉丝机
mower	割草机
oil pumping machine	抽油机
harvester, reaper	收割机
stem	阀杆
winepress	葡萄榨汁机
power supply	电源
milking machine	挤奶机
automatic	自动的

2. 食品类

soup	汤
bill of fare, menu	菜单，菜谱
main course	主菜
roast	烤
dessert	甜食
bake	烘
snack	点心，小吃
ingredients	配料
fast	禁食
net weight	净重
diet	节食
edible after opened	开袋即食
banquet	宴会
appetizing	美味的

3. 医药类

composition, main ingredients	主要成分
description	说明，描述
properties	性质，特性
actions	主治
pharmacology	药理作用
indication	适应症
precaution	注意事项
warnings	警告
adverse reaction	不良反应
usage	用法
specification	规格
contraindication	禁忌
expiry (date)	使用期限
side effect, adverse events	副作用

4. 化学类

whiten	使变白
shampoo	洗发露
smoothen	使光滑

cosmetics	化妆品
cleanse	清洗
rub, apply	搽
formulate	配制
cream	膏
moisturizer	滋润剂
mousse	摩丝
rash	皮疹
insecticide	杀虫剂
whitening essence	净白精华
washing powder	洗衣粉
moisturizing lotion	润肤露
correction fluid	涂改液

5. 电子产品类

audio amplifier	音频放大器
counter	计数器
definition	分辨率
fidelity	保真度
filter	过滤，滤波，过滤器，滤波器
mixer	混合器，混频器
modulator	调制器
anode	阳极
cathode	阴极
diode	二极管
generator	发电机
integrated circuit	集成电路
magnetic field	磁场
rectifier	整流器
resistor	电阻器
bus	总线
central processing unit	中央处理器
decoder	译码器
instruction register	指令寄存器

Task 6

Business Documents

Warm-up: Have a Try

Try to translate the following sentences into Chinese

1. Document from third party acceptable.

2. Relative documents will be mailed as soon as they are ready.

3. In case documents presented with discrepancies, a discrepancy fee of US$15.00.

4. The freight charges include airfreight, handling pick-up, airport terminal, documentation charges, etc.

5. We usually make payment by irrevocable letter of credit, negotiable against shipping documents.

6. All documents should be packed into a bag sent to issuing bank by DHL.

7. Getting the goods ready, making out the documents and booking the shipping space—all this takes time.

8. The customs shall, after verification, release the same on the strength of the quarantine certificates issued, or the stamps on the customs declaration forms affixed, by the port animal and plant quarantine office.

9. Produce the list and invoice of purchased provisions and freshwater when doing formalities for ship exit quarantine.

10. This advice constitutes a documentary credit issued by the above bank and should be presented with the documents / drafts for negotiation / payment / acceptance, as applicable.

Background: Learn Something About Business Documents

1. 商务单证词语特点分析

1) 运用不同词形体现不同交际功能

与中文不同，英语是注重形式的语言，能直接从谓语的形式上判断时态，而商务单证将这一特点体现得淋漓尽致。

例 1. signed commercial invoice in _____ original(s) and in _____ copy(copies) indicating.

参考译文：已签字的商业发票正本 _____ 份，副本 _____ 份。

原句没有直接要求说此商业发票必须签字，却用一个 sign 的过去分词简洁明了地表示祈使功能，表达敦促、劝说、祈求等意愿。

2) 名词翻译中透露人际关系

虽然国际商务信用证体现的是百分之百的信息功能，但在翻译中还应对部分名词进行意译，以体现它的部分人际功能。

当涉及对方银行时，英语可能直接表达成"issuing bank"，但如果翻译者看懂双方关系后，可将其翻译成"贵行"，而不是"开证行"。

信用证中的"applicant"和"beneficiary"，它们的字面意思是"申请人"和"受益人"，但在实际翻译中译者如果隶属于卖方，可以根据各方关系把它们分别译为"贵公司"和"我公司"，这样就会让读者一目了然，简化了其中的人际关系。

3) 正式、书面语词汇

鉴于商贸英语的功能特点，经常使用非常正规，甚至旧体的书面语词汇，有许多词汇不仅口语中不用，甚至在新闻、文学或其他语体中也极少使用。在翻译时也应尽量保持词汇方面的风格，有些古体词汇不妨结合汉语的习惯，用文言词语进行翻译。

4) 旧体词汇

为使文本更好地体现法律的严肃、庄重，具有法律责任的商贸文书中经常使用一些旧体词汇，在翻译时虽无须逐字对译，但在整体上应把握其语体风格，选择较古雅的词汇，不妨在译文中灵活、适当使用一些文言文的结构，同时要参照汉语法律文本的语体风格进行翻译。

5) 同、近义词重复

法律性文件中常重复意思相同或者相近的词，中间用"and""or"或者"and/or"连接。

重复意义基本或者完全相同的词，表示强调。例如 all and any, goods and chattels, by and between, null and void, terms and conditions 等，翻译时可以省略其中之一。

重复的两个词项具有包含关系。例如，在"This contract is made and signed…"这一合同常用的开头句式中"made"中已经包含了"signed"的含义，所以常省略其中之一，译成"本合同由……签订"。

2. 商务单证语句的语法特点

商业单证（表格除外）的句子较长，每句话都表达一个完整的意思，句子之间很少有关联词。为了达到准确的目的，法律性文献中常重复关键词，很少使用代词。商业单证中均以完整句子为主，陈述句居多，信函中偶尔使用疑问句和祈使句。句子结构大致相同，具有相同或者类似的深层逻辑结构，翻译时应注意其逻辑关系的表达。商务单证法律文件中名词的使用频率非常高，名词短语的结构极其复杂，环环相扣。在动词运用方面，各种单证中常用动词非谓语形式。情态动词"shall"的使用频率非常高，以表达法律所规定的义务和权利。翻译时可选用恰当的表达情态的词汇来表达这种意义。

例 2. Insurance to be effected by the seller on behalf of the buyer for 110% of invoice value against all risks, premium to be for buyer's account.

参考译文：由买方委托卖方按发票金额110%代为投一切险，保险费由买方负担。

例 3. The buyer shall open through a bank acceptable to the seller an l/c to reach the seller 30 days before the month of shipment, stipulating that 50% of the invoice value available against clean draft at sight while the remaining 50% on D/P at sight. The full set of the shipping documents of 100% invoice value shall accompany the collection items and shall only be released after full payment of the invoice value, the shipping documents shall be held by the issuing bank at seller's disposal.

参考译文：买方须通过卖方所接受的银行于装运月份前30天开立以卖方为受益人的不可撤销即期信用证，规定50%发票金额凭即期支票支付，其余50%发票金额即期付款交单。100%发票金额的全套装运单据随附托收项下，于买方付清发票的全部金额后交单。如买方不付清全部金额，则装运单据须由开证行掌握凭卖方指示处理。

例 4. All disputes arising in connection with this contract or the execution there of shall be settled amicably through negotiation. In case no settlement can be reached, the case under dispute shall be submitted to China International Economic and Trade Arbitration Commission for arbitration. The arbitral award is final and binding upon both parties. Arbitration fee shall be borne by the losing party.

参考译文：凡有关本合同或执行本合同而发生的一切争执，应通过友好协商解决。如不能解决，则应提请中国国际经济与贸易仲裁委员会进行仲裁。该仲裁委员会做出的仲裁是最终的，甲乙双方均受其约束，费用由败诉一方承担。

Discussion: Talk About How to Do the Task Well

进行商务单证的翻译时，要注意三个对等，即：语义对等、语境对等和风格对等。

1. 语义对等

语义对等，顾名思义，就是指在翻译过程中用合理、准确的词语将单证译成汉语，以达到准确、无误地传达单证信息的功能，即信息对等的功能。然而，英语与汉语又是两种完全不同的语言，英语一词多义、一词多性，灵活丰富，因此，要准确翻译单证，译者就必须准确选择一个最契合的词义。如何才能达到语义的完全对等呢？在处理多义词时，我们要结合语境选出一个适当的意思。

例 5. We shall credit you... account with... bank on receipt of your authenticated wire confirming all the terms and conditions of the credit have been complied with (L/C Terms).

此句中有两个 credit，经分析可知：第一个 credit 是动词"贷记……"的意思，第二个 credit 是名词，代指信用证。

参考译文：一旦收到你行的加押电报，且与信用证全部条款相符，我行将贷记你行在某某银行的某某账户。

另外，词组在单证中也有特殊的含义。

例 6. The certificate of inspection would be issued and signed by authorized applicant of L/C before shipment of cargo, whose signature is subject to our final confirmation.

参考译文：发货前由申请人授权开立并签署的检验证书，其签字须待我方最终确认。

这是一条软条款，意在发生对进口人不利的情况时，限制这份信用证的实际生效。这里的 subject to 意为"有待于，须经……的，以……为条件"之意，而不是意为"受……约束，受……管制"。

当然，我们在单证中还会碰到特殊的词——缩略语，如 FOB（离岸价）、CIF（到岸价）、CFR（成本加运费价）、FCA（货交承运人），这些缩略语只有在商务英语语境中才有意义。

2. 语境对等

同一个词在不同的语境下,翻译出来的意思显然是不尽相同的。那么商务单证作为一种被普遍接受的、用于进出口业务的保证文件,已经形成了其特有的语言特点,翻译中要力求做到语境、信息对等,从而避免某些词义的细小变化而带来的巨大损失。单证具有法律文书的语言特色,用词严谨、正规、严肃、专业性强,是对不熟悉的贸易双方之间交易的一种保障。所以,我们在翻译商务单证时,也必须力求表达出它严谨、正规、严肃、专业性强的一面,而不能对其原文直译,以致失去商务单证本身的特点。翻译商务单证,就必须熟悉它背后所隐藏的各种小语境(例如具体情景语境、文化语境和个人语境等),深入体会在当前的语境中它的每句话,甚至每个单词,这样才能使译文与原文所传达的信息对等,以维护各方利益。

1) 具体情景语境

下面A、B两组句子中,同一词在不同语境下具有不同含义。

例7.

A1:The full set of shipping documents shall accompany the collection (托收) draft and only be released after full payment of the invoice value.

A2:Freight-collected. (运费到付)

B1:This documentary credit is subject to (受……约束) the Uniform Customs and Practice for Documentary Credits (1993Revision) International Chamber of Commerce (publication No.500).

B2:This Proforma Invoice is subject to (有待于,须经……) our last approval.

2) 文化语境

在商务单证翻译过程中要做到文化信息的对等,就要求译者对双方的文化有比较好的理解。这一点在单证中有关产品描述的翻译中有着重要体现,例如"twin beds""Queen-size/ King-size bed"等字眼,如果没有对英语文化的较好了解,我们很难把它们翻译成"一对单人床""特大号床";即使简单的"pillow"一词,在美语中很多时候指的是"靠垫",而非"枕头"。所以,单证翻译还要充分考虑文化因素,否则不但达不到对等的效果,还会译得不伦不类,甚至贻笑大方。

3) 个人用语习惯

因为译者本身的能力和思维存在差异,所以难免会产生以个人经历及所学知识为依据的翻译,从而使意思与原文不符。因此,作为译者要尽量避免这样的情况,尽力使译文传达"地道、准确"的源语信息。

3. 风格对等

商务英语最大的特点是格式化和规范化,它具有术语性、专业性、简约性等特点,翻译成汉语时也应保留这些特点。

1) 使用术语体现正式和专业性

单证英语拥有数量可观的专业词汇，带有很强的专业性，并且词义专一，例如：stock（存货）、repeat order（重复订购）、confirmed L/C（保兑信用证）。

2) 用短语表达，体现简洁

在商务口语和书面语中，尽量避免拖沓、烦琐的语言，因而常常出现非完整句的表现形式，例如 Partial Shipments Allowed（允许分批装运）；另外，还要注意分词的使用，例如 loading on Board（装船）。

3) 单证英语在句式上的两个主要特点

(1) 多用被动语态体现正式和命令语气。

例 8. The documents must be presented for negotiation within 15 days after the date of the transport document but within the validity of the credit.

参考译文：在单证有效期内，必须在装运单据签单后 15 天之内交单议付。

(2) 使用定语从句体现简洁正式。

例 9. As per attached sheets which form an integrate part of this L/C.

参考译文：货物如附页，此附页构成本信用证不可分割的一部分。

Follow-up: Do It Yourself

Translate the following sentences and paragraphs into English or Chinese

(1) The letter of credit is the written promise of a bank undertaken on behalf of a buyer to pay the seller the amount specified in the credit. That means if the documents presented by beneficiary constitute a complying presentation, the issuing bank must be in the first place to make payment to the beneficiary instead of the buyer.

(2) A bill of lading is a title document in the sense that the legal owner of the bill of lading is the legal owner of the goods. The carrier will only release the goods against surrendering the original bill of lading. When a bill of lading is transferred, the ownership over the goods has also been transferred.

(3) It is evident that documents which stand for the goods, certify performance of the traders, become the basis for making payment in international trade payment. Meanwhile, it is essential for the traders to make sure that documents are exactly in conformity with the terms and conditions of L/C.

(4) 收到单证严格相符的单据后，我们（开证行）授权贵行向我总行索偿，5 个工作日起息，SWIFT 通知我行，费用由贵方承担。

(5) 因办各项手续的有关单证送交不及时、不完备或者不正确，使承运人的利益受到损害的，托运人应当负赔偿责任。

(6) 签署发票一式五份，证明货物是根据 2004 年 3 月 11 日编号为 12345 的合同发货的，并注明信用证号码和布鲁塞尔税则分类号码，显示正本发票和一份副本随附原套单证。

Homework: Practice Makes Perfect

Translate the following document into Chinese

CATHAY BANK
777 NORTH BROADWAY, NEW YORK, USA
PHONE 625-4700 / CABLE ADDRESS: CATHBANC

☐ CONFIRMATION OF TELEX/ CABLE PRE-ADVISED   DATE: MAY 5, 1996   TELEX NO. 4720688 ITT

IRREVOCABLE DOCUMENTARY CREDIT	CREDIT NUMBER 96/0500-FTC	ADVISING BANK'S REF. NO.

ADVISING BANK:
SHANGHAI A J FINANCE CORPORATION
59 HONGKONG ROAD   SHANGHAI 200002, CHINA

APPLICANT:
CATHAY PACIFIC TRADING CO.
1-18 ITHACA STREET ELMHURST   NEW YORK 11373

BENEFICIARY:
LEAD IMPORT & EXPORT CORPORATION
HENGTONG ROAD 144   SHANGHAI, CHINA

AMOUNT:
USD 1 17,227.52   (US DOLLARS FIFTY THREE THOUSAND FIVE HUNDRED AND SEVENTY NINE   ONLY)

EXPIRY DATE: JUNE 15TH, 1996   **FOR NEGOTIATION IN CHINA**

GENTLEMEN:
WE HEREBY OPEN OUR IRREVOCABLE LETTER OF CREDIT IN YOU FAVOR WHICH IS AVAILABLE BY YOUR DRAFT AT 45 DAYS' SIGHT FOR FULL INVOICE VALUE ON US ACCOMPANIED BY THE FOLLOWING DOCUMENTS:
+ SIGNED COMMERCIAL INVOICE AND 3 COPIES
+ PACKING LIST AND 3 COPIES, SHOWING THE INDIVIDUAL WEIGHT AND MEASUREMENT OF EACH ITEM.
+ ORIGINAL CERTIFICATE OF ORIGIN AND 3 COPIES ISSUED BY THE CHAMBER OF COMMERCE.
+ FULL SET CLEAN ON BOARD OCEAN BILLS OF LADING SHOWING FREIGHT PREPAID CONSIGNED TO ORDER OF CATHAY BANK 777 N. BROADWAY, NEW YORK, USA NOTIFY APPLICANT
+ INSURANCE POLICY OR CERTIFICATE FOR 130 PERCENT OF INVOICE VALUE COVERING: RISK (A) AS PER I.C.C. DATED 1/1/1982.
+ BENEFICIARY'S CERTIFICATE IN DUPLICATE CERTIFYING THAT EACH PIECE HAS BEEN PRINTED WITH "MADE IN CHINA"

COVERING SHIPMENT OF:
288 CARTONS CHAMPION BRAND BASKETBALL (SO252 SIZE 5 96 CARTONS, SO262 SIZE 7 96 CARTONS, KS241 S SIZE 7 99 CARTONS) IN ACCORDANCE WITH SALES CONFIRMATION 96S-0421 DATED APRIL 21, 1996.

☒ FOB/ ☐ CFR/ ☒ CIFC3 / ☐ FAS NEW YORK, USA

SHIPMENT FROM SHANGHAI	TO NEW YORK, USA	LATEST JUNE 30, 1996	PARTIAL SHIPMENTS PROHIBITED	TRANSSHIPMENT PROHIBITED

DRAFTS TO BE PRESENTED FOR NEGOTIATION WITHIN 15 DAYS AFTER SHIPMENT, BUT WITHIN VALIDITY OF CREDIT.
ALL DOCUMENTS TO BE FORWARDED IN ONE COVER, BY AIRMAIL, UNLESS OTHERWISE STATED UNDER SPECIAL INSTRUCTIONS.
SPECIAL INSTRUCTIONS: ALL BANKING CHARGES OUTSIDE THE UNITED STATES ARE FOR ACCOUNT OF BENEFICIARY
+ ALL GOODS MUST BE SHIPPED IN ONE 20' CY TO CY CONTAINER AND B/L SHOWING THE SAME
+ THE VALUE OF FREIGHT PREPAID HAVE TO SHOW ON BILLS OF LADING
+ DOCUMENTS WHICH FAIL TO COMPLY WITH THE TERMS AND CONDITIONS IN THE LETTER OF CREDIT SUBJECT TO A SPECIAL DISCREPANCY HANDLING FEE OF US$35.00 TO BE DEDUCTED FROM ANY PROCEEDS.

DRAFT MUST BE MARKED AS BEING DRAWN UNDER THIS CREDIT AND BEAR ITS NUMBER; THE AMOUNTS ARE TO BE ENDORSED ON THE REVERSE HEREOF BY THE NEGOTIATING BANK.

WE HEREBY AGREE WITH THE DRAWERS, ENDORSERS AND BONA FIDE HOLDER THAT ALL DRAFTS DRAWN UNDER AND IN COMPLIANCE WITH THE TERMS OF THIS CREDIT SHALL BE DULY HONORED UPON PRESENTATION AT THE OFFICE OF CATHAY BANK, NEW YORK, USA.

THIS CREDIT IS SUBJECT TO THE UNIFORM CUSTOMS AND PRACTICE FOR DOCUMENTARY CREDITS(1993 REVISION) BY THE INTERNATIONAL CHAMBER OF COMMERCE PUBLICATION NO. 500.

Yours Very Truly,

_____   _____
AUTHORIZED SIGNATURE   AUTHORIZED SIGNATURE

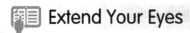 **Extend Your Eyes**

中英文对照单证常用表达

1. 发票 (Invoice) 常用表达

Invoice(INV.)	发票
Contract(CNT.)	合同
Unit Price	单价
Description Goods	货物描述
Amount(AMT)	总额
Model	规格、型号
Total Amount	总价
Size	尺寸
Packages (PKGS)	件数
Quantity	数量
Gross Weight(G.W.)	毛重
Made in / Origin	原产国
Net Weight(N.W.)	净重
Port of Loading(P.O.L.)	装货港
Insurance	保险
Destination Country	目的国
Extras	杂费
Port of Destination(P.O.D.)	指运港 / 目的港
Commission	佣金
Freight	运费
Rebate/allowance/Discount	折扣
in duplicate	一式两份
in triplicate	一式三份
in quadruplicate	一式四份
in quintuplicate	一式五份
in sextuplicate	一式六份
in septuplicate	一式七份
in octuplicate	一式八份
in nonuplicate	一式九份
in decuplicate	一式十份

2. 装箱单 (Packing List) 与重量单常用表达

Packing List	装箱单
Packages (PKGS)	件数
Document Attached (DOC.ATT.)	所附单证
Documents(DOC(S))	单证

packing list detailing the complete inner packing specification and contents of each package
载明每件货物之内部包装的规格和内容的装箱单

Packing List Detailing...	详注……的装箱单
Packing List Showing in Detail...	注明……细节的装箱单
Weight List	重量单
Weight Notes	磅码单(重量单)
Detailed Weight list	明细重量单
Weight and Measurement List	重量和尺码单

3. 提单 (Bill of lading) 常用表达

Bill of loading(B/L)	提单
Carrier	承运人
Shipper	托运人
Consignee	收货人
Notify Party	被通知人
Air Way Bill(A.W.B.)	空运提单
Port of Call(P.O.C)	停靠港
Air Freight Bill(A.F.B.)	空运提单
Port of Discharge(P.O.D)	卸货港
Port of Loading(P.O.L)	装货港
Ocean Vessel Voy. No.	船名及航次
Port of Transfer	转运港
Port of Arrival(P.A)	到达港
Via	经过
Port of Destination(P.O.D.)	目的港
in transit to	转运到

full set shipping (company's) clean on board bill(s) of lading marked "Freight Prepaid" to order of shipper endorsed to... Bank, notifying buyers 全套货物装船后，提单应注明"运费付讫"，根据托运人指示，背书给……银行，通知买方

bills of lading made out in negotiable form 做成可议付形式的提单

clean shipped on board ocean bills of lading to order and endorsed in blank marked "Freight Prepaid" notify: importer (openers, accountee) 清洁已装船的提单空白抬头并空白背书，注明"运费付讫"，通知进口人（开证人）

full set of clean "on board" bills of lading/cargo receipt made out to our order/to order and endorsed in blank notify buyers M/S... Co. calling for shipment from China to Hamburg marked "Freight prepaid" / "Freight Payable at Destination" 全套清洁"已装船"提单/货运收据做成以我（行）为抬头/空白抬头，空白背书，通知买方……公司，要求货物自中国运往汉堡，注明"运费付讫"/"运费在目的港付"

bills of lading issued in the name of... 提单以……为抬头

bills of lading must be dated not before the date of this credit and not later than Aug. 15, 1977 提单日期不得早于本证的日期，也不得迟于 1977 年 8 月 15 日

bill of lading marked notify: buyer, "Freight Prepaid" "Liner terms" "received for shipment" B/L not acceptable 提单注明通知买方，"运费预付"按"班轮条件"，"备运提单"不接受

non-negotiable copy of bills of lading 不可议付的提单副本

4. 包装量词常用表达

case, C	箱	plastic bag	塑料袋
carton, Ctn.	纸箱	5-ply paper bag	五层纸袋
cardboard	纸板箱	polythelene net	尼龙绳网袋
wooden case	木箱	zippered bag	拉链袋
three-plywood case	三夹板箱	cask	桶（小桶）
box, Bx.	盒	drum	圆桶
wooden box	木盒	keg	小圆桶
iron box	铁盒	barrel	琵琶桶
plastic transparency box	塑料透明盒	wooden cask	木桶
bag(sack)	袋	plastic drum	塑料桶
jute bag gunny bag	麻袋	iron drum	铁桶
bale	包	pallet	托盘
packet	小包	pair	双
bottle	瓶	dozen	打
flask	长颈瓶	ream	令
jar	罐（坛子）	gross	罗
vial	药水瓶	bolt(piece)	匹

carboy	大玻璃瓶	yard	码
can	罐	roll	卷
tin	听	block	块
basket	篮（篓、筐）	bundle	捆
pannier	盖篮	unit	辆
container	集装箱	in nude	裸装
nude with iron wire bundle	铁丝捆裸装	in bulk	散装

5. 度量衡常用表达

克	gram, g.	码	yard, yd.
千克	kilogram, kg.	英尺	foot, ft.
公担	quintal, q.	英寸	inch, in.
公吨	metric ton, m.t.	平方米	square metre, sq.m.
长吨	long ton, l.t.	平方英尺	square foot, sq.ft.
短吨	short ton, sh.t.	平方码	square yard, sq.yd.
英担	hundredweight, cwt.	立方米	cubic metre, cu.m.
美担	hundredweight, cwt.	立方英尺	cubic foot, cu.ft.
磅	pound, lb.	升	litre, l.
两（常衡）	ounce, oz.	毫升	millilitre, mL.
两（金衡）	ounce, oz.t	加仑	gallon, gal.
司马担	picul	蒲式耳	bushel, bu.
米	metre, m.	克拉	carat, car.
千米	kilometre, km.	马力	horse power, h.p.
厘米	centimetre, cm.	千瓦	kilowatt, kw.
毫米	milimetre, mm.	公吨度	Metric ton unit, m.t.u.

6. 汇票 Draft(Bill of Exchange) 常用表达

Available By Drafts At Sight	凭即期汇票付款
Draft(s) To Be Drawn at 30 Days Sight	开立 30 天的期票
Sight Drafts	即期汇票
Time Drafts	远期汇票

7. 保险单（或凭证）Insurance Policy (or Certificate) 常用表达

Free From Particular Average (F.P.A 或 FPA)	平安险
With Particular Average (W.P.A 或 WPA)	水渍险（基本险）
All Risk	一切险（综合险）

Total Loss Only (T.L.O.)	全损险
War Risk	战争险
Cargo(Extended Cover) Clauses	货物（扩展）条款
Additional Risk	附加险
From Warehouse To Warehouse Clauses	仓至仓条款
Theft, Pilferage And Non-Delivery (T.P.N.D.)	盗窃提货不着险
Rain Fresh Water Damage	淡水雨淋险
Risk Of Shortage	短量险
Risk Of Contamination	沾污险
Risk Of Leakage	渗漏险
Risk Of Clashing & Breakage	碰损破碎险
Risk Of Odour	串味险
Damage Caused By Sweating And/Or Heating	受潮受热险
Hook Damage	钩损险
Loss And/Or Damage Caused By Breakage Of Packing	包装破裂险
Risk Of Rusting	锈损险
Risk Of Mould	发霉险
Strike, Riots And Civil Commotion (S.R.C.C.)	罢工、暴动、民变险
Risk Of Spontaneous Combustion	自燃险
Deterioration Risk	腐烂变质险
Inherent Vice Risk	内在缺陷险
Risk Of Natural Loss Or Normal Loss	途耗或自然损耗险
Special Additional Risk	特别附加险
Failure To Delivery	交货不到险
Import Duty	进口关税险
On Deck	舱面险
Rejection	拒收险
Aflatoxin	黄曲霉素险
Fire Risk Extension Clause-For Storage Of Cargo At Destination Hongkong, including Kowloon, or Macao	出口货物到香港（包括九龙在内）或澳门存仓火险责任扩展条款
Survey In Customs Risk	海关检验险
Survey At Jetty Risk	码头检验险
Institute War Risk	协会战争险
Overland Transportation Risks	陆运险

Overland Transportation All Risks	陆运综合险
Air Transportation Risk	航空运输险
Air Transportation All Risk	航空运输综合险
Air Transportation War Risk	航空运输战争险
Parcel Post Risk	邮包险
Parcel Post All Risk	邮包综合险
Parcel Post War Risk	邮包战争险
Investment Insurance(Political Risks)	投资保险（政治风险）
Property Insurance	财产保险
Erection All Risks	安装工程一切险
Contractors All Risks	建筑工程一切险

8. 产地证 (Certificate of Origin) 常用表达

Stating	证明
Evidencing	列明
Specifying	说明
Indicating	表明
Declaration Of	声明
Certificate Of Chinese Origin	中国产地证明书
Certificate Of Origin Shipment Of Goods Of Origin Prohibited	
产地证，不允许装运……的产品	
Declaration Of Origin	产地证明书（产地声明）
Certificate Of Origin Separated	单独出具的产地证
Certificate Of Origin "Form A"	"格式 A"产地证明书
Generalized System Of Preference	
Certificate Of Origin Form "A"	普惠制格式"A"产地证明书

9. 检验证书 (Inspection Certificate) 常用表达

Certificate Of Weight	重量证明书
Certificate Of Inspection certifying quality & quantity in triplicate issued by CIBC.	
由中国商品检验局出具的品质和数量检验证明书一式三份	
Phytosanitary Inspection Certificate	植物检疫证明书
Plant Quarantine Certificate	植物检疫证明书
Fumigation Certificate	熏蒸证明书
Certificate Stating That The Goods Are Free From Live Weevil	
无活虫证明书（熏蒸除虫证明书）	

Sanitary Certificate	卫生证书
Health Certificate	卫生（健康）证书
Analysis Certificate(通常为 Certificate of Analysis)	分析（化验）证书
Tank Inspection Certificate	油仓检验证明书
Record Of Ullage And Oil Temperature	空距及油温记录单
Certificate Of Aflatoxin Negative	黄曲霉素检验证书
Non-Aflatoxin Certificate	无黄曲霉素证明书
Survey Report On Weight Issued By CIBC.	中国商品检验局签发之重量检验证明书
Inspection Certificate	检验证书
Inspection And Testing Certificate Issued By CIBC.	中国商品检验局签发之检验证明书

Business Contract

Warm-up: Have a Try

Try to translate the following contract into Chinese

Sales Contract

No. :
Signed at:
Date:
Seller:
Address
Tel:
Fax:

E-mail:
Buyer:
Address:
Tel:
Fax:
E-mail:

The undersigned Seller and Buyer have agreed to close the following transactions according to the terms and conditions set forth as below.

1. Name, Specifications and Quality of Commodity:

2. Quantity:

3. Unit Price and Terms of Delivery:

 (The terms FOB, CFR, or CIF shall be subject to the International Rules for the Interpretation of Trade Terms (INCOTERMS 2000) provided by International Chamber of Commerce (ICC) unless otherwise stipulated herein.)

4. Total Amount:

5. More or Less:_____%.

6. Time of Shipment:

Within _____ days after receipt of L/C allowing transhipment and partial shipment.

7. Terms of Payment:

By Confirmed, Irrevocable, Transferable and Divisible L/C to be available by sight draft to reach the Seller before _____ and to remain valid for negotiation in China until _____ after the Time of Shipment. The L/C must specify that transshipment and partial shipments are allowed.

The Buyer shall establish a Letter of Credit before the above-stipulated time, failing which, the Seller shall have the right to rescind this Contract upon the arrival of the notice at Buyer, or to accept whole or part of this Contract non-fulfilled by the Buyer, or to lodge a claim for the direct losses sustained, if any.

8. Packing:

9. Insurance:

Covering_____Risks for_____110% of invoice value to be effected by the _____.

10. Quality/Quantity discrepancy:

In case of quality discrepancy, claim should be filed by the Buyer within 30 days after the arrival of the goods at port of destination; while for quantity discrepancy, claim should be filed by the Buyer within 15 days after the arrival of the goods at port of destination. It is understood that the Seller shall not be liable for any discrepancy of the goods shipped due to causes for which the Insurance Company, Shipping Company, other Transportation Organization /or Post Office are liable.

11. The Seller shall not be held responsible for failure or delay in delivery of the entire lot or a portion of the goods under this Sales Contract in consequence of any Force Majeure incidents which might occur. Force Majeure as referred to in this contract means unforeseeable, unavoidable and insurmountable objective conditions.

12. Dispute Resolution:

Any dispute arising from or in connection with this Contract shall be submitted to China International Economic and Trade Arbitration Commission for arbitration which shall be tried in Nanjing and conducted in accordance with the Commission's arbitration rules in effect at the time of applying for arbitration. The arbitral award is final and binding upon both parties.

13. Notices：

All notice shall be written in _____ and served to both parties by fax/e-mail /courier according to the following addresses. If any changes of the addresses occur, one party shall inform the other party of the change of address within _____ days after the change.

14. This Contract is executed in two counterparts each in Chinese and English, each of which shall be deemed equally authentic. This Contract is in _____ copies effective since being signed/sealed by both parties.

The Seller: The Buyer:

Background: Learn Something About Business Contract

英文中的合同contract一词定义如下：A contract is a promise enforceable at law. The promise may be to do something or to refrain from doing something.（合同是具有法律约束力的承诺，该承诺可以是保证做某事或保证不做某事）(The New Encyclopaedia Britannica, 15th edition, published by Encyclopaedia Briannica, Inc. 1977, Vol. 5, p124)

1. 商务合同的格式

国际商务合同种类繁多，标的各异，但就其结构来说，一般由三个部分组成：前言或首部(Head)、正文或主体(Body)、结尾或尾部(End)。

1) 前言一般包括以下几点内容

(1) 合同名称。

合同一般写作Contract，如果是正本则在右上方注明Original，副本则注明Copy。比如购买合同Purchase Contract，销售合同Sale Contract，租赁合同Lease

Contract，运输合同 Shipping Contract。

(2) 合同编号。

通常合同的编号是由年份、公司代码及部门代号等构成的。比如 03CMEC、DA006，这个编号中 03 指 2003 年；CMEC 是 China Machinery Export Company(中国机械出口公司)的缩写；DA 是 Department A (A 部)；006 指第六份文件。即中国机械出口公司 A 部 2003 年第六份合同。

(3) 签约日期。

(4) 签约地点。

(5) 买卖双方的名称、地址和联系方式。

(6) 套语。

前言的语言呈现格式化的特点，中英文都有其对应的句子模式，比如：This contract is signed by and between the Buyer and the Seller according to the terms and conditions stipulated below.（这份合同是买卖双方之间根据以下条款而签订的。）

英汉合同前言范例如下。

例 1. This contract is made this 29th day of March, 2008 in Shanghai, China by and between ABC Corporation, China (hereinafter referred to as "Seller"), a _____ Corporation having its principal office in Shanghai, China who agrees to sell, and XYZ Corporation (hereinafter referred to as "Buyer"), a _____ Corporation having its principal office in New York, N.Y., USA, who agrees to buy the following goods on the terms and conditions as below.

参考译文：本合同由中国 ABC 公司，_____ 总公司设于上海(以下简称卖方)与美国 XYZ 公司，_____ 总公司设于美国纽约州纽约市(以下简称买方)于 2008 年 3 月 29 日订立于中国上海，双方同意按下列条件买卖下列货物。

2) 正文

正文再现合同的主要内容，通常包括以下几个方面。

一是签订合同的依据和目的；

二是合同内容的基本条款，包括标的、数量、质量、规格、发货装货方式、运输方式、交接货地点、验收办法、价款、酬金及结算方式和时间等；

三是合同当事人的经济责任或法律责任；

四是合同的有效期限；

五是合同份数及保存；

六是合同附件，包括图纸、材料项目、表格、担保书、有关协议及实物样品等。附件是合同的组成部分，与合同具有同等法律效力。

3) 结尾

结尾是合同的签署。要写明签订合同的双方或多方单位全称、法人代表姓名与委托代理人姓名，并加盖公章，法人代表及委托代理人亦签名盖章。同时还要写明单位地址、电话、电挂、开户银行、账号及邮政编码等，并注明签约的年、月、日。结尾也常使用程式化的语言表达。

合同结尾范例如下。

例2. 本合同一式二份，以中英文书就，两种文本具有同等效力，签字后每方各持一份。

参考译文：This contract is made out in two originals in both English and Chinese. Both versions are equally valid. Each Party keeps one original of the two after the signing of the contract.

例 3. Any amendment and/or supplement to this contract shall be valid only after the authorized representatives of both parties have signed written documents, forming integral part of the Contract.

参考译文：本合同的任何修改和/或补充，只有在双方授权的代表在书面文件上签字方有效，并成为本合同不可分割的一部分。

2. 涉外商务合同语言特点

1) 多用正式或法律上的用词

例 4. At the request of Party B, Party A agrees to send technicians to assist Party B to install the equipment.

参考译文：应乙方要求，甲方同意派遣技术人员帮助乙方安装设备。assist 较 help 正式。

例 5. In case one party desires to sell or assign all or part of its investment subscribed, the other party shall have the preemptive right.

参考译文：如一方想出售或转让其投资之全部或部分，另一方有优先购买权。法律用词 assign 较 transfer 正式。

例 6. The term "effective date" means the date on which this Agreement is duly executed by the parties hereto.

参考译文："生效期"指双方合同签字的日子。法律用词 execute 较 sign 正式。

2) 语言力求严谨，明白无误

例 7. The following documents shall be deemed to form and be read and construed as an integral part of this Contract.

参考译文：下列文件应被认为、读作、解释为本合同的组成部分。

例 8. This Contract can only be altered, amended or supplemented in accordance with documents signed and sealed by authorized representatives of both parties.

参考译文：本合同只能按照双方授权代表签名盖章的文件进行修改或增补。

例 9. All activities of ABC Co. shall be governed by the laws, decrees and pertinent rules and regulations of China.

参考译文：ABC公司的一切活动必须受中国的法律、法令和有关规章条例的管辖。

3) 多用现在时，少用将来时，尽管很多条款规定的是合同签订以后的事项

例 10. Licensee may terminate this Contract 90 days after a written notice thereof is sent to Licensor upon the happening of one of the following events.

参考译文：当有下列事件之一发生，被许可人提前90天向许可人发送书面通知后，可以终止合同。

例 11. The patent described in Article 2 is not issued within 30 days from signing this Contract.

参考译文：第二条规定的专利未在签约后30天之内发布。

4) 直接表达方式用得多，间接表达方式用得较少

例 12. This Article does not apply to bondholders who have not been paid in full. (用得少)

参考译文：本条款不适用于尚未全部偿付的债券持有者。

例 13. This Article applies only to bondholders who have been paid in full. (用得多)

参考译文：本条款只适用于已全部偿付的债券持有者。

5) 英文合同多用情态动词"shall"，汉语使用能愿动词"必须""应该"等

"shall"代替"will"或"should"可以加强语气和强制力。合同中，shall 并非单纯表示将来时，而常用来表示法律上可强制执行的义务，具有约束力，宜译为"应""应该""必须"；will 无论是语气还是强制力都要比 shall 弱，宜译为"将""愿""要"；should 通常只用来表示语气较强的假设，比如"万一"。汉语合同中往往使用与英文情态动词相当的能愿动词"(必)须""应(该)"等，根据上述英文的特点，这些能愿动词就往往可以译成 shall，而表示允许、可以等意思的"可(以)""能(够)"往往译成 may。

例 14. This Contract shall become effective upon and from the date on which it is signed.

参考译文：本合同自签字日生效。

例 15. 除第三方应负责的索赔，买方应对卖方发出索赔通知，有权对卖方提出索赔。

参考译文：Except those claims for which the third party is liable, the Buyer shall give a notice of claims to the Seller and shall have the right to lodge claims against the Seller.

6) 汉语多用主动语态，英语多用被动语态

例 16. Party B is hereby appointed by Party A as its exclusive sales agent in Singapore. (不宜)

参考译文：乙方被甲方委托为在新加坡的独家销售代理商。

例 17. Party A hereby appoints Party B as its exclusive sales agent in Singapore. (适宜)

参考译文：甲方委托乙方为在新加坡的独家销售代理商。

例 18. 本文件的交付时间应符合受方工程计划的进度要求。

参考译文：All technical documents shall be handed over in accordance with the requirements of the recipient's schedule for the project.

7) 英文合同尽量使用一个动词，避免使用"动词＋名词＋介词"的同义短语

例 19. Party A shall make an appointment of its representative within 30 days after signing the Contract.

参考译文：甲方应于签约后 30 天内指派其授权代表。

宜用 appoint 代替 make an appointment of。

例 20. Party A will give consideration to Party B's proposal of exclusive agency.

参考译文：甲方愿意考虑乙方独家代理的建议。

宜用 consider 代替 give consideration to。

Discussion: Talk About How to Do the Task Well

鉴于合同的性质特点和功能作用，翻译时，译者应做到译文语言逻辑严谨而完整，措辞准确而规范，并且一定要避免因漏译、错译和误译而带来的纠纷和损失。这也就要求译者除应具备良好的英、汉语水平外，还应具有一定的相关专业的知识和严谨认真的态度。具体说来，在翻译合同时要注意以下几点。

1. 力求措辞清晰、准确，避免歧义

词语是合同构成的基本单位，对词义的正确理解和选择是合同翻译的前提和基础，翻译合同时应结合专业特点和上下文对有关词汇进行推敲、选择和确定。了解与掌握极易混淆的词语的区别是极为重要的。

1) abide by 与 comply with

例 21. 双方都应遵守合同的规定。

参考译文：Both parties shall abide by the contractual stipulations.

例 22. 双方的一切活动都应遵守合同规定。

参考译文：All the activities of both parties shall comply with the contractual stipulations.

abide by 与 comply with 都有"遵守"的意思。但是当主语是"人"时，须用 abide by；当主语是物时，则用 comply with。

2) and/or

例 23. 如果上述货物对船舶和（或）船上其他货物造成任何损害，托运人应负全责。

参考译文：The shipper shall be liable (负责任) for all damage caused by such goods to the ship and/or cargo on board.

and/or 体现两种可能：一是 and 所体现的两种可能同时发生的情况，另一个是 or 所体现的两种情况中只有一种发生，两种可能都是符合合同的规定的。

3) no (not) later than (+date)

例 24. 本合同自签字之日一个月内，即不迟于 12 月 15 日，乙方须将货物装船。

参考译文：Party B shall ship the goods within one month of the date of signing this Contract, i.e. no later than December 15.

no (not) later than (+date) 即"不迟于某月某日"，其中 no later than (+date) 的意思更加肯定，意思为"绝对不能迟于某月某日"。

4) ex 与 per

例 25. 由"维多利亚"轮运走 / 运来 / 承运的最后一批货将于 10 月 1 日抵达伦敦。

参考译文：The last batch per/ex/by S.S. "Victoria" will arrive at London on October 1. (S.S. = Steamship)

源自拉丁语的介词 ex 与 per 有各自不同的含义。英译由某轮船"运来"的货物时用 ex，由某轮船"运走"的货物用 per，而由某轮船"承运"用 by。

5) in 与 after

例 26. 该货于 11 月 10 日由"东风"轮运出，41 天后抵达鹿特丹港。

参考译文：The goods shall be shipped per M.V. "Dong Feng" on November 10 and are due to arrive at Rotterdam in 41 days. (M.V.= motor vessel)

当英译"多少天之后"的时间时，往往是指"多少天之后"的确切的一天，所以必须用介词 in，而不能用 after，因为介词 after 指的是"多少天之后"的不确切的任何一天。

6) on/upon 与 after

例 27. 发票货值须货到付给。

参考译文：The invoice value is to be paid on/upon arrival of the goods.

当英译"……到后，就……"时，用介词 on/upon，而不用 after，因为 after 表示"之后"的时间不明确。

7) by 与 before

例 28. 卖方须在 6 月 15 日前将货交给买方。

参考译文：The vendor shall deliver the goods to the vendee by June 15 (or: before June 16).

"before June 16"说明含 6 月 15 日在内，如果不含 6 月 15 日，就译为 by June 14 或者 before June 15。英语表达"在某月某日之前"，如果包括所写日期时，就用介词 by；如果不包括所写日期，即指到所写日期的前一天为止，就要用介词 before。

8) 有些词汇在合同文本中的意思与其原来的意思有所不同

例 29. In the absence of such statement, the commercial documents will be released only against payment.

参考译文：如无此项说明，商业单据将仅凭付款交付。

句中 release 在此不是"释放、解除"之意，而是"交付（凭证、单据）"的意思；against 也不是"反对"之意，而是"针对"的意思。

例 30. Both Party A and Party B agree that a technology transfer agreement shall be signed between the Joint Venture Company and Party X (or a third party) ...

参考译文：甲、乙双方同意，由合营公司与X方（或第三方）签订技术转让协议……

例句中的 Party A 和 Party B 指合同当事人，在合同中只能翻译成"甲方"和"乙方"。类似的还有如 the Seller(卖方)、the Buyer(买方)；the Transferor(转让方)、the Transferee(受让方)等。

9) 同一个单词在不同的合同文本中所表达的意思也有差别

译者应根据专业特点和搭配关系等方面来判断确定具体的词义。

例 31. If Party A insists on its original quotation, Party B will have to cover its requirements elsewhere.

参考译文：如果甲方坚持原报价，乙方则只能从其他地方购进所需货物。

例 32. Party B shall cover the goods with particular average.

参考译文：乙方将对该货物投保水渍险。

例 33. In order to cover our order, we have arranged with the Bank of China, Dalian Branch, a credit for USD 86,000.

参考译文：为支付我方订货款项，我方已委托中国银行大连分行开立 86,000 美元的信用证。

动词 cover 一般是做"包括、囊括"的意思讲，但在以上三个例句中，不但不能按原来的意思翻译，而且在各句中由于所属领域范围不同，其所表达的意思也是不同的，在例 1 句、例 2 句、例 3 句中分别表示"购进货物""投保险""偿付"的意思。

2. 注意规范组句

翻译合同时，应注意分析句子结构，厘清思路，规范组句，以实现顺畅而清晰的表达。

例 34. We hereby certify to the best of our knowledge that the foregoing statement is true and correct and all available information and data have been supplied herein, and that we agree to provide documentary proof upon your request.

参考译文：我们保证就我们了解的上述声明真实无误，并提供了全部现有的资料和数据，应贵方要求，我们同意出具证明文件。

这个句子由 that 引导的两个并列宾语从句为 certify 的宾语。翻译时应厘清思路，正确理解，做到清楚表达。

3. 了解相关的专业知识

在合同文本的翻译中，相关的专业知识也是正确理解和表达的基础，因此译者熟悉和了解相关的专业知识，特别是一些习惯表达和专业术语，显得非常重要，因为在合同翻译中出现的问题大多与缺乏专业知识有关。

例 35. The lead Partner submits a copy of the short term cash flow which covers the period September 1997 to February 1998. Mr. Marchesini highlights the main items of the cash flow which are the Endowment fund and the Advance Payment as far as the Receipt is concerned and the down payment for TBMs and plants, purchase of fixed assets and the advance payment to subcontractors for the Expenditures.

这段文字中有一些财经术语，即 cash flow（资金流动、现金流量）、endowment fund（留本基金、捐赠基金）、advance payment（预付款）、receipt（收款、收入）、down payment（分期付款的定金）、fixed asset（固定资产）、expenditure（支出款、消费额）。这些财经术语是翻译本段文字的关键，如果不熟悉，就会出现翻译错误。

4. 有关金额的数字（特别是货款总金额）一律用汉语的大写形式表达

例 36. 乙方（聘方）须每月付给（甲方）受聘方 500 美元（大写：伍佰美元整）。

参考译文：Party A shall pay Party B a monthly salary of $500 (SAY FIVE HUNDRED US DOLLARS ONLY)。

"大写"可以译为：word number，或者 say；而"整"译作 only。且金额数字必须紧靠货币符号，不留空格，如应该写作：Can$891,568(Can$ 是指加拿大元)，而不能写成：Can$ 891, 568。

5. 有关价格、品质、交货的方式和时间地点、违约责任等方面的词句要准确、详细

例 37. 自 9 月 20 日起，甲方已无权接受任何订单或收据。

参考译文：Party A shall be unauthorized to accept any orders or to collect any account on and after September 20.

例 38. 我公司的条件是，3 个月内，即不得晚于 5 月 1 日，支付现金。

参考译文：Our terms are cash within three months, i.e., on or before May 1.

6. 有关指称应保持一致

例如，在合同或者协议中如果将"销售方(the Seller)"定义为"甲方(Party A)"，在下文中就应该一直使用"甲方(Party A)"的指称方式，避免一会儿使用"销售方(the Seller)"，一会儿使用"甲方(Party A)"。

7. 古体词的翻译

尽管古体词在现代英语口语和一般书面语中极少使用，但在商务合同等法律文体

中，古体词却大量出现，充分体现出其庄重严肃的文体风格。这些古体词主要为 here, there, where 等前缀加上 after, by, in, of, on, to, under, upon, with 等词构成。举例如下。

hereafter = after this time 今后

hereby = by means/reason of this 特此

herein = in this 此中，于此

hereinafter = later in this contract 在下文

thereafter = afterwards 此后，后来

thereby = by that means 因此，由此，在那方面

therein = from that 在那里，在那点上

thereinafter = later in the same contract 以下，在下文

whereby = by what, by which 由是，凭那个

wherein = in what, in which 在哪里，在哪点上

8. 合同中特殊用语的翻译

1) WHEREAS 鉴于

正式而重要的合同，尤其是英美法系的合同，多用它在前文中引出签约背景和目的，起连词作用。

例 39. WHEREAS the Employer is desirous that manpower can be rendered available for the construction of High-Rise Residential Complex in Baghdad, Iraq.

参考译文：鉴于雇主欲请劳动力建造伊拉克巴格达的高层住宅综合大楼。

例 40. WHEREAS the Contractor is desirous to provide the manpower for the Works.

参考译文：鉴于承包人想为此工程提供劳动力。

2) WITNESS 证明

在合同前文中常用作首句的谓语动词。

例 41. This Agreement, made by ...
WITNESSES
WHEREAS..., it is agreed as follows.

参考译文：
本协议由……签订
证明：鉴于……特此达成协议如下。

3) IN WITNESS WHEREOF 作为所协议事项的证据

该短语常用于合同的结尾条款。

例 42. IN WITNESS WHEREOF, the parties have executed this Contract in duplicate by their duly authorized representatives on the date first above written.

参考译文：作为所协议事项的证据，双方授权代表于上面首次写明的日期正式签

订本协议一式两份。

4) IN CONSIDERATION OF 以……为约因/报酬

约因是英美法系的合同有效成立要件之一，没有则合同不能依法强制履行。但是，大陆法系的合同则无此规定。

例 43. Now therefore, in consideration of the premises and the covenants herein, contained, the parties hereto agree as follows.

参考译文：兹以上述各点和契约所载条款为约因，订约双方协议如下。

例 44. In consideration of the payment to be made by Party A to Party B, Party B hereby covenants with Party A to complete the building in conformity with the provisions of the Contract.

参考译文：乙方特此立约向甲方保证按合同规定完成工程建设，以取得甲方所付的报酬。

5) NOW, THEREFORE 兹特

此短语用于 WHEREAS 条款之后引出具体协议事项的常用开头语，并与其后的 hereby 结合。如果无 WHEREAS 条款，则本短语可省略。

例 45. NOW, THEREFORE, it's hereby agreed and understood as follows.

参考译文：兹特协议和谅解如下。

例 46. NOW THESE PRESENTS WITNESS.

兹特立约为据。

本句话也是用于 WHEREAS 条款之后引出具体协议事项。

6) PRESENTS = the present writings 是主语，WITNESS 是谓语

例 47. NOW THESE PRESENTS WITNESS that it is hereby agreed between the parties hereto as follows.

参考译文：兹特立约为据，并由订约双方协议如下。

7) IN THE PRESENCE OF 见证人

本短语只在有见证人时使用。在订约双方当事人签名的下方由见证人签名作证，一般是相关的律师 (Attorney) 或公证处 (Notary Public)。

例 48. IN THE PRESENCE OF the parties hereto have hereunder set their respective hands and seals.

参考译文：作为协议事项的证据，订约双方各自签名盖章如下。

Follow-up: Do It Yourself

Translate the following sentences into Chinese or English

(1) The Contractor shall be responsible for the true and proper setting-out of the Works in relation to original points, lines and levels of reference given by the Engineer in writing

and for the correctness, subject as above-mentioned, of the position, levels, dimensions and alignment of all parts of the Works and for the provision of all necessary instruments, appliances and labor in connection therewith.

(2) Upon successful completion of the tests the Purchaser shall sign a Plant Acceptance Certificate evidencing such completion and listing any agreed Deficiencies to be corrected by CAE within such period as may be agreed with the Purchaser.

(3) The Purchaser shall be able at all times to account for all copies of the Proprietary Software which are required to be made to permit its efficient use in its intended function.

(4) 双方本着平等互利的原则，经友好协商，依照有关法律，同意按照本合同的条款，建立经销关系。

(5) 经销商储存并运输经销产品的设施应保证经销产品处于良好状态，并应符合供应商关于产品储存和运输条件的合理要求。

Homework: Practice Makes Perfect

1. Translate the following contract into Chinese

Contract of Business

No. 005327

Date: May 18, 2002

Buyers: Peter Company Limited (Co. Ltd.)

       18 Lincoln Street,

       London, U.K.

Sellers: John Hayde, Inc.

       20 Maiden Lane,

       New York, N. Y. , U. S. A.

This Contract is made by and between the Buyers and the Sellers; whereby the Buyers agree to buy and the Sellers agree to sell the under-mentioned goods on the terms and conditions stated below:

    Name of Commodity- Printed Cotton Sheeting

    Specifications: No. 127

               30's × 30's, 68 × 60

               35.36 inch in width

               40 yards per piece

    Quality: As per sample submitted by Peter Company Limited (Co. Ltd.) on March 9,

2002.

　　　　Quantity: 40,000 yards

　　　　Price: $ 6.6 per yard CIF London

　　　　Amount: $264,000.00

　　　　Shipment: Shipment with the first ten-day period of June 2002. Partial shipments are not allowed.

　　　　Destination: London

　　　　Terms of payment: In order to cover the order, a credit for 100% value of goods will be arranged with the Bank of London against the commercial bills.

　　　　This Contract is made in duplicate and each party shall keep one copy. This Contract shall come into force after the signature by the authorized representatives of both parties.

　　　　Buyers: Peter Company Limited (Co. Ltd.)　Sellers: John Hayde, Inc.

　　　　Manager: (signature)　　　　　　　　　　　Manager: (signature)

2. Translate the following contract into English

售货合同

　　合同编号：

　　签订地点：

　　签订日期：

　　买方：

　　卖方：

　　双方同意按下列条款由买方出售下列商品：

(1) 商品名称、规格及包装	(2) 数量　(3) 单价　(4) 总值
	（装运数量允许有 ____ %的增减）

　　(5) 装运期限：

　　(6) 装运口岸：

　　(7) 目的口岸：

　　(8) 保险；由 _____ 方负责，按本合同总值110%投保 _____ 险。

　　(9) 付款：凭保兑的、不可撤销的、可转让的、可分割的即期有电报套汇条款/见票/出票 _____ 天期付款信用证，信用证以 _____ 为受益人并允许分批装运和转船。该信用证必须在 _____ 前开到卖方，信用证的有效期应为上述装船期后第15天，在中国 _____ 到期，否则卖方有权取消本售货合约，不另行通知，并保留因此而发生的一切损失的索赔权。

(10) 商品检验：以中国 _____ 所签发的品质/数量/重量/包装/卫生检验合格证书作为卖方的交货依据。

(11) 装运唛头：

(12) 其他条款。

① 异议：品质异议须于货到目的口岸之日起 30 天内提出，数量异议须于货到目的口岸之日起 15 天内提出，但均须提供经卖方同意的公证行的检验证明。如责任属于卖方者，卖方于收到异议 20 天内答复买方并提出处理意见。

② 信用证内应明确规定卖方有权可多装或少装所注明的百分数，并按实际装运数量议付 (信用证之金额按本售货合约金额增加相应的百分数)。

③ 信用证内容须严格符合本售货合约的规定，否则修改信用证的费用由买方负担，卖方并不承担因修改信用证而延误装运的责任，并保留因此而发生的一切损失的索赔权。

④ 除经约定保险归买方投保者外，由卖方向中国的保险公司投保。如买方需增加保险额及/或需加保其他险，可于装船前提出，经卖方同意后代为投保，其费用由买方负担。

⑤ 因人力不可抗拒事故使卖方不能在本售货合约规定期限内交货或不能交货，卖方不负责任，但是卖方必须立即以电报通知买方。如果买方提出要求，卖方应以挂号函向买方提供由中国国际贸易促进委员会或有关机构出具的证明，证明事故的存在。买方不能领到进口许可证，不能被认为系属人力不可抗拒范围。

⑥ 仲裁：凡因执行本合约或有关本合约所发生的一切争执，双方应以友好方式协商解决；如果协商不能解决，应提交中国国际经济贸易仲裁委员会，根据该委员会的仲裁规则进行仲裁。仲裁裁决是终局的，对双方都有约束力。

⑦ 附加条款 (本合同其他条款如与本附加条款有抵触时，以本附加条款为准)。

（略）

卖方：　　　　　　　　　　　　　　买方：

Extend Your Eyes

商务合同常用词组

for and on behalf of the first party	甲方代表
the employer	雇主
capacity	职位
in the presence of	见证人

address	地址
for and on behalf of the second party	乙方代表
the contractor	承包人
agreement and contract	协议与合同
agency agreement	代理协议
agreement on general terms and conditions on business	一般经营交易条件的协议
agreement on loan facilities up to a given amount	商定借款协议
agreement on fixing price	共同定价协议
agreement on import licensing procedure	进口许可证手续协议
agreement on reinsurance	分保协议
agreement to resell	转售协议
bilateral agreement	双边协议
bilateral trade agreement	双边贸易协议
commercial agreement	商业协定
compensation trade agreement	补偿贸易协议
distributorship agreement	销售协议
exclusive distributorship agreement	独家销售协议
guarantee agreement	担保协议
international trade agreement	国际贸易协议
joint venture agreement	合营协议
licensing agreement	许可证协议
loan agreement	贷款协议
management agreement	经营管理协议
multilateral trade agreement	多边贸易协议
operating agreement	经营协议
partnership agreement	合伙契约
supply agreement	供货合同
trade agreement	贸易协议
written contract	书面协议
ad referendum contract	暂定合同
agency contract	代理合同
barter contract	易货合同
binding contract	有约束力合同
blank form contact	空白合同

commercial contract	商业合同
cross licence contract	换许可证合同
exclusive licence contract	独家许可证合同
ex contract	由于合同（按合同）
export contract	出口合同
firm sale contact	确定的销售合同
formal contract	正式合同
forward contract	期货合同
illegal contract	非法合同
import contract	进口合同
indirect contract	间接合同
installment contract	分期合同
international trade contract	国际贸易合同

商务合同常用句型

1. Any event or circumstance beyond the control of the Parties shall be deemed an event of Force Majeure and shall include, but not be restricted to, fire, storm, flood, earthquake, explosion, war, rebellion, insurrection, epidemic and quarantine restriction.

双方无法控制的事件或情况应视为不可抗力事件，这包括但不限于火灾、风灾、水灾、地震、爆炸、战争、叛乱、暴动、传染病及瘟疫。

2. The Seller shall sell and the Buyer shall buy the following described property upon the terms and conditions hereinafter set forth within this contract.

按照合同中所提之条款条件，卖方将出售而买方将购进以下商品。

3. Party A acknowledges and agrees that the technology it will receive from Party B during the term of this Contract shall be kept secret and confidential.

甲方承认并同意在合同期内由乙方提供的技术应属保密。

4. This agreement is made and entered into by and between Party A and Party B.

该合同由甲方和乙方共同制定。

5. The Buyer reserves the right to investigate or inspect at any time whether the products, qualifications, or facilities meet the Contract requirements.

买方保留随时对产品、质量或设施是否符合合同要求进行检查的权利。

6. If the Seller determines the performance has not been completed satisfactorily and in conformance with this Contract, the performance bond may be retained by the Seller until the Seller can determine damages caused by the lack of performance.

卖方如果确定履行情况不令人满意或与合同不符，在他能够确定履行不善所造成的损失之前可以扣留履约保证金。

7. The date of registration of the cooperative venture company shall be the date of the establishment of the board of directors of the cooperative venture company.

合资公司登记注册之日，为董事会正式成立之日。

8. The amendment of the contract or other appendices shall come into force only after a written agreement has been signed by Party A and Part B and approved by the original examination and approval authority.

只有在甲方和乙方共同签署书面协议，并且经原审批机构批准，合同及其他附件的修订才能生效。

9. This Contract shall be written in English in four copies. Each party shall keep two copies.

本合同应以英文写成，一式四份，双方各持两份。

10. In case a third party brings a charge of infringement, licensor shall be responsible for dealing with the third party and bear full legal and financial responsibilities which may arise.

若第三方起诉侵权，出让方应负责处理第三方事务，并承担全部相应的法律和财政责任。

11. Licensor guarantees that licensor is legitimate owner of the know-how supplied by licensor to licensee in accordance with the stipulations of the contract, and that licensor is lawfully in a position to transfer the know-how to licensee.

出让人担保自己合法拥有按合同规定由他转让给受让人的该项技术，把该项技术转让给受让人是合法的。

12. Party A shall bear all expenses for advertising and publicity.

甲方应承担所有广告和推销费用。

13. The employer may ask bidders individually for clarification of their tenders, including breakdowns of unit prices.

业主可要求投标者就其标书做出解释，包括单位价格细目表。

14. The Contractor shall supply to the Engineer four copies of all Drawings, Specification and other documents.

承包商应向工程师提供所有的图纸、规格和其他文件，一式四份。

15. During the validity of this Agreement, Party A refrains from offering the above-mentioned goods to other merchants with ports in Country X as ports of destination, while Party B undertakes to refrain from purchasing, pushing sales off or acting as agents for the commodity of other suppliers the same as or similar to that stated in Article 2 and guarantees

not to transship in any way the said goods supplied by Party A to any area, where exclusivity or sale agency has been granted by Party A.

在本协议有效期内，甲方不得将上述商品提供给以 X 为目的港的其他商人，而乙方不得购买、促销或代理与第二条规定的产品相同或相似的其他供应商的产品，并且保证不将甲方提供的上述商品转运到甲方指派独家代理人或销售代理人的任何地方。

16. If any loss or damage happens to the Works, or any part thereof, or materials or Plant for incorporation therein, during the period for which the Contractor is responsible for the care thereof, from any cause whatever, other than the risks defined in Clause 53.1.1, the Contractor shall, at his own cost, rectify such loss or damage so that the permanent Works conform in every aspect with the provisions of the Contract to the satisfaction of the Engineer.

在承包商负责照管期间，如果工程或其任何部分，或所用材料或设备对公司造成任何损失或损坏，除第 53.1.1 条规定的风险外，不论出于何种原因，承包商须出资对这些损失或损坏进行弥补，以使永久工程在各方面都符合合同的规定，达到工程师满意的程度。

17. If, before the Time for completion of the whole of the Works or, if applicable, any Section, a Taking-Over Certificate has been issued for any part of the Works or of a Section, the liquidated damages for delay in completion of the remainder of the Works or of that Section shall, for any period of delay after the date stated in such Taking-Over Certificate, and in the absence of alternative provisions in the Contract, be reduced in the Proportion which the value of the Part so certified bears to the value for the whole of the Works or Section, as applicable.

在整个工程或区段的竣工期限之前，如果已对工程或区段的任何部分签发了移交证书，在合同中无替代条款的情况下，该工程或区段剩余部分拖到该移交证书注明的日期之后尚未完工，由此产生的违约赔偿金应该按已签发部分的价值在整个工程或区段的价值中占的比例减少。

18. Prior to commencement of any work under this Contract and during the period of the Contract, the Purchaser shall provide proof of insurance coverage required by this Contract.

在本合同各项目开工之前以及在合同期间，买方应按合同要求出具保险范围证明。

19. The measurement, gross weight, net weight and the cautions such as "Do not stack up and down" "Keep away from moisture" "Handle with care" shall be stenciled on the surface of each package with fadeless pigment.

在每件包装上必须用不褪色颜料印上尺寸、毛重、净重以及"请勿倒置""保持干燥""小心轻放"等警示语。

20. The Seller shall be liable for any damage and loss of the goods attributable to the inadequate or improper packing.

由于包装不当造成的货物缺损由卖方负责。

21. Licensee agrees that licensee shall keep the know-how supplied by licensor under secret and confidential conditions within the validity period of the Contract.

受让人同意在合同有效期内对出让人提供的技术保密。

22. In the course of arbitration, the contract shall be continuously executed by both Parties except the part of the contract which is under arbitration.

在仲裁过程中，除仲裁中的那部分合同外，其他部分应由双方继续执行。

23. In two visits to the United States, Jamaica's Prime Minister, in response to the World Bank's repeated urges, suggested the message to the US policy makers for the good of both countries, particular in the matter of bilateral monetary affairs.

在世界银行的反复催促下，为了牙买加和美国的利益，特别是双边金融事务方面的利益，牙买加总理两次访美时都向美国决策者提出了这些建议。

24. All disputes arising from the performance of this Contract shall, through amicable negotiations, be settled by the Parties hereto.

由此合同履行而导致的所有争议都应由双方友好协商解决。

25. The Seller may terminate this Contract by oral or written notice to the Purchaser upon its beach as determined by the Seller or at other times when deemed necessary by the Seller. Upon such notice, the Purchaser shall cease all operations on and immediately leave, and not return to, the Seller's property unless otherwise provided by the Seller.

卖方确定买方违约或认为有必要终止合同时，可以用口头或者书面通知买方的方式终止此合同。一收到这一通知，若卖方没有其他规定，买方就应停止一切工作并立即离开卖方的房地产并不得返回。

26. Party A and Party B agree to jointly form a Co-operation Venture Company to introduce the Patent and engage in production cooperation in accordance with the technical know-how specified in the Patent.

甲乙双方同意双方共同成立一家合作经营企业来引进专利，并按专利提供技术进行合作生产。

27. The Sellers shall not be held responsible if they fail, owing to force Majeure cause or causes, to make delivery within the time stipulated in this Sales Contract or can not deliver the goods.

因不可抗力原因使卖方不能发货或在本销售合同规定的期限内交货，卖方不负责任。

28. It will also have its own offices, associates or agents in the countries with which it trades.

它在与它进行贸易的国家里也拥有办事处、合伙人或代理商。

29. Except in cases where the insurance is covered by the Buyer as arranged, insurance is to be covered by the Sellers with a Chinese insurance company.

除按约定由买方投保外，其他的由卖方向中国保险公司投保。

30. The Equipment and Material which are carefully and properly packed in the best and stable condition according to the figures and characteristics of the Equipment and Material may be expected to withstand long-distance sea and inland transportation and numerous handlings.

这些设备和材料按其形状和特性精心包装，固定牢实可靠，可望经受长途海上和内陆运输和反复装卸。

31. The Buyer shall establish a Letter of Credit before the above-mentioned time, failing which, the Seller shall have the right to rescind this Contract upon the arrival of the notice at Buyer, or to accept whole or part of this Contract non- fulfilled by the Buyer, or to lodge a claim for the direct losses sustained, if any.

买方须在上述日期前开立信用证，否则卖方有权通知买方取消合同，或接受买方未履行的合同的全部或部分，并就遭受的直接损失提出索赔。

32. The manufacturer desires to appoint some overseas agents for its business abroad, who will work on commission.

厂商想指定一些海外代理负责其国外业务，他们的工作报酬按佣金支付。

33. It is necessary for us to conduct amicable negotiation on the quality discrepancy, which may help sustain our long-term cooperation.

我们必须就质量异议进行友好协商，这有助于维持我们的长期合作。

34. I am contacting you because I can help you improve the pulling power of your advertising without increasing your advertising budget.

我们与贵方联系是因为我们可以帮助贵方提高广告的吸引力而不增加广告预算。

35. Where there is any quality discrepancy, the seller needs to look into it right away.

倘若有质量异议，卖方需要立即调查。

36. The Seller may, when it deems it reasonable and in the best interest of the Seller, allow the Purchaser to continue performance under the Contract.

若卖方认为合理且符合卖方最佳利益，可以允许买方继续履行合同。

37. No modification of this Contract or waiver of its terms and conditions shall be effective unless they are made in writing and signed by the parties.

合同修订或条款条件取缔以双方书面形式签字为准。

本合同有效期从合同生效之日算起共 10 年，有效期满后，本合同自动失效。

38. The contract shall be valid for 10 years from the effective date of the contract to the expiry of the validity term of the contract, on which the contract shall automatically become void.

买卖双方经协商同意按下列条款成交。

39. The underlined Seller and Buyer have agreed to close the following transaction according to the terms and conditions set forth as follows.

若买方提出索赔，凡属品质异议须于货到目的口岸之日起 30 天内提出，凡属数量异议须于货到目的口岸之日起 15 天内提出。

40. In case of quality discrepancy, claim should be filed by the Buyer within 30 days after the arrival of the goods at port of destination; while for quantity discrepancy, claims should be filed by the Buyer within 15 days after the arrival of the goods at port of destination.

买方应用不可撤销信用证支付该卖方运费。

41. The delivery payment shall be paid by Buyer to Seller under an irrevocable letter of credit.

本合同为中英文两种文本，两种文本具有同等效力。

42. This contract is executed in two counterparts each in Chinese and English, each of which shall be deemed equally authentic.

因乙方违背本合同的规定而产生的违约金、损坏赔偿金和其他相关费用，甲方可在保证金中抵扣。

43. In case Party B breaches this contract, Party A has right to deduct the default fine, compensation for damage or any other expense from the deposit.

本合同附件是本合同的有效组成部分，与本合同具有同等法律效力。

44. Any annex is the integral part of this contract. The annex and the contract are equally valid.

由于一般公认的人力不可抗拒原因而不能交货或装船延迟，卖方不负责任。

45. The seller shall not be held responsible for late delivery or non-delivery of the goods owing to generally recognized "Force Majeure" causes.

一切因执行本合同所发生与本合同有关之争执，双方应友好协商解决。

46. All disputes in connection with this Contract or the execution thereof shall be amicably settled through amicable negotiation.

本合同采用一次性支付使用费的方式，计价的货币为美元。

47. The amount of the payable Royalty for the Program will be a one-time charge. The currency shall be in US dollars.

48. The royalties shall be calculated on the basis of Net Selling Price of such products.
版税应该根据产品的销售净价计算。

49. Owner shall have no obligation to grant extension if delays were not excusable delays, or otherwise resulted, directly or indirectly, from the Contractor's breach of this Contract.
如果是无理由的，或者直接或间接由承包商违约造成无法如期竣工，业主没有义务予以宽限。

50. It is the responsibility of the Owner to take reasonable steps to provide a work area free of household obstructions, and to remove or protect household items in areas where it may be reasonably anticipated by the Owner that they may be subject to dust, damage or vibrations.
业主有责任采取合理措施保证居家环境畅通无阻，并且搬掉或者保护可能受尘、受损、受震动的用品。

51. Seller shall deliver each shipment to the applicable place of delivery on or before the applicable delivery date set forth in the project schedule.
卖方应该在工程计划表中所规定的交货日期之日或之前发送每批货物。

52. This Contract shall terminate and expire automatically upon the full performance or discharge of all the obligations of the parties hereunder.
双方全部责任一经履行完毕，该合同自动终止。

53. Immediately after completion of loading of goods on board the vessel the Seller shall advise the Buyer by cable of the contract number, name of goods, quantity or weight loaded, invoice value, name of vessel, port of shipment, sailing date and port of destination.
货物装船后卖方应该立即发电报告知买方合同号、品名、装运数量或重量、发票金额、船名、装运港、起航日期以及目的港。

54. In case the quality, quantity or weight of the goods be found not in conformity with those stipulated in this Contract after re-inspection by the China Commodity Inspection Bureau within 60 days after arrival of goods at the port of destination, the Buyer shall return the goods to or lodge claims against the Seller for compensation of losses upon the strength of Inspection Certificate issued by the said Bureau, with the exception of those claims for which the insurers or owners of the carrying vessel are liable.
货到目的口岸 60 天内经中国商品检验局复验，如发现品质或数量或重量与本合同规定不符时，除属于保险公司或船方负责者外，买方凭中国商品检验局出具的检验证明书向卖方提出退货或索赔。

55. It is mutually agreed that for the quality of the contracted goods in this category, the Inspection Certificate issued by the China Commodity Inspection Bureau after inspection the goods within 90 days from the date of arrival at the port of destination shall be taken as final and binding upon both parties.

双方同意本合同所订立此类商品之品质应以货物到达目的口岸后 90 天内经中国商品检验局检验并以该局所签发之检验证为最终依据，双方均应遵守之。

56. If insurance for additional amount and/or other insurance terms are/is required by the Buyer, prior notice to this effect must reach the Sellers before shipment and is subject to the Sellers' agreement, and the extra insurance premium shall be for the Buyers' account.

买方如需增加保险额及或需加其他保险，可于装船前提出，经卖方同意后代为投保，其费用由买方负担。

57. The Parties, adhering to principle of equality and mutual benefit and through friendly consultation, desire to exert all their efforts in co-operating with each other and agree to jointly invest to set up a joint venture enterprise TEDA, Tianjin, P.R. China for the purpose of expanding international economic cooperation and technological exchange on a mutual beneficial and profitable basis.

双方本着平等互利原则通过友好协商，愿尽全力相互合作，共同投资，在中华人民共和国天津市经济技术开发区建立合资经营企业；在互惠互利的基础上，扩展国际经济合作和技术交流。

Meeting Minutes

 Warm-up: Have a Try

Try to translate the following Meeting Minute into Chinese

April 8, 2010

Subject: Routine Meeting of the Domestic Sales Team

Present: ...

Chairperson: James Wang

Secretary: Jane Lee

Apologies for absences:...

Discussion:

The minutes of the previous meeting were accepted without comment. The participants then proceeded to discuss the following points.

1. Report on a Market Survey by Johnson Wang

Mr. Wang reported back on his investigation into the production problems the company had been experiencing at the time of the last meeting. He reported that these had now been completely overcome, and stated that production was now back at its expected level.

2. Other business

Mr. Han reported that the local fire officer would conduct an inspection prior to the renewal of the Safety License.

Resolved: that Mr. Charlotte Sun with the help of the secretary is to see it that everything is up to requirements.

3. Letter to Mr. Sullivan

Resolved: that a letter expressing the team's regret at Mr. Sullivan's continued ill health be sent by the secretary with the team's best wishes for a speedy recovery.

4. Date of next meeting

There being no other business, the next meeting was provisionally set for Tuesday, May 11. The meeting adjourned at 11:30 p.m.

Signed:

Background: Learn Something About Meeting Minutes

1. 会议记录概述

会议记录 (Minutes of Meeting) 就是客观、详细地记录会议情况的文件，如会议的时间、地点及讨论的问题等。会议记录应该忠于事实，简明扼要，抓要点。

1) The use and requirements of minutes of a meeting

The minutes of a meeting are the official record of all business matters that happen at a meeting and write down basic contents of a meeting so that we can further research work and summarize the important experience for the future. So the minutes are required to:

a. Keep accurate: Write down others' speech accurately. No matter whether it is the detailed record or outline record, the original meaning must be faithful and we can't add our personal view or opinion.

b. Keep main points: Whether it should be detailed or simple depends on the importance of decision. Generally speaking, we should take down the views of important resolving and proposing concretely. For some general explanations, it is enough to catch the simple meaning. In a word, it is necessary for us to keep main points whether the decision is important or not.

c. Remain the same from the beginning to the end: This means that the minutes recorders must write down the main points responsibly and seriously from the beginning to the end.

会议记录就是把会议报告、发言记录下来，帮助我们今后了解情况。会议记录是进一步研究工作、总结经验的重要材料。因此会议记录要求如下。

a. 准确：要如实地记录别人的发言，不论是详细记录，还是概要记录，都必须忠实原意，不得添加记录者的观点、主张。

b. 要点不漏：记录得详细与简略，要根据情况而定。一般地说，决议、建议、问题和发言人的观点、论据材料等要求记得具体、详细。一般情况的说明，可抓住要点，略记即可。

c. 始终如一：这是指记录人从会议开始到会议结束都要认真负责，贯穿始终。

2) The format of minutes of a meeting

The format of minutes of a meeting is uncomplicated and usually includes four parts: the heading of the meeting, the basic situation of the meeting, the body of minutes and the ending.

a. The heading of the meeting usually includes: the name of the meeting; the time, date; the place of the meeting and the chairperson.

b. The basic situation of the meeting includes: attendees, absentees, agenda and minutes recorder.

c. The body of minutes is the main part of minutes, including reports by officers, old and new business, solutions, the date and agenda of next meeting, the names of those who make motions and those who make second motions, the results of all votes, adjournment time, etc.

d. The usual ending consists of the complimentary close respectfully submitted, the handwritten and typewritten signature of the minutes recorder.

Of course, you can omit some parts of them according to the character of different meetings.

After the minutes have been transcribed in rough draft form, the chairperson, who will make changes, as considered necessary before they are distributed to members, should review them.

会议记录通常包括四部分：会议标题、会议基本情况、会议记录正文和结尾。

a. 会议标题通常包括会议名称，开会日期与时间，开会地点以及开会主持人。

b. 会议基本情况包括会议出席人、缺席人、议事日程以及会议记录人。

c. 会议记录正文是会议记录的主要部分，包括各位领导的报告、新旧业务、决议、下次会议的召开日期和议事议程、提议人、附议人姓名、表决结果以及休会时间等。

  d. 通常结尾部分为结尾礼词 (respectfully submitted)，记录人的手写和打字签名。

  当然，可以根据不同的会议有所节选。会议记录写好后，先由会议主持人过目，作必要的改动，再分发给相关人等。

2. 会议纪要的一般格式

(1) 标题 (Heading)。
(2) 出席会议人员 (Attendants)。
(3) 未出席会议人员 (Non-attendants)。
(4) 特邀与会者 (Special Attendants)。
(5) 有关上次会议纪要的评论 (Endorsement of Minutes)。
(6) 旧事项及新议题 (Items of old and new business)。
(7) 下次会议地点、时间、日期 (Place, time and date of next meeting)。
(8) 会议主持人及记录人员签名 (Signatures of Chairperson and Secretary)。

Discussion: Talk About How to Do the Task Well

1. 会议记录词汇翻译

  会议记录一般用比较中性的词汇和语调，不可带有主观性；翻译时应注意措辞，使会议记录显得比较正式。

  A. 避免缩略语，用其全称。

不用	常用
aren't	are not
She's	She is, She has

  B. 避免缩写，用完整拼写。

不用	常用
Dept.	Department
Corp.	Corporation

  C. 避免使用人称，用非人称术语。

不用	常用
Our idea	the company's proposal
We wanted	the corporation required
Your letter to us	the correspondence received

2. 英文会议记录中被动语态的汉译

1) 为显示客观性，英语会议发言人常常使用被动语态

例1. It was moved, seconded, approved unanimously that a leaflet be printed to solicit new membership.

参考译文：有人建议印制宣传小册来招募新的会员，得到附议和多数通过。

例2. These recommendations were discussed in detail by the speaker and by several members of the audience.

参考译文：发言者和几名听众对这些提议进行了详细讨论。

例3. The minutes of the last meeting, having been previously circulated, were approved and signed by the Chairman as a correct record.

参考译文：上次会议的会议记录已事先传阅，该会议记录已被确认通过并由主席签字。

例4. It was agreed that the next meeting will be held on 1st July, 2009, at 10:00 a.m. in the conference room.

参考译文：全体一致同意下次会议于2009年7月1日上午10时在会议室举行。

例5. The Chairman announces that Mr. Li Haixia has been elected Sales Manager.

参考译文：主席宣布李海霞当选为销售经理。

2) 翻译为汉语时一般要转变为被动语态

(1) 译成祈使句。

例6. You are requested to submit your report as the date of meeting is approaching.

参考译文：由于会议日期临近，谨请提交报告。

(2) 谓语译成宾语。

例7. The production has been greatly increased.

参考译文：产量有了很大的提高。

(3) 主语译成宾语。

例8. These computers would be very large and bulky if vacuum tubes were used.

参考译文：如果使用真空管，这些计算机就会又大又笨。

(4) 用不定人称句。

例9. I was supposed to learn something about market.

参考译文：有人建议我了解一下市场情况。

(5) 用无人称句。

例10. I was told that the goods will be shipped next week.

参考译文：我听说下周装运货物。

(6) 译出"被"字。

例11. About three-fourths of the surface of the earth is covered with water.

参考译文：大约四分之三的地球表面被水覆盖着。

(7) 译成"由""受""所""给""用""让"等。

例 12. The American trade delegation was given a hearty welcome.

参考译文：美国贸易代表团受到热烈欢迎。

(8) 译为"得"。

例 13. The documents must be made clear.

参考译文：单据必须制得清清楚楚。

(9) 译为"加以""予以""为……所"。

例 14. It has to be stressed that shipment must be effected within the prescribed time limit, as a further extension will not be considered.

参考译文：必须强调，货物装运必须按期进行，任何进一步延期的要求将不予考虑。

(10) 译为"是……的"。

例 15. This idea was put forward by the manager.

参考译文：这个意见是那位经理提出来的。

3. 会议记录中用正式语言替代与会者发言时的口头语

例 16. Wang: I'm sure, after appointing a local agent, the sales will be boosted.

Mr. Wang said they could boost the sales after they appointed a local agent.

例 17. Manager: So we all agreed that the plan should be canceled? Good!

会议记录： It was agreed that the plan should be canceled.

4. 使用过去时态为主，以汇报的形式撰写

The meeting was held on ...(date) at ...(time) in/at ...(place)

Minutes of last meeting were approved and signed.

The draft/documents of ...were discussed/approved/signed.

The documents of ... were distributed and read.

Several appointments and dismissals were announced at the meeting.

A was appointed to replace B.

... was appointed/promoted to ...

... was nominated for

例 18. Mr. Wang acknowledged that further research was necessary, and offered to undertake this research. It was agreed that once it is clear that a market does exist, the production can proceed.

参考译文：王先生指出，还需要进一步调查，并提出要承担这项调查工作。会议同意，一旦证实市场确实存在，可以批准生产。

Follow-up: Do It Yourself

1. Translate the following words into Chinese

(1) call to order (2) adjourn (3) preside
(4) second (5) resolution (6) agenda
(7) minutes (8) chairperson (9) present
(10) absent

2. Translate the following sentences

(1) The minutes of the last meeting, having been previously circulated, were approved and signed by the Chairman as a correct record.

(2) The meeting suggested inviting experts from Canada to give a training course to all the employees of the company.

(3) Mr. Zhang volunteered to arrange for estimates to be obtained on the cost of repairs, and report back at the next meeting.

(4) The meeting adjourned at 8:45 p.m.

(5) There being no further business, the chairperson closed the meeting.

(6) 人事部经理陈明强先生未能出席。

(7) 会议记录修正后被一致通过，并由主席签字。

(8) 全体一致同意下次会议于 2009 年 7 月 1 日上午 10 时在会议室举行。

(9) 主席指出本委员会无权做出这个决定。

(10) 下午 2 点半在工会会议室召开会议，讨论国内市场销售中出现的问题。

Homework: Practice Makes Perfect

Write a meeting minute with the following information

情况介绍：

作为 Slate & Johnson 箱包公司劳资协调委员会的秘书，你要为 2015 年 9 月 23 日的每月例会做一份会议记录。请根据下边几个要点用英文写一份完整的会议记录。

开会时间：下午四点；开会地点：员工餐厅

主持人：Mr. Falk

出席者：Mr. Baum, Ms. Dulugatz, Mr. Fenster, Ms. Liu, Ms. Sun；缺席者：Ms. Penn

会议内容：秘书宣读前次会议记录（8 月 21 日），主持人就其中的部分内容做了修正，应该是 Ms. Dulugatz 而不是 Ms. Penn 对仓库里的员工专用洗手间做调查，修正被通过；Mr. Fenster 对办公室员工所做的调查进行总结，他将就其写一份报告递交董事会。

下次会议：10月20日（时间、地点相同）

会议结束时间：下午五点十五分

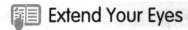 **Extend Your Eyes**

会议记录常用词汇

call to order	宣布开会
minutes approved	通过上次会议记录
verbatim notes	逐字记录
narrative notes	叙述性记录
outline notes	概要性记录
preside	做会议主席，负责主持
adjournment	休会，闭会
second	赞成，支持，附和
submit	提交
transcribe	写下，记录
attendant/participant	出席者
schedule	安排，计划
staff	全体职员
material	材料
data	数据
regular meeting	例会
group meeting	小组会议
annual meeting	年会
put off, delay	推迟，拖延
arrange	安排
item	项目
motion; proposal	提议
status report	状况报告
nomination	提名
presentation	陈述
premise	前提
agree	同意
disagree	不同意

support	支持
oppose	反对
doubt	怀疑
attitude	态度
advisory committee	顾问委员会,咨询委员会
advisory opinion	顾问意见
adjourn	延会
agenda	议程
amendment	修正
appointment	任命
assembly	大会
ballot	选票
board of directors	董事会
budget committee	预算委员会
casting vote	决定票
chairman	主席
clarification	澄清
comment	评论
committee of experts	专家委员会
committee, commission	委员会
congress	代表大会
consensus	意见
constitution, statutes	章程
consultant	顾问
deadlock	僵局
decision	决定
declaration, statement	声明
draft resolution	决议草案,提案
drafting committee	起草委员会
executive council, executive board	执行委员会
executive secretary	执行秘书
factual report	事实报告
first draft, preliminary draft	草案初稿
former chairman	前主席 (美作 past chairman)
full powers	全权

full-fledged member	全权代表
garden party	游园会
general committee, general officers, general bureau	总务委员会
general debate	长时间的讨论
governing body	主管团体
head of delegation	代表团团长
honorary president	名誉主席
interim chairman	临时主席
item on the agenda	议程项目
lie on the table	被搁置
life member	终身成员
member as of right	法定代表
member	成员
membership	成员资格
memorandum	备忘录
minutes, record	记录
motivations	表明动机
motion	提议
operative part	生效部分
other business	其他事项
plenary meeting	全会
precis writer	记录（员）
presidency, chairmanship, chair	主席团
procedure	程序
proposal	建议
representative	代表

会议记录常用表达法

1. 该委员会听取了某报告或建议。
The committee heard/noted/recognized/recorded that...
2. 该委员会决定最好采取某措施。
The committee agreed/conceded/concurred/decided/found/resolved(to) that...
3. 该委员会决定最好不采取某措施。
The committee declined/agreed not/refused/rejected(to) ...

4. 该委员会得到某指示或建议。

The committee was advised/informed/instructed/notified/(that) /(to) ...

5. 该委员会决定等待一段时间。

The committee deferred/postponed/shelved/tabled ...

6. 参加会议的成员有：

The following members were in attendance(or present) :

7. 没有出席会议的委员有：

The following members were not in attendance(or present or apologies for absence) :

8. 被邀请来列席会议的成员或仅就某个事项被邀请参加的成员有：

Present by invitation：

Present by invitation for Item Three：

9. 宣读并通过了上次会议的议程。

The minutes of the last meeting were read and approved.

10. 会上做出了几项任免。

Several appointments and dismissals were announced at the meeting.

11. 财务主管做如下报告。

The treasurer gave the following report.

12. 与会者一致提议聘请……

The meeting suggested inviting...

13. 张经理自愿在下次会议上汇报有关情况。

Mr. Zhang volunteered to report back at the next meeting.

14. 晚上8点45分休会。

The meeting adjourned at 8:45 p.m.

15. 没有其他事项，主席宣布会议结束。

There being no further business, the chairperson closed the meeting.

16. 会议主席要求财务主管做报告。

The president requested the treasurer's report.

17. 20张赞成票，5张反对票，2张弃权票。

There were 20 affirmative votes, 5 negative votes and 2 abstentions.

18. 双方签署了之前的会议纪要。

The minutes of previous meeting were signed by both parties.

Application Documents for Going Abroad

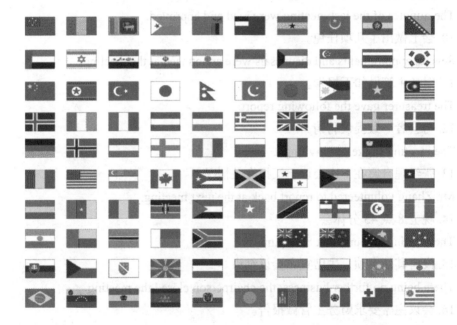

Warm-up: Have a Try

Try to translate the following recommendation letter into Chinese

Dear Sir/Madam,

Being a professor in Shanghai Finance and Economics University, I had given six lectures to Hua Sheng as an auditing teacher when she studied accountancy there as her second major, and had been her supervisor when she worked as an intern in my credit rating company. She had listened to me so attentively that many of the cases we studied in class were applied to her work effectively.

  I was really impressed by Hua Sheng's performance during her five-week internship. In order to be more competent in the field of credit rating, she volunteered to assume more tasks, and further offered to work overtime with other regular employees. However hard the tasks were, she always managed to fulfill them with flying colors. Such devotion to her career even as an intern is rarely seen in her peers. As she had done well in her accounting major, with an average score of 85 for the core courses, in addition to her remarkable learning ability, Hua Sheng was capable of doing some of the basic businesses in the company, and thus understanding the know-how of accounting more profoundly. She visited and researched fifteen companies in all, big or small, home or abroad, within the twenty-five weekdays. I could see a clear mind and a strong logic in her participation in writing credit rating reports. She was able to accomplish her own assignments independently while at the same time communicating smoothly and cooperating excellently with all of the five teachers, who had given her some instructions during the internship, further she had raised a few profound questions in the specialty of credit rating. All in all, her work was highly appraised by everyone in the company.

Yours truly,
×××

Background: Learn Something About Application Documents for Going Abroad

  在商务活动或留学申请中，我们都会用到一些文书，这些文书文件都需要从中文翻译成英文，以便对方查阅。在各种出国文书中，推荐信、个人陈述和简历是最为重要的组成部分。

1. 出国文书的特点

1) 突出重点，主线明确

  清楚有力地表达您的求学动机和学习学术能力。在国内有一种错误的观点，要"煽情"才能有效果。有的留学申请人就通过描述不相干活动展示"独特"的性格，或是学术上感觉没有什么可写的，就写自己考试时克服了重重困难，如何考取了好成绩！这是根本不着边际的写法，会让录取者发掘不到你的特点。要知道，你是要在很短的时间内，清楚地用几百字告诉招生教授你是入学(奖学金)非常合格的人选，盲目"煽情"完全不需要。

2) 结构简单，衔接紧密

  留学文书其实是你个人的广告！要重点突出，形象鲜明。仔细想想，留下深刻印象的广告哪个不是简明而富有创意的？许多申请人往往想把自己的全部优点都写出来告诉教授，觉得这样才能全面地展现自己。但是，"Simple is the best"，试想一下，招生教授天天都要做大量的教学工作，还要抽出时间阅读数量可观的留学申请资料，只有那种简单有力的文章才能 HIT THE TARGET，让人印象深刻！

3) 符合西方思维习惯

文化的差异导致东西方在什么是美德和优缺点的看法上不尽相同。在以往的经历中发现，有些留学申请人表达出来的"优点"实际上在西方人看来是缺点，反映申请人对学术问题毫无主见；而有些申请人认为不好的东西恰恰是西方人所欣赏的，认为这些能表明申请人充满个性。所以申请人要了解如何以西方人的思维方式取舍你的申请素材，把有益的亮点有选择性地挑选出来，在适当的篇幅里展示出来。

2. 出国文书常见句型

出国文书写作是一项高度系统化、专业化的工程，其质量的高低直接影响出国申请的成败。出国简历、个人陈述、推荐信等材料的撰写有各自的规律和特点，出国简历侧重简洁的文字、严密的逻辑；个人陈述需要出色的主题和巧妙的谋篇布局；推荐信需要有针对性地体现申请人鲜明的特点等。

1) 推荐信常见句型模板

(1) There's no doubt about it... 毫无疑问

例 1. There's no doubt about it, she will be an excellent researcher.

参考译文：毫无疑问，她将成为一位优秀的科研工作者。

例 2. There's no doubt about it, she is more intelligent and diligent than others.

参考译文：毫无疑问，她要比其他的学生聪明和勤奋许多。

(2) be powerful enough to do

例 3. He is powerful enough to influence the other members of the class/committee.

参考译文：他有足够的力量影响班级/委员会的其他成员。

(3) be + adj. + without being+adj.

例 4. He is capable without being aggressive, modest without being affected.

参考译文：他很能干，但不是逞强好胜，谦逊但不是做作。

2) 个人陈述常见句型

例 5. I have an excellent track record in...

参考译文：在……方面我有过杰出的记录。

例 6. I have had experience working with...

参考译文：在……方面我有过工作经验。

例 7. I am a bright, articulate professional with excellent...skills and...abilities.

参考译文：我是一个拥有杰出的……技能和……能力的朝气蓬勃、能言善辩的专业人员。

例 8. With the solid knowledge base derived from these research efforts and experiences, I have embarked on the process of developing...

参考译文：我在研究和实践中积累了扎实的知识，我已经开始着手发展……

例 9. Throughout my career, I have been fortunate to represent quality merchandise and services and have learned just how to present them in their most favorable aspects.

参考译文：在我的职业中，我有幸作为商品质量和服务的代表，并且已经学到该如何呈现它们最佳的方面。

例 10. I'm a responsive and responsible listener, maintaining a gracious and empathetic attitude, creatively troubleshooting, thoroughly researching options and making well-thought-out recommendations designed to establish and enhance customer/client relationship.

参考译文：我是一个敏锐和负责任的倾听者，保持亲切和深入体察的态度，创造性地消除疑难，彻底地研究各种可能性并提出有助于建立及提高顾客/当事人关系的成熟意见。

3) 个人陈述结尾段常见句型

例 11. I look forward to hearing from you. Thank you for your consideration.

参考译文：我期待您的回音。谢谢您的考虑。

例 12. I believe that my professional experience would make me a valuable asset to your organization.

参考译文：我相信我在职业上的经验会成为你们机构有价值的财富。

例 13. I fervently request more than your cursory consideration; I request your time to verify my claims. Your time will not be wasted.

参考译文：我热切地请求您认真考虑；请求您花时间证实我的诉求。您的时间不会被浪费的。

例 14. I'm organized and detail-oriented, work well under pressure and on deadline, enjoy working with a variety of people, and have a great attitude.

参考译文：我思路清晰、细致有序，能在压力下和期限内很好地工作，能够和各种人合作，工作态度认真。

Discussion: Talk About How to Do the Task Well

在翻译出国文书的过程中，仅仅将中文转换成英文是不够的，我们要注意翻译的技巧和语言的正式性，一定要符合目的地国家的写作和阅读习惯。这里要求的不仅是准确，还有对目的地国家文化、风俗、习惯的了解，从而留下好的印象，达到顺利完成行程的目的。

申请人如何讲述非常重要——用清晰、准确的方式表达思想。因此在翻译过程中，要牢记，在一所充斥着高素质候选人的学校里，决策的依据并非是数据和公式。个人自述帮助招生办做出理性的但最终还是主观的判断。举例如下。

(1) "I am interested in English literature." 这句话表达不够清楚，而 "I was concentrated on Milton and Shakespeare in college"，就明白地说出了申请人的志趣及专业研究的范围。

(2) "I received extensive training in physics." 这句话不够详细，"My training was in the area of particle physics." 就具体多了。

(3) "I was very active as a student representative"，最好说明曾经做什么：如主办演讲、沟通学生与校方之间的意见等。

(4) "I am attracted to your department by its brilliant faculty." 应说明对教授的认知是从何而来，如在何处读到某教授的文章而愿受教于他，或某位教授正在从事一项重要研究，与自己欲攻读的研究领域相同等；表达对所申请系所的课程、教师和特性有些了解，依学校不同而提及对某位任教于该校的教授、新课程或该校的某个学位感兴趣。

(5) 不要用语意模糊的句子，如 "Your esteemed school"——应代以学校的名字；"I will return to serve my country"——应明确说出所要从事的到底是什么工作。

(6) 避免用深奥的词汇，尽量以简单容易的文字来表达，也就是说尽量使用一般书面语甚至口语中的常用词汇，句型则比口语要更正式一些。例如，As my teachers have commented, I am goot at independent thinking and like to ask "why".

(7) 态度诚恳认真，不卑不亢。不用为自己的弱点道歉，譬如托福成绩不高等；也不要表现得过分自信，重要的是给学校一个专业的、认真的印象。例如，My intense interest is civil engineering, a subject that combines engineering science with construction technology and social value. It provides me a good opportunity to express my idea, display my creativity! 第一句话简单一个同位语结构 "a subject that... social value" 道出自己对所学专业的独到看法，第二句话虽然没有使用褒奖自己的任何形容词，但两个动词短语 "express my idea" 和 "display my creativity" 显示出了自己具备进一步进行本学科研究的潜质——独立的思维和创造力。

Follow-up: Do It Yourself

Translate the following recommendation letter

Recommendation

Gary Chen

CEO

××× Digital Inc, Beijing, China

Tel: +8613921298225

Email: garychen@digi100.cn

To Whom it may concern,

It has been a great pleasure for me to work with Miss Shen Ling, who had been a marketing project manager with our company between the year 2005 and 2007.

As a marketing project manager of our company, Shen is responsible for a number of job duties ranging from promoting our company products to exploring and establishing business relationship with potential clients.

Apart from being a good team member, Shen also displayed outstanding initiative and approached her work thoughtfully and intelligently. She also impressed me of ability of time and work management, and was more than capable of taking up extra responsibilities.

Above all, Shen Ling is so excellent that I do not hesitate to introduce her to you. If you need other information about this young lady, I will be very happy to be contacted.

Faithfully yours,
Gary Chen

Homework: Practice Makes Perfect

1. Translate the following Curriculum Vitae into Chinese

Curriculum Vitae

Personal Details

Name:	× × ×
Age:	40 years old
Marital Status:	Married
Sex:	Male
Date of Birth:	13th Feb, 1970
Country of Origin:	Malaysia
Address (Home):	
Personal Email Address: peterchang@yahoo.com	

Education

Name of College	Qualification	Year and Duration
abc University	degree	1989—1992
Ielts	English exam	1989
xyz college	diploma	1985—1988

Work Experience

Company	Position	Year and Duration
123 company	senior marketing manager	2006—present
KKK company (Shanghai)	sales manager	2002—2006
333 company	admin executive	1997—2002

Work Experience

123 company

Explored new markets and business. In charge of forming new business department within the existing company. Establish links for cooperation with local University and to set up new company in China.

KKK Company (Shanghai)

Managed 22 centres through Central China, and also two other related subsidiaries. Successfully revived a dormant company resulting in an immediate increase of 15.6 million in the subsidiary company's turnover. Increased the company potential turnover yearly by another 12.5 million (2003).

TTT company

In charge of daily administrative work.

2. Translate the following passage into English

我以教务处主任的身份及我多年教书育人的经验向您推荐我校学生李霞。

李霞在我校读书已有近四年的时间了。自入校起，她就表现出了与其他学生不同的综合素质。她对于各科学习都有极大的热情，在英语方面的突出表现更是让所有老师都惊叹不已。她有超出同龄人的组织管理能力、逻辑思维能力强，更善于独立解决问题。在课堂上她思维敏捷，学习自主性强，成绩优异。在课外活动中，也经常见到她积极参与的身影。是一个不折不扣的全面发展的模范学生。在生活中，她开朗热情，为人友善，乐于助人，是老师们的得力助手，同学们的好榜样。

她同时还担任学生会社团部文学社社长。她思考问题缜密细致，沟通及语言表达能力极强。文学社的各项活动都举办得有声有色，极大地丰富了同学们的业余生活，也锻炼了她自己的各方面的能力。

李霞是一个积极进取的学生，她立志要到国外去读商科。我们所有老师都为她有如此远大的志向而感到高兴。同时，我也相信无论她身处何地都会尽她最大的努力去做到最好，她的未来将不可限量。

如果您需要她更多的信息，请方便时随时联系我。

 **Extend Your Eyes**

出国文书常用词汇

education	学历
educational background	教育程度
educational history	学习履历
curriculum	课程
major	主修
minor	副修
educational highlights	课程重点部分
curriculum included	课程包括
specialized courses	专门课程
courses taken	所学课程
courses completed	完成的课程
special training	特别训练
social practice	社会实践
part-time jobs	业余工作
summer jobs	暑期工作
vacation jobs	假期工作
refresher course	进修课程
extracurricular activities	体育活动
recreational activities	娱乐活动
academic activities	学术活动
social activities	社会活动
rewards	奖励
scholarship	奖学金
"Three Goods" student	"三好"学生
excellent League member	优秀团员
excellent leader	优秀干部
student council	学生会
off-job training	脱产培训
in-job training	在职培训
educational system	学制

academic year	学年
semester	学期（美）
term	学期（英）
president	校长
vice-president	副校长
academic dean	教务员
monitor	班长
vice-monitor	副班长
commissary in charge of studies	学习委员
commissary in charge of entertainment	文娱委员
commissary in charge of sports	体育委员
commissary in charge of physical labour	劳动委员
Party branch secretary	党支部书记
League branch secretary	团支部书记
commissary in charge of organization	组织委员
commissary in charge of publicity	宣传委员
degree	学位
post doctorate	博士后
doctor (Ph.D)	博士
master	硕士
bachelor	学士
graduate student	研究生
abroad student	留学生
returned student	回国留学生
foreign student	外国留学生
undergraduate	大学肄业生；（尚未取得学位的）大学生
senior	大学四年级学生；高中三年级学生
junior	大学三年级学生；高中二年级学生
sophomore	大学二年级学生；高中一年级学生
freshman	大学一年级学生
guest student	旁听生（英）
auditor	旁听生（美）
government-supported student	公费生
commoner	自费生

extern	走读生
day-student	走读生
intern	实习生
aliss	别名
pen name	笔名
date of birth	出生日期
house number	门牌
health condition	健康状况
bloodtype	血型
short-sighted	近视
far-sighted	远视
color-blind	色盲
ID card	身份证
date of availability	可到职时间
available	可到职
membership	会员、资格
president	会长
director	理事
standing director	常务理事
secretary-general	秘书长
society	学会
association	协会
research society	研究会

Task 10

Business Travel

📖 Warm-up: Have a Try

Try to translate the following passage into Chinese

Travel has always been an important part of doing business. From train trips to commercial flights, people have long understood the importance of travel to making new connections. What is changing, however, is the way journeys are made. As technology opens the door to a more connected world, global business travel is becoming increasingly common. This presents travelers with both advantages and disadvantages. While all the information needed to travel safely is in a mobile phone, a forgotten charger can spell disaster. It all comes down to details, and that's why a comprehensive itinerary is more important than ever when it comes to taking a business trip.

Background: Learn Something About Business Travel

商务旅行出发之前需要了解旅行的目的、同行人员、地点、时间、商务活动参与者等基本情况，并且有必要做好准备工作事宜，例如，制定商务旅行计划表，预订机票、车船票，预订酒店，预支差旅费或明确差旅费的限额，准备必要的文件资料，以及整理用品等。

1. 商务旅行计划表的制定

下表是津玛特公司总经理一行赴新西兰的奥克兰与恒天然公司开展洽谈的 6 日商务之旅的计划书。

Business Travel Itinerary of TJ-Mart Company Mission led by GM, Calvin White 6 Days from Tianjin, China to Auckland, New Zealand via Beijing		
Date	Cities	Itinerary
(Sun.) Sept 11 Day 1	Tianjin/ Beijing	• 18:00 Company shuttle to Beijing-Capital International Airport (Driver: Li Ming) • Dinner at the airport • Mid-night flight to Auckland • CA783 00:25-17:10
(Mon.) Sept 12 Day 2	Auckland	• 17:10 Arrival at Auckland International Airport • Taxi to Crowne Plaza Auckland • Check in at Crowne Plaza Auckland (Reserved Room 1236, 0836, 0838, 0840) • 20:00 Welcome dinner of the Fonterra Cooperative Group at Crowne Plaza (business attire)
(Tue.) Sept 13 Day 3	Auckland	• Morning Visit to the Farm • Afternoon Visit to the dairy plant • Dinner with representatives of Fonterra at a local restaurant
(Wed.) Sept 14 Day 4	Auckland	• Morning Preliminary negotiation with Fonterra (to reach Letter of Intent) • Lunch at a local restaurant • Farewell Dinner with representatives of Fonterra at a local restaurant

续表

Date	Cities	Itinerary
(Thu.) Sept 15 Day 5	Auckland	• Morning Free time • Afternoon 14:00 Check out • Taxi to Auckland International Airport • Evening flight to Beijing NZ3889 19:00-05:10
(Fri.) Sept 16 Day 6	Beijing/ Tianjin	• 05:10 Arrival at Beijing-Capital International Airport • Company shuttle to Tianjin (Driver: Li Ming)

Note：1. It is early Spring in Auckland.
　　　2. Clock time in Auckland is 4 hours ahead of Beijing Time.

一份清清楚楚的商务旅行计划表 (Business Travel Itinerary) 主要包括六项内容：日期、时间、地点、交通工具、具体事项、备注。

1) 日期 Date
指某月、某日、星期几。

2) 时间 Time
一是指旅行出发、返回时间，包括因商务活动需要到两个或两个以上的国家或地区的抵离时间和中转时间；二是指旅行过程中各项活动或工作时间；三是指旅行期间就餐、休息的时间。

3) 地点 Cities/ Places
一是指旅行抵达的目的地（包括中转的地点），目的地的名称既可以详写，即哪个国家、哪个地区、哪个公司，也可以略写，即直接写到达的公司名称；二是指旅行过程中开展的各项活动或工作的地点；三是指食宿地点。

4) 交通工具 Transportation
一是指出发、返回的交通工具；二是指商务活动使用的交通工具。

5) 具体事项 Activities
一是指商务活动内容，如访问、洽谈、会议、宴请、娱乐活动等；二是指私人事务活动。

6) 备注 Notes
记载需要注意的事项，诸如抵达目的地需要中转、中转站的名称，休息时间，飞机起飞的时间，或需要中转时转机机场的名称、时间，或某国家为旅客提供了特殊服务等，或展开活动时，要注意携带哪些有关文件契约，就餐时应该遵守对方民族习惯的注意事项。

2. 机票的预订

各大航空公司均向广大用户提供机票预订服务。游客可以通过网站、固定电话、手机客户端等渠道预订机票。下图以在线预订机票为例,展示了机票预订的操作:输入出发地、目的地、离港时间、出行人数、舱位类型以及优惠码等信息,进行查询;然后根据查询结果,对满意的航班进行预订。

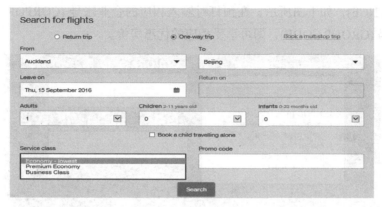

Return trip 往返机票
One-way trip 单程机票
Service class 舱位选择
Economy-lowest 经济舱
Premium Economy 豪华经济舱
Business Class 商务舱
Promo code 优惠码

3. 酒店的预订

游客可以通过互联网、电话、手机客户端等多种方式获得酒店预订服务。预订时,需要综合考虑酒店所处的街区、周边建筑物、品牌、星级、价位、开业时间、最近装修时间、用户评价以及酒店的房型、床型、房内配置、有线和无线网络配置等相关信息。

下图显示的是奥克兰皇冠假日酒店在线预订的内容。

在页面上输入入住时间(CHECK IN)、退房时间(CHECK OUT)和人数(ADULTS)，然后进行查询。

经常进行商务旅行的客人、政府官员、大集团客户通常都会有各种优惠价(RATE PREFERRENCE)，如下图所示，在预订时输入相应的企业账号(CORPORATE ID)或者集团代码(GROUP CODE)，即可享受相应的优惠房价。

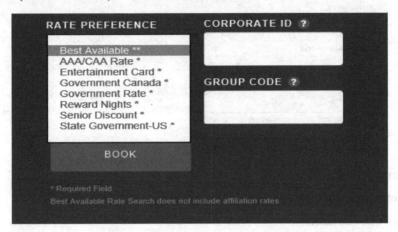

根据查询结果，选择合适的房间类型(ROOM PREFERRENCE)，如下图所示。

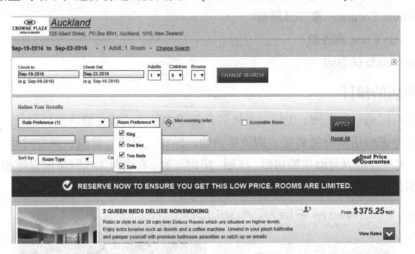

King 大床房

One Bed 单人房

Two Beds 双床房

Suite 套房

Non-smoking hotel 无烟房

同一房间会有不同的价格，如下图页面上显示的分别是IHG优乐汇会员价(YOUR RATE BY IHG ®Rewards Club)、商旅套餐价(BUSINESS SUCCESS PKG)、食宿同享价(Stay and Dine)和家庭之旅优惠价(FAMILY GETAWAY)。

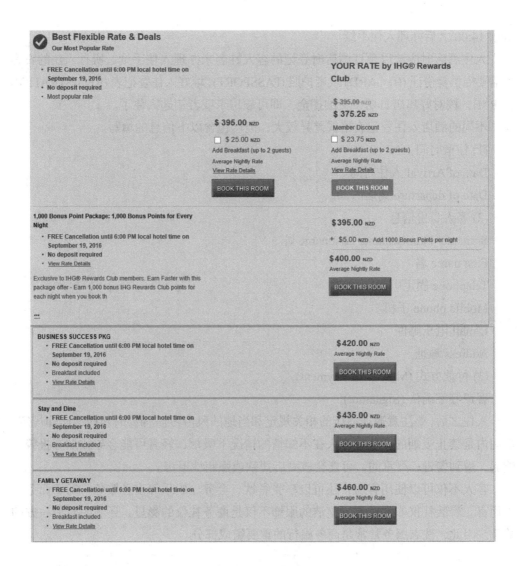

价格明细有必要仔细研读，因为其中注明了免费取消 (FREE Cancellation) 预订的条件，是否需要担保金 (deposit)，以及此价格是否包含早餐等具体的项目。

4. 候机与登机

考虑到时间成本，远途的商务旅行大多选择飞机作为交通工具。坐飞机需要比起飞时间提前 1 小时以上到机场，办理登机手续。领取机票、办理登机牌 (BOARDING PASS)、检查和托运行李一般需要 30 分钟左右的时间，而正常情况下航空公司都要求提前 30 分钟过安检候机。因此，提前 1 小时到达机场才能给自己多一份从容，以免耽误重要的行程。

5. 酒店的入住和服务

酒店入住一般是到店当日 14：00 之后，如果在 14：00 之前到酒店，可以寄存行李，等候14:00之后办理入住手续。

  入住酒店时应该以预订酒店时登记的客人姓名来办理入住手续。所有入住的宾客均需要提供身份证(ID CARD)或者护照(PASSPORT)，填好入住登记表(REGISTRATION FORM)，核对好离店日期，交纳押金，即可领房卡或者钥匙入住了。

  不同的酒店入住登记表格式差异较大，但均包含以下信息的填写。

(1) 住宿时间

Date of Arrival 入住时间

Date of departure 离店时间

(2) 客人身份信息

Surname/ Family name/ Last name 姓

First name 名

Telephone 固定电话

Mobile phone 手机

E-mail 电子邮件

Address 地址

(3) 付款方式 (Method of Payment)

客户签字确认 (Signature)

  入住之后，要注意遵守酒店的相关规定和当地的风俗习惯。例如，新西兰法律规定，房间内是禁止吸烟的。某些客人在不知情的情况下吸烟，轻者可能会导致烟雾报警器响起，遭到警告；严重的，可能会被酒店罚款或强制性退房。

  客人不仅可以使用客房，还可以享受餐饮、会务、娱乐等多种服务。对于商务人士而言，着装礼仪非常重要。整洁的服饰不仅是商务礼仪的彰显，还表明对另一方的尊重。因此，洗衣服务常常是商务旅行的重要组成部分。

LAUNDRY SERVICE			
Please Dial Guest Service Extension			
Name:_____	☐ Tick which is applicable		
Room Number:_____	LAUNDRY	DRY CLEANING	PRESSING
Date:_____			
Laundry Picked Up At:___	☐ Normal service	☐ Express service	
To Be Returned At:_____	☐ On Hanger	☐ Folded	
Voucher Number:_____	Guest Signature:		
Total Number:_____			
Total Amount:_____			

Normal service: Garment collected before 12:00, room will be returned the day by 19:00. Garment collected after 12:00, room will be returned the next day by 12:00.

Express service: Garment returned within 4 hours from the collection time, 100% additional charge.

LAUNDRY(L) / DRY CLEANING(D) / PRESSING(P)

Guest Count			Hotel Count			Gentlemen	Rate L/D/P	Amount	Guest Count			Hotel Count			Ladies	Rate L/D/P	Amount
L	D	P	L	D	P				L	D	P	L	D	P			
						TUXEDO	45/85/35								EVENING DRESS	45/85/35	
						OVERCOAT	45/85/35								OVERCOAT	45/85/35	
						SUIT- 3 PCS	45/85/35								SUIT- 3 PCS	45/85/35	
						SUIT- 2 PCS	38/75/28								SUIT- 2 PCS	38/75/28	
						PYJAMAS-2PCS	35/70/28								PYJAMAS-2PCS	35/70/28	
						TRACKSUIT-2PCS	35/70/28								TRACKSUIT-2PCS	35/70/28	
						JACKET	30/65/20								DRESS- 1 PIECE	30/65/20	
						SWEATER	28/60/18								SWEATER	28/60/18	
						DOWN COAT	40/80/30								DOWN COAT	40/80/30	
						DOWN JACKET	35/70/28								DOWN JACKET	35/70/28	
						JEANS	25/55/18								BLOUSE	20/50/14	
						TROUSERS	20/50/14								WAISTCOAT	18/35/10	
						SHORTS	18/35/10								JEANS	25/55/18	
						SHIRT	20/50/14								SKIRT	20/50/14	
						WAISTCOAT	18/35/10								SHORTS	18/35/10	
						TIE	15/33/8								SCARF	15/33/8	
						UNDERPANTS	10/30/6								UNDERPANTS	10/30/6	
						SOCKS	10/30/6								STOCKING	15/33/8	
						HANDKERCHIEF	10/30/6								SOCKS	10/30/6	
															HANDKERCHIEF	10/30/6	
						NORMAL TOTAL									NORMAL TOTAL		
						PLUS EXPRESS									PLUS EXPRESS		
						TOTAL									TOTAL		

REMARKS: All articles sent for laundering are accepted by the Hotel at the owner's risk. Although the Management will exercise reasonable care, the Hotel cannot hold responsible for any damage resulting from the laundry process for loss of buttons or for anything left in the pockets of garments. In the event that any article is damaged due to hotel negligence, compensation will be limited to five (5) times the charge fee of laundering or dry cleaning the said item. All claims must be made within 24 hours after delivery. Please indicate number of articles in guest count column. Failing to do so, the Hotel count shall accepted as correct in case of discrepancy in the count, we will try to contact you, and if you are not available, the Hotel count must be accepted as correct. Shirt and blouse will be returned on hanger unless otherwise requested.

6. 酒店的退房

一般情况下，酒店退房时间是离店当日当地时间 12: 00 之前，超时会加收房费。注意，星级酒店在提供良好服务的同时也会收取服务费和相关的税款。退房时，请注意看清楚房费是否包含税费。

7. 商务英语中接待客户的技巧

1) 妥善安排会面的约定

—— I'd like to make an appointment with Mr. Lee.

当你计划到海外出差，顺道拜访客户时，必须先以书信通知对方。出国以前再以电传或电话向对方确认访问的日期和目的。如果是临时决定的拜访，也要通过对方的秘书安排，告诉她，"I'd like to make an appointment with Mr. Lee."（我想和李先生约见一次）。让对方对你的造访有所准备，才会有心情和你洽谈。

2) 向商务会谈的另一方表示善意与欢迎

—— I will arrange everything.

如果沟通是由你发起，提供商务会谈的另一方一切的方便，能使沟通一开始便在友善和谐的气氛下进行。尤其是当你的沟通对手是远道而来的，你热心地告知他，"I will arrange everything."（我会安排一切），不但表现出你的诚意，也能使他在不必顾虑食宿等琐事的情况下，专心与你进行沟通。

3) 资料须充实完备

—— We have a pamphlet in English.

具体的物品通常比口头描述更有说服力。当客户听到你说"We have a pamphlet in English."（我们有英文的小册子），或"Please take this as a sample."（请将这个拿去当样品）时，一定会兴趣大增，进而问你许多和产品有关的问题。如果你平时资料搜集得全面，便能有问必答。这在商务沟通上是非常有利的。

4) 清楚地说出自己的想法与决定

—— I mean it.

如果在沟通场合中，你无法翔实地说出心中的意念，不仅会使对方听得满头雾水，说不定还会让对方认为你对实际情形根本不了解，而失去和你沟通的兴致。"I mean it."（我是认真的；不是开玩笑），"From my perspective, I will..."（如果是我的话，我会……）。

5) 询问对方的意见

—— What is your opinion?

每个人都希望自己的意见受到重视。当你和他人进行沟通时，除了说出自己的想法以外，随时可加上一句"What is your opinion?"（你的意见是……），或"I'd like to hear your ideas about the problem."（我想听听你对这个问题的看法），不但让对方感觉受到重视，更能使你们因思想的交流而逐渐达成协议。

6) 说"不"的技巧

—— No, but...

在商务沟通上，该拒绝时，就应该斩钉截铁地说"No."，拐弯抹角地用"That's

difficult"（那很困难），或 "Yes, but..."（好是好，可是……）来搪塞，会令对方觉得你答应得不够干脆，而不是在委婉地拒绝。如果你说 "No，but..."，对方便清楚地知道你是拒绝了，但似乎还可以谈谈。这个时候，你因为已先用 "No" 牵制对方，从而站在沟通的有利位置上了。

Discussion: Talk About How to Do the Task Well

1. 正确选择词义

词义精当，是指译者对原文每一个词都译得恰如其分。当然，怎样才算是"恰如其分"，这是个相对标准，但我们在翻译实践中，务必高标准、严要求、精益求精。

1) 一词多义

一词多义是语言的普遍现象。因此，根据不同语境正确选词是翻译最基本的一项技能。我们来看几个例子。

例 1.

(1) Service is not included in the room rate.

(2) The world's tropical forests are disappearing at an even faster rate than experts had thought.

(3) His heart rate was 30 beats per minute slower.

(4) The film was rated G, so you can introduce it to kids.

(5) Well, at any rate, let me thank you for all you did.

以上五个句子都涉及"价格低"这一概念，但若要译得贴切，却可能需用不同词来表达。

参考译文：

(1) 服务费不包括在房价里。

(2) 世界上热带森林消失的速度比专家们预想的还要快。

(3) 他的心率每分钟慢了 30 次。

(4) 这部电影被评为大众级，可以推荐给小朋友们。

(5) 好吧，不管怎样，还是要感谢你所做的一切。

2) 词义引申

在英汉互译中，有时会遇到某些词在词典上难以找到贴切具体上下文的词义，如生搬硬套，译文往往语意不清，甚至导致误解。在这种情况下，需要根据上下文和逻辑关系，从该词固有的基本含义出发，进一步加以引申。

例 2.

(1) To cover our shipment, we would request you to establish a commercial letter of credit in our favour for the contracted amount through an American Bank.

(2) We enclose a list showing our present availabilities.

(3) The arrivals do not conform to the sample. You must have shipped the wrong parcel.

(4) It is one of the most useful of the household conveniences.

(5) We insist that international trade should not be a one-way street.

以上五个句子中"shipment""availabilities""arrivals""conveniences"和"one-way street"，如查词典，它们基本含义可分别是"装运（货）""可得到东西""到达（的东西）""便利（设施）"和"单行道"。如果将这些词义直接放入译文，显然不能充分表达原文含义，应该进一步将这个例子中的词的引申意义翻译出来，分别译为：(1) 所运输的货物、(2) 可提供的产品、(3) 我方收到的货物、(4) 家庭用品、(5) 单方受益。

2. 翻译活用技巧

有人误以为，所谓合乎标准翻译，就是在把一种语言转换为另一种语言时，做到"不增、不减、不改"。翻译实践告诉我们，由于两种语言表达方式有异，适当翻译往往都是"既增、又减、还改"。灵活运用这些技巧，可以帮助我们在实际翻译时妥善解决内容与形式之间矛盾，使译文做到内容忠实、文字通顺、行文简洁、明确易懂。

1) 增词

增词，根据具体上下文，可增加动词、形容词、名词或其他词类，但在什么时候增加什么词，才能恰到好处，而不超出一定界限，则需要悉心体会。

例 3. It's more expensive than it was last time but not as good.

参考译文：价钱比上次高，但质量却比上次差。（增补原文省略部分，原句后半句完整形式应该是：...but it's not as good as it was last time.）

2) 减词

由于两种语言表达习惯不同，翻译时如果一字不漏照搬，往往会显得累赘、拖沓、冗杂，或不合行文习惯，甚至产生歧义。采取减词的译法可以使译文言简意赅。

例 4. 我在此诚挚地感谢恒天然公司的威廉约翰逊先生。

参考译文：I'd like to take a moment to offer my sincere thanks to William Johnson of Fonterra Cooperative Group. （"take a moment"是英语中的惯用语，却不符合中文的说话习惯，直译会影响句子的顺畅，省略这部分既不会影响句子的原意，又符合中文的习惯。）

3) 改译

例 5. 我公司经营举世闻名的贝雕工艺品；色彩艳丽、种类繁多的人造花卉；令人爱不释手的小工艺品；体态生动、活泼的各式玩具；款式新颖、穿着舒适的各种工艺鞋；稀有名贵的钻石珠宝；技艺精湛、巧夺天工的玉石雕刻；格调高雅的抽纱工艺品等。

参考译文：Our famous products include shell carvings, a variety of artificial flowers, small craft articles, lively toys, fashionable and comfortable craft shoes, rare jewelry, meticulous jade carvings and sophisticated embroideries.

原文中的"色彩""种类""体态""款式""穿着""技艺"和"格调"等词从信息角度而言都属于冗余信息,这是汉语排比结构的行文特点,译为英文时不必一一译出,译文将有些冗余信息的表达重新整合,做适当的改写,以符合英美人的审美习惯。

Follow-up: Do It Yourself

1. Translate the following sentences into Chinese

(1) If your company has a preferred corporate account with us, please provide the account number here. This will allow us to display your company's preferred rates.

(2) Please put all your metal objects such as coin, cell phone, chewing gum, cigarettes and anything with Aluminum foil into the basket.

(3) I'm sorry to tell you that it's a flammable item that cannot be taken with you into the airplane.

(4) Have your bags been in your possession the whole time?

(5) You've been selected for additional screening.

(6) You are invited to attend the welcome dinner of the Fonterra Cooperative Group at Auckland Crowne Plaza at 8 o'clock this evening.

(7) I would like to introduce Mark Sheller, the Marketing Department Manager of our company.

(8) Let me introduce you to Mr. Li, general manager of our company.

(9) Mr. Smith, this is our General manage, Mr. Zheng, this is our Marketing Director, Mr. Lin. And this is our RD Department Manager, Mr. Wang.

(10) If I'm not mistaken, you must be Miss Chen from France.

(11) Do you remember me? Benjamin Liu from Marketing Department of PVC. We met several years ago.

(12) Is there anyone who has not been introduced yet?

(13) It is my pleasure to talk with you.

(14) Here is my business card. / May I give you my business card?

(15) May I have your business card? / Could you give me your business card?

2. Translate the following passages into Chinese

(1) All articles sent for laundering are accepted by the Hotel at the owner's risk.

Although the Management will exercise reasonable care, the Hotel cannot hold responsible for any damage resulting from the laundry process for loss of buttons or for anything left in the pockets of garments. In the event that any article is damaged due to hotel negligence, compensation will be limited to five (5) times the charge fee of laundering or dry cleaning the said item. All claims must be made within 24 hours after delivery. Please indicate number of articles in guest count column. Failing to do so, the Hotel count shall accepted as correct in case of discrepancy in the count, we will try to contact you, and if you are not available, the Hotel count must be accepted as correct. Shirt and blouse will be returned on hanger unless otherwise requested.

(2) Rates are per room, per night and are subject to availability at participating hotels. Offer includes accommodation for two adults and one child, with buffet breakfast for a minimum length of stay of 2 nights or more. Extra bed is available subject to local hotel policy. If you book 2 rooms the hotel will endeavour to provide adjoining rooms (Subject to availability) . Rates also qualify for IHG Rewards Club points. Ticket to the local attraction will be provided by individual hotels and may vary. Extra tickets for local attraction can be bought from the hotel if needed. Please note that the Auckland Hop On Hop Off Explorer does not include entry to any attractions and these will be at the bearers cost.

Homework: Practice Makes Perfect

1. Translate the following dialogue into Chinese

Johnson 和小王来到酒店。Johnson 先生入住，小王担任翻译，并协助他完成入住手续。

1) 有预订情况下的入住

Johnson:　　Good morning, I have a reservation under the name of Johnson.

Hotel staff: Ok, I've found it. Checking out on the 27th?

Johnson:　　That's right.

Hotel staff: Can I take a credit card for the deposit?

Johnson:　　Yes, sure. Also, I'd like a non-smoking room please.

Hotel staff: Certainly, sir. Here's your key. Your room is on the 7th floor and on the left. Room 8781. Check out is at 12:00 noon.

2) 无预订情况下的入住

Johnson:　　Hello, I'd like to check in please.

Hotel staff: Certainly. Can I have the name please?

Johnson:　　Mr. Johnson.

Hotel staff: OK, are you checking out tomorrow?

Johnson: Yes, I am.

Hotel staff: Will you need a wake-up call, sir?

Johnson: Yes please. At 6:30am.

Hotel staff: OK then, your room is 8502 on the fifth floor. Breakfast is served between 6:30am and 9:00 am. Enjoy your stay.

Guest: Thank you.

2. Translate the following dialogue into English

接机后的次日，小王在公司里，为 Johnson 介绍自己的老板——孙先生。

小王： 孙先生，让我为你介绍加拿大 Lanston 的业务经理——William Johnson 先生。(孙先生先伸出手，两人握手) Johnson 先生，这是 Steven，孙先生，Cast 公司的总经理。

孙先生： 多次电话、传真往返之后，非常高兴终于见到您，Johnson 先生 (先递出名片)，请收下我的名片。

Johnson： 谢谢您，孙先生。也请收下我的名片 (递上自己的名片)，叫我 William 就行了。(两个人都看了一下对方的名片，放入皮夹而非口袋中。)

Johnson： 孙先生，他看起来是个有为的青年，很难找到像他这样有才干、有热忱的人。

孙先生： 他确实在公司表现不凡，请叫我 Steven 就行了。

Johnson： Steven，你可以简单地告诉我天津零售市场的现况吗？

孙先生： 唔，由于每人的平均收入不断地增高，市场的发展领域似乎偏向于高价位商品。

Johnson： 此地的零售走入高价位了？天津的发展比我想象的要快多了。

孙先生： 没错，现在的天津和我小时候完全不一样了，这里发展得非常快速。

Johnson： 你想这种趋势还会维持下去吗？

孙先生： 我不觉得有什么不行！虽然是有一些问题，但我们仍愿意勤奋工作，而且现阶段工资仍不算太高。

Johnson： 到目前为止，我所看到的一切都令我印象深刻，真的十分深刻。

 **Extend Your Eyes**

常用商务旅行词汇

en-suite	套房
family suite	家庭套房
twin room	带两张单人床的双人房间
double room	带一张双人床的双人房间
advance deposit	定金
reservation	订房间
registration	登记
rate sheets	房价表
tariff	价目表
cancellation	取消预定
imperial suite	皇室套房
presidential suite	总统套房
suite deluxe	高级套房
junior suite	简单套房
mini suite	小型套房
honeymoon suite	蜜月套房
penthouse suite	楼顶套房
unmade room	未清扫房
on change	待清扫房
valuables	贵重品
porter	行李员
luggage/baggage	行李
registered/checked luggage	托运行李
light luggage	轻便行李
baggage elevator	行李电梯
baggage receipt	行李收据
trolley	手推车
storage room	行李仓
briefcase	公文包
suit bag	衣服袋
travelling bag	旅行袋

shoulder bag	背包
trunk	大衣箱
suitcase	小提箱
name tag	标有姓名的标签
regular flight	正常航班
non-scheduled flight	非正常航班
international flight	国际航班
domestic flight	国内航班
flight number	航班号
airport	机场
airline operation	航空业务
alternate airfield	备用机场
landing field	停机坪
international terminal	国际航班候机楼
domestic terminal	国内航班候机楼
control tower	控制台
jetway	登机道
air-bridge	旅客桥
visitor's terrace	迎送平台
concourse	中央大厅
loading bridge	候机室至飞机的连接通路
airline coach service	航空汽车服务处
shuttle bus	机场内来往大巴

Business Report

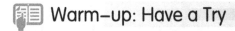 Warm-up: Have a Try

Try to translate the following business report into Chinese

Final Report on This Year's Costume Fair in Paris
To: John Brown, the Managing Director
From: Lily Jones, the Marketing Department
Date: April 14, 2009

INTRODUCTION:

This year's Costume Fair was held in the Paris International Exhibition Hall from April 6 to 12, 2009. The week-long exhibition attracts more than 8,000 exhibiters from all over the world, among which our company ranks the first in the field of environmentally-friendly textile manufacturers from China. We feel so excited to see so many famous and outstanding brands of costumes and at the same time, the fierce competition equally touches us deeply.

FINDINGS:

Since this is the first time for us to attend such big and high-level costume fair, we find that there is huge space for us to improve:

• Our slogan is lack of creativity and novelty, and is drowned among all those original and attractive brands, big or small.

• The promotion appeal does not match with our products; the theme of being environmentally-friendly fails to come up remarkably.

CONCLUSIONS:

During this exhibition, we feel it's so important and vital to participate in such fairs, so as to know the latest trend in the costume field and to learn from other manufacturers.

RECOMMENDATIONS:

Based on the experience from this fair, we'd like to make the following suggestions:

• Change our slogan. We should come up with a new and suitable slogan, both with creativity and novelty, to distinguish our products with other similar brands.

• Change the marketing strategies. The promotion campaign should emphasize the theme of being environmentally-friendly, for instance, adding more green colors in the design of new costumes.

Background: Learn Something About Market Investigation

商务报告是指针对某种特殊的、有意义的商务目的，向一个人或多个人提供的公正、客观和有计划的事实陈述。按种类划分，常见的有：事件调查报告 (Investigative Reports)、意见调查报告 (Survey Reports)、周报告 (Weekly Reports)、月度报告 (Monthly Reports)、进展报告 (Progress Reports) 等。在撰写商务英语报告时，应确保报告内容准确无误 (Accurate)、简明扼要 (Brief)、结构清晰 (Clear)、建议明确果断 (Decisive)，故简称 ABCD 原则。

英语商务报告的文体结构如下。

(1) Title (题目)。

报告的标题应尽可能概括报告的内容，因为它是整篇报告的信息浓缩，而且标题应该准确、客观，不应像报刊文章标题那样为了吸引读者的注意力而别出心裁。此外，标题应该是名词短语或动名词短语。如以下几例。

Report on Improving the Training Methods of HDC
Report on the Proposed Incentive Scheme
Report on the Adoption of Flex-time Working Systems

(2) Transmittals（报告传达书，包括作者姓名和单位、呈送对象、日期）。

(3) Contents（目录）。

Table of Contents
1. Introduction·· 3
1.1 Gives background
1.2 States purpose&scope
1.3 Outline main argument and structure
2. Findings··· 4
2.1 Finding One
2.2 Finding Two
2.3 Discussion
3. Recommendations··· 5
4. Conclusions·· 7

(4) Summary（总结、提要、摘要、概要）。

尽量限制段落的数量，一般可用三段式：报告的目的、报告的调查结果和结论、报告的建议。

摘要写作的时态用一般现在时，因为报告已经存在。

如"This report shows"属于正确表达，而"This report will show"则不妥。

(5) Introduction（引言、导言、导语、序言）。

在导言部分，扼要地说明一下报告的写作背景和主旨。此外，还应该注明报告提交给何人、是何时提交的。如果是事件调查报告应首先说明事件的经过，包括事件发生的日期、时间、地点、情况叙述等。以下是导言部分写作的常见句型。

• The report examines/explains...
• The purpose of this report is to...investigate/evaluate/study...
• The objective of this report is to...recommend/analyze/give...
• The aim of this report is to...feedback/estimate/assess...
• Enclosed is a report about...

(6) Findings(body)（正文）。

报告的调查结果部分是报告建议的依据，其内容应当准确无误，结构清晰，语言流畅、衔接。这部分内容的每一个段落都应当有一个明确的主题句，一般放在段首，这样便于读者摄取这部分的信息。以下是这部分主题句写作的常见句型。

• The findings of the investigation indicate that...

• It was proposed/found/felt/discovered that...

• It was generally the case that...

• Most people thought/suggested that...

• A number of people mentioned that...

• Several changes were put forward.

• Several staff members expressed the view that...

若报告中需提供图表统计数据或描述行情走势，撰写人应当熟悉这方面写作的常用句型，以下就是该方面写作的一些典型句子结构。

• The table/chart/graph/diagram/figure/statistics shows/describes/illustrates that...

• As it can be seen from the table/chart/figure...

• It is clear/apparent from the table/chart/graph/diagram/figure/statistics that...

• The number of...increased/jumped/rose suddenly/rapidly/dramatically from...to...

• The number of...decreased/dropped/fell greatly/significantly/sharply from...to...

• The number of...fluctuated slowly/slightly between...to...

• The number of...remained steady/stable(stayed the same) between...to...

• There was a(very) sudden/rapid/dramatic/significant increase/jump/rise in the number of...from...to...

• There was a(very) sharp/steep/steady/gradual/slow/slight decrease/drop/fall in the number of...from...to...

• The monthly profit/figures peaked in December at 10%.

• The monthly profit/figures reached a peak/a high(point) in December at 10%.

• The monthly profit/figures bottomed out in December at 10%.

• Sales witnessed a great rise/increase/drop/fall between...to...

(7) Conclusions（结论）。

It was decided/agreed/felt that...

No conclusions were reached regarding...

也可直接陈述结论，举例如下。

According to the findings above, it can be concluded that...

From the table shown, it can be concluded that...

Therefore, it can be concluded that...

(8) Recommendations（建议、意见）。

Our findings suggest that...

We would recommend that...

It is suggested/recommended that...

The following are the recommendations...

Based on the conclusion/analysis above, we recommend that/it can be concluded that...

With reference to the facts/advantages stated above, the following recommendations can be made...

Something is recommended.

A change of attitude is recommended.

A more professional attitude will need to be encouraged through training.

On the basis of the results, I have the following recommendations:

On the basis of the analysis, it is reasonable to have the following recommendations:

(9) References（参考资料）。

(10) Appendices（附录、附件）。

Discussion: Talk About How to Do the Task Well

商务报告为了达到有效的交流目的，其语言特点是 reader-oriented（以读者为导向）、clear（清晰）、accurate（准确）、concise（简洁）、objective（客观）、vivid（生动）。翻译的时候同样要遵循这些特点。

1. 商务英语报告的用词特点

进行英语商务报告写作时要尽可能使用简单和人们熟悉的词汇，举例如下。

Formal	Informal	Formal	Informal
anticipate	expect	endeavor	try
ascertain	find out	interrogate	ask

2. 商务英语报告句式特点

1) 段落要有主题句 (topic sentence)

一个好的主题句可以显示段落的结构和内容，使读者更容易读懂报告内容。首句如果不是主题句，读者可能会错过作者的要点和真正的意图，没有好的主题句也会使段落的句子间缺乏统一性。

例 1. The purpose of this report is to compare the terms and conditions of managerial-grade staff in this company with those of staff employed at Transpacific Shipping.

参考译文：此报告的目的就是将该公司管理人员的待遇条件和跨太平洋海运工作人员的条件进行比较。

句式使用了不定式做表语，直切主题，使读者迅速理解报告主要内容。

2) 在行文过程中要使用好逻辑过渡词汇或者信号词

段落中概念间的逻辑联系是继续前面的想法，还是提出更为重要的观点，需依靠信号词汇来完成。比如表达对比关系的：in contrast, on the other hand；表达转折关系的：but, however, nevertheless, on the contrary；表达因果关系的：as a result, because, consequently, for this reason, therefore 等。

例 2. Therefore, I'd like to make the following recommendations for your reference.

参考译文：因此我提出以下建议供您参考。

3) 强调主谓语的重要性和在一个句子中的地位

为充分发挥主要主语和谓语动词的力度，将主谓语放在突出的位置，同时将要表达的核心意思放在主谓语中。

例 3. 我们之所以建议计算机化是因为它能够缩短获取数据的时间，同时能够获取更精确的数据。

参考译文 1：The reason we are recommending the computerization of this process is because it will reduce the time required to obtain data and will give us more accurate data.

该句翻译遵循了汉语原句的结构，使用了主系表 +because 引导的表语从句，但作为商务报告句式，则显得啰唆。因此在译文 2 中使用了更简洁的主从句式，直接引出建议，然后用原因状语从句表达因果。

参考译文 2：We are recommending the computerization of this process because it will save time and give us more accurate data.（改进）

4) 可利用平行句组织松散句

有些句子从语法的角度看是正确的，但杂乱无章，很难让人抓到核心。

例 4. The goal of the new planning process is to provide headquarters with more accurate information about the long-range needs of each division so that they can be reviewed and coordinated at the corporate level to ensure that capital is allocated fairly in accordance with coherent overall strategy.

句子中虽然使用了一些连接词，如 so that, in accordance with 等，但并没有很好地组织起一个句子内所要传达的几个概念，可以将上述句子利用几个平行句改写如下。

The goals of the new planning process are to gather accurate information about the needs of each division, to review these needs at the corporate level and to allocate capital fairly according to an overall strategy.

Follow-up: Do It Yourself

Translate the following business report into Chinese

(1) Following your instruction, we examined the cause of the decline in sales of

Shanghai Branch.

(2) In this report, I present the data collected for improving our new series products.

(3) Therefore, I'd like to make the following recommendations for your reference.

(4) 在进行全面比较之后，我们决定采用第三方案。

(5) 我在十二个可选方案中选择了第三个，因为它的可行性比其他的大。

(6) 这份报告将提供您所需要的信息，以帮助您决定是否该投资 ABC 公司。

Homework: Practice Makes Perfect

Translate the following English passage into Chinese

Subject：On the Re-investment of This Year's Profit

Introduction

This report sets out to examine how the company should re-invest this year's profits.

Alternatives

The areas under consideration are:

a) the purchase of new computers

b) the provision of language training courses

c) the payment of special bonuses

Evaluation

1. New computers

The majority of company computers are quite new and fast enough to handle the work done on them. Consequently, new computers would not be recommended.

2. Language training courses

The company aims to increase exports, particularly in Spain and France. Therefore, language training courses would be an excellent idea for those employees who deal with business partners and customers overseas. Besides, training courses would increase motivation. Staff would enjoy the lessons and perceive that the company is investing in them. Therefore, language courses would be a option.

3. Special bonus payment

Although special bonus payments would have a beneficial impact on motivation, they would have no direct effect on the company's operation. There are also potential problems concerning the selection of staff eligible for the payments and the setting of a precedent for future payments. Therefore, bonus payments would not be advisable.

Conclusions

1. Purchasing new computer is not necessary at present.

2. Special bonus payment may result in problem.

3. Language training courses are good for both company's operation and empolyees' motivation.

Recommendation

It is felt that the best solution for both the company and staff would be to invest in language training. It is suggested that the company should organize courses in French and Spanish. Those employees who have contact with partners should be assured of places but other interested members of staff should also be allowed to attend.

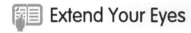# Extend Your Eyes

商务报告常用表达

industry quota	行业配额
market conditions	市场状况
research report	研究报告
market scale	市场规模
utilizing habits	使用习惯
purchasing process	购买过程
purchasing flow	采购流程
flow analysis	流程分析
sales revenue	销售收入
research objectives	研究目的
result delivery	结果提交
research scope	调研范围 / 调查范围 / 研究范围
budget	费用预算
schedule	时间安排
market research	市场调查 / 市场调研 / 市场研究
research objects	研究对象 / 调查对象
case research	案面研究
in-depth interview	深访
interview	面访
telephone interview	电话访问
data collection	数据采集
data analysis	数据分析
report writing	报告撰写
working plan	工作方案

project training	项目培训
follow-up research	追踪调查
competitive brand	竞争品牌
brand planning	品牌规划
market share	市场占有率
sales performance	销售业绩
sampling	抽样
development trend	发展趋势
driving forces	驱动因素/推动因素
supply end	供应端
sales amount	销售额
sales volume	销售量
production capacity	生产能力
major products	主打产品
sales share	销售份额
value chain	价值链
direct sales	直销
distribution sales	分销
advance rate	加价率
sales network	销售网络
producer price/ex-factory price	出厂价
purchase price	进货价
growth rate	增长率
price/performance ratio	性价比
brand popularity	品牌知名度
product reliability	产品可靠性
enterprise nature	企业性质
major methods	主要方法
quota sampling	配额抽样
peak season of sales	销售旺季
brand image	品牌形象
sample formation	样本构成
report description	报告说明
brand capability	品牌性能
competition research	竞争研究
high-end	高端
mid-high end	中高端

low-end	低端
competition structure	竞争格局
sales scope	销售范围
production scale	生产规模
key regions	重点区域
promotion objects	推广对象
development strategy	发展战略
consumption research	消费研究
general analysis	总体分析
industrial features	行业特征
total sales volume	总销量
price trend	价格走势
profit trend	利润走势
promotion policy	推广政策
management policy	管理政策
sales profit	销售利润
consumption concept	消费观念
sales strategy	销售策略
cost accounting	成本核算
profit margin	利润空间
inspection report	检测报告
enterprise credit	企业信誉
sales analysis	销售分析
demand quantity	需求量
sales channel	销售渠道
sales chain	销售链
project effectiveness	项目成效
market prospects	市场前景
consumption volume	消耗量
market capacity	市场容量
investment research	投资研究
commercial environment	商业环境
the third party logistics	第三方物流
core competence	核心竞争力
customer expectations	客户期望
customer complaints	客户抱怨
investment prospects	投资前景

market forecast	市场预测
promotion strategy	促销策略
specialized research	专项调研
market potentials	市场潜力
comprehensive performance	综合绩效
proposal	计划书
comprehensive report	综合报告
report format	报告格式
project proposal	项目计划书
rules and standards	法规标准
price advantage	价格优势
representative enterprise	代表企业
price fluctuation	价格波动
market promotion	市场推广
after-sales service	售后服务
bonded zone	保税区
current status	现状
delivery period	供货周期
sales modes	销售格局
general agent	总代理
gross profit	毛利率
profit return	返点
project bidding	项目竞标
discount rate	折扣度
penalty measure	处罚措施
authorized manufacturer	授权制造商
R&D ability	研发能力
external resources	外部资源
customer satisfaction	客户满意度
executive report	执行报告
maintenance cost	维护成本
first line brand	一线品牌
second line brand	二线品牌
production conditions	生产状况
shopping centers	商场
best seller	畅销产品
manufacturing enterprise	生产企业

end user	最终用户 / 终端用户
purchasing right	采购权
idle funds	资金闲置
bargain price	成交价格
bad debts	坏账
annual report	年度报告
investment and financing	投资融资
cost structure	成本费用构成
capital operating status	资产运行情况
profitability ability	盈利能力
debts repayment ability	偿债能力
merger and reorganization	兼并与重组
leading enterprise	龙头企业
macro economy	宏观经济
monthly report sample	月报样本
formal report	正式报告
memorandum report	备忘录式报告
letter report	书信式报告
periodic report	定期报告
investigation report	调查报告
progress report	进展报告
feasibility report	可行性报告
audit report	审计报告
proposal report	建议报告

Corporate Profile

Warm-up: Have a Try

1. Put the following Chinese into English

索迪斯集团由皮埃尔·白龙先生创建于1966年,1983年在巴黎证券所上市,2000年于纽约股票交易所上市,总部设在法国巴黎。

今天,凭借40余年的丰富经验以及在世界五大洲的成功经营,索迪斯联盟已成为世界上最大的从事餐饮服务及综合后勤管理的跨国公司。作为《财富》杂志全球500强公司,截至2005年年底,索迪斯联盟在全球拥有员工32.4万人,在76个国家中设立了超过2.4万个合作项目。

2. Put the following English into Chinese

The Haier Group was founded in 1984 with headquarters in Qingdao, Shandong Province, PRC. At its initial stage, Haier produced only a single model of refrigerators, but today it is one of the World's leading white goods manufacturers. Haier has manufactured home appliances in over 15,000 different specifications under 96 categories. Haier products are now sold in over 100 countries around the globe. Haier has over 240 subsidiary corporations, over 110 design centers and trading companies and over 50,000 employees throughout the World. Haier's focused industries include technology, manufacturing, trade and financial services. Haier's product categories range from refrigerators, refrigerating cabinets, air conditioners, washing machines, televisions, mobile phones, home theatre systems, computers, water heaters, DVD players, among which 9 are ranked market leaders in China, and 3 are ranked among the top 3 worldwide in their respective industries.

Background: Learn Something About Corporate Profile

公司介绍是公司面向目标客户、消费者及全社会提供的公司基本信息的书面概述，公司为树立自己的形象，用较为生动的语言对自己的现状、历史、组成、业务范围、业务特色等进行介绍，从而达到宣传自己的目的。一份相对完整的公司简介结构如下。

1. 标题：公司全称，后面可加"简介"或不添加。
2. 正文：正文是公司简介的主体部分，一般包括四部分内容。

第一部分：用精练简短的文字概括介绍公司基本情况。

(1) 公司的发展历程：公司的注册时间、发展速度、重要的成绩和荣誉称号。
(2) 公司所属行业及主打产品。
(3) 公司的注册资本和资质等级等。
(4) 公司规模：部门构成、员工数量及员工素质。
(5) 公司的法律性质——独资公司、合伙公司或合作经营公司。

第二部分：应承接上文，对公司经营的主营产品(服务)进行重点介绍，内容如下。

(1) 公司的经营范围和服务类型，公司主要产品的介绍。
(2) 公司的经营业绩和成功范例。
(3) 公司服务的特点和优势，如售后服务的承诺。

第三部分：介绍公司的文化特色和发展愿景，包括公司的发展目标、理念、宗旨、使命、愿景、寄语等，以期树立良好的公司形象，具体分为以下几点。

(1) 公司的发展方向、运作模式。
(2) 公司的经营理念。
(3) 公司的发展战略。

(4) 公司的社会贡献。

(5) 公司获得过的荣誉奖项。

第四部分：具体、准确地介绍公司的经营地址、联系方式，如电话、传真、网址等。

另外，公司简介通常随附图片若干张，如公司全景、干净卫生的办公场所、精神饱满的员工、奖项证书等。

无论是英文公司简介，还是中文公司简介，都具有呼唤功能和信息功能，旨在唤起读者对公司的好感，然后采取投资该公司、购买该公司产品或服务等行动，但由于汉英两种语言的差异，中英文公司简介在用词、句式和篇章结构等方面各有其特点，翻译时要遵循一定的翻译策略和原则。

Discussion: Talk About How to Do the Task Well

1. 中英文公司简介的语言差异

1) 中英文公司简介的行文差异

在中英两种文化中，读者思维方式和价值观念存在差异，中英文公司简介的文体特征也不尽相同。在内容上，中文公司简介重信息功能，主要通过提供尽可能详细的信息，让读者对该公司有更深入的了解。在语篇特征上，中文公司简介喜用夸张，常有笼统、抽象的套话，辞藻华丽，经常引经据典，并喜用对仗、排比修辞手段，以渲染效果。

例1. 在中国经济高速发展的伟大进程中，它容纳百川，汇成大海的壮阔。在一片创造神话、抒写千年梦想的热土上，它上下求索，承载着历史的重托。1986年8月16日，联塑集团的诞生，宣告了一个童话与奇迹的诞生，从此它以横空跃世的雄姿，以锐不可当的气势，致力于改善给水排水管道的环保卫生，致力于保障人民身体健康和提高人们的生活品质。

英文公司简介则是信息功能和呼唤功能并重，旨在通过提供信息去"煽情"和"诱说"，从而促使读者做出积极的反应。

例 2. Our customer service always follows the principle of "Customer Satisfaction is the Ultimate Goal". We have set up customer service branches in more than 20 key cities in China. These include Beijing, Shanghai, Guangzhou, Harbin, Hohhot, Lanzhou, Haikou, etc. We have always set up commercial representation and service agencies in Europe, America, Oceania, Africa, the Middle East, Southeast Asia and other areas. We are always ready to give you first-rate service and support.

中文公司简介中常用大量的修饰语，国内一些厂家在宣传自己的产品时喜欢用"国内一流""国际领先"和"顶尖"等语汇，同时汉语句式表达重视音韵和词汇的对仗工整。相比之下，英文公司简介的语言表达趋于直白，注重事实和客观性，文体朴实，用词具体，重在信息的提供。国外消费者更倾向于接受那些经过国际权威机构标准认证的产品，他们不太接受国内一些宣传材料中那些文体夸张，带有笼统、抽象的套话。

由于汉英两种语言中公司简介具有不同的文体特征，因此在将中文公司简介译成英语时，译者不应按照中文原文的行文方式去翻译，而应根据译文所要实现的预期功能，结合英语文化读者的思维方式和价值观念去翻译。在保证实现译文预期功能的前提下，译者应对中文原文进行语篇重构，即以语篇为中心，采用增删和改译等策略，对原文信息内容进行取舍和重组。

例 3. 某中国公司在介绍产品时这样表达："我们的产品质量一流，畅销国内外。"

如果将以上这句话简单翻译为 "Our products are the first-rate quality and they are very popular both in domestic market and World market."这样的译文往往会让英文读者产生反感，如果将 "first-rate quality" 的意思扩展一下，用获得国内同类产品权威机构认证的证书来表示，即可达到想要宣传的效果。另外，所谓的 "... are very popular both in domestic market and World market"，还不如用一些具体的国家和地名来描述自己产品的销售范围更实在和清楚。

2) 不同文化的语义差异

比如英汉两种语言中都有"龙"的概念，却反映了两种迥异的文化特征。在英语文化中，"dragon"（龙）是个喷毒火、身长双翼、凶残暴虐的怪物，很难让西方读者联想起在汉语言文化中的那种对"龙"的帝王尊严的象征。因此，涉外公司对外宣传材料中出现的一些与"龙"有关的时髦词语，如"龙头公司""龙头产业"和"一条龙服务"等在英译时均不出现"dragon"为好。

事实上，除了词语在不同文化里含义有别外，东西方不同的价值观往往也会影响宣传的效果。许多国内宣传广告译文中原封不动地照搬中华民族的价值观，虽然这种宣传早已被国人熟悉，但往往很难让译文读者接受。例如，当前中国正处于经济高速发展时期，一些国内广告借助媒体就以"先进的设备和技术""最新的科学方法"等表达方式来包装产品。但是西方发达国家早已步入以技术密集型为主体的高科技生产体系，那里的人们更渴望回归自然。鉴于此，译者应利用跨文化知识，在有利于宣传效果的前提下，针对原文进行合理的取舍。

2. 公司简介的翻译策略与方法

1) 增 / 省译法

在将中文公司简介翻译成英文时，要根据西方人的表达习惯和思维方式，化繁为简，采取省译法来简化语句和结构，以达到突出文章事实和重点的目的。

例 4. ……诞生于 20 世纪末的虎豹集团，信守孜孜以求、永不言退的发展理念，在市场经济的大潮中，任凭浊浪排空，惊涛拍岸，独有胜似闲庭信步的自信，处变不惊，运筹帷幄。尽握无限商机于掌间，渐显王者之气于天地……虎豹人以其特有的灵气，极目一流，精益求精，集世界顶尖服装生产技术装备之大成。裁天上彩虹，绣人间缤纷，开设计之先河，臻质量之高峰，领导服装潮流，尽显领袖风采……

这段公司外宣资料运用了很多汉语中的四字、五字、六字结构，辞藻优美，在汉语读者中能引起美的享受。但如果把此段文字直译成英语，会使崇尚简洁、明快为美的英语读者感到厌恶，也很难达到公司对外宣传的目的。根据英语公司简介的风格特点和英文读者的审美标准，翻译时可运用省译的翻译方法。

参考译文：Founded in the late 1990s, the Hubao Group is determined to succeed in new times if socialist market economy. The Hubao Group has a high standard of quality and is well equipped with the World's most advanced technology. They are taking the lead in designing new fashions and maintaining high quality products...

该译文精练明快，既传译了原文的主要信息，又迎合了西方读者的审美心理，能够达到有效宣传的目的。

中文的宣传类材料中的主观描写、虚夸之词较多，中国悠久的历史、灿烂的文化也常集中体现在宣传材料中，如历史人物、典故、神话、诗赋、成语、地名、历史年代等，为了让英文读者更好地理解原文，有时需要在翻译时稍微增加一些解释，但是又不能增加太多，否则翻译就变成了阐释，如何恰如其分地增译，需要在大量的翻译实践中去总结经验。

例5. 大乘寺坐北朝南，院墙按八卦建造。

参考译文：The Great Mahayana Temple faces south with its walls shaped after the Eight Diagrams combinations of three whole or broken lines formerly used in divination.

例6. 林子的边上原来有一个洞，传说白娘子曾经在这里修炼。

参考译文：Near the forest, there once was a cave, which was said to be the very place Lady White, the legendary heroine of The Story of the White Snake, cultivated herself according to Buddhist doctrine.

以上例5和例6分别在译文中增加了"八卦"和"白娘子"的简明扼要的解释，既不显得累赘，又有利于英文读者的理解。

2) 逻辑重构法

汉语思维以直觉、具体和圆式为特征，因此，汉语公司外宣资料常采用"旁敲侧击""含而不露"的归纳推理法；西方文化注重线性的因果思维，因而，他们偏爱开门见山、直入主题的演绎推理法。因此，在进行两种语言转换时，需要对译文进行逻辑重构，迎合读者的审美心理，达到译文的预期目的。示例如下。

例7. 山海关啤酒厂坐落在风景优美的避暑胜地、历史名城——山海关。素有"龙头"之称的万里长城的东部起端，由此伸向大海。该厂始建于1982年，后经二次扩建和技术改造，如今已形成了具有年产8万吨啤酒和9千吨麦芽的生产能力，是我国啤酒行业的骨干公司之一。

上述文字属归纳式的行文方式，最后才提到中心信息"骨干公司之一"。把此段文字译成英语的话，需要对之进行逻辑重组，因为英语是信息功能突出的语言，喜欢直入主题，逻辑条理清楚。译文通过调整句序，将重点信息置于句首，突出了信息功能，增加了译文的移情功能和呼唤功能。

参考译文：Shanhaiguan Brewery is a key enterprise brewing beer in China. It is located in Shanhaiguan, a picturesque summer resort and historical town, where the East End of the Great Wall extends to the sea. Since its founding in 1982, Shanhaiguan Brewery has been technically transformed and expanded to the present scale with an annual capacity of 80,000 tons of beer and 9,000 tons of malt.

3) 合句法

汉语企业简介常有警句和大量零句，句式呈多样化，一个短句接一个短句，是典型的流散型句式，然而英语讲求结构的完整和严密，句式以长句为主、短句为辅，因此，中文企业简介英译时常常需要把一个由数个零句组成的汉语句子缩合成完整严密的英语长句。

例8. 彩虹集团公司下属20多家公司，总资产达8亿人民币……

参考译文：There are altogether 20 sub-companies under Rainbow Group Ltd. with a total asset of 8.7 billion RMB...

例8的原文两个分句各自有自己的主语，中间用一个逗号分隔，英语译文将逗号处理为with引导的短语，将中文的两个分句合成了英语的一个单句，结构严谨，符合英语的行文风格。

例9. 招商宾馆是一家外商投资的高级涉外宾馆，毗邻中国出口商品交易会，面临风景秀丽的流花湖花园。

参考译文：CHINA MERCHANTS HOTEL is a foreign-venture hotel, situated next to Guangzhou Trade Fair and facing to the beautiful Liuhua Lake.

例9的中文原句有三个分句，中间用逗号相隔，主语统一为"招商宾馆"，英语译文将后两个分句分别处理为过去分词短语(situated...)和现在分词短语(facing...)，这是英语中典型的书面用语，显得正式、严谨。

Follow-up: Do It Yourself

Translate the following sentences and paragraphs into English / Chinese

(1) Throughout our businesses, we have established a reputation for product innovation, quality, design and value.

(2) Our strong brand names and new product development capabilities enjoy worldwide recognition.

(3) Our products and services are marketed in more than 100 countries, and we have manufacturing operations in eleven countries, including three in China.

(4) Black & Decker is a global marketer and manufacturer of quality power tools, hardware, household appliances, plumbing and building products used in and around homes and for commercial applications.

(5) October 2009, Ting Hsin International Group, accompanied by Japan's Waseda University(日本早稻田大学) announced jointly an investment of 26.4 million U.S. dollars to high scholarship, funding Chinese top students for International Training in world famous universities.

(6) 摩托罗拉是世界财富百强公司，拥有全球性的业务和影响力，2005年的销售额为353亿美元。

(7) 自1990年起，公司已连续三年在中国进出口额最大的500家外贸企业中进入前30位。

(8) 公司拥有雄厚的技术力量，大、中专毕业以上的技术、管理人才占员工总数的30%以上，并与国内多家科研机构建立了紧密型的合作关系。

(9) 十多年来，本公司一贯以优质的产品、卓越的服务为宗旨，备受国内外大客户的支持、拥护与信赖。

(10) 珠海迪蒙贸易有限公司是经珠海市外经委批准成立的具有进出口经营权的法人企业。

Homework: Practice Makes Perfect

1. Translate the following paragraph into Chinese

In China, Unilever sponsored 9 hope schools and launched the "Unilever Hope Star" project in universities, helping 200 poor students for the 4-year college tuition. We also set up scholarship in Fudan University to reward students with excellent performance. Since 1996, we launched "Zhonghua" teeth protection campaigns across the whole country. In 2000, we launched a tree-planting campaign in more than 10 provinces in China to increase people's awareness of environmental protection.

2. Translate the following paragraph into Chinese

Motorola has been a global leader in innovation in telecommunications. In China, Motorola has invested US$600 million in R&D, building 17 R&D centers and labs in Beijing, Tianjin, Shanghai, Nanjing, Chengdu and Hangzhou. The number of R&D staff is about 3,000 now.

Motorola China R&D Institute has now become one of the world-class R&D bases at Motorola. It has also evolved the largest R&D institute global companies with have ever set up in China.

3. Translate the following paragraph into English

中钞国鼎拥有一支锐意进取、理想高远的高素质队伍，他们是一群乐于奉献的灵魂舞者，在创意与设计的世界中舞蹈，在文化与经济的领域中翱翔。正是这样一支队伍，演绎了中钞国鼎三年间飞速发展的惊世传奇。

4. Translate the following paragraph into English

天津市外国企业专家服务有限公司面向外商驻津代表机构、三资企业以及国有或民营企业提供以人力资源服务为核心业务，在天津市人力资源服务市场中占据了重要的份额，2003年和2004年连续两年荣获天津市优秀企业的称号。

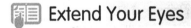 Extend Your Eyes

公司简介常用词汇

be founded in ...(time/place)	于……(时间、地点)开业
made an initial public offering of shares on...	在……上市
a global Fortune 100 company	世界财富百强公司之一
state-owned	国有
collective-owned	集体所有
private-owned	私有
joint venture	合资公司
foreign-funded enterprise	外资公司
cooperative enterprise	合作公司
wholly foreign-owned enterprise	独资公司
consistent efforts and contributions	不懈地努力进取
expand business	扩大业务(范围)
guiding principle	指导原则
since the earliest days of establishment	创建初期
aim principally at	以……为首要目标
diversely import, export and reexport	经营各种进口、出口和转口业务
adopt a consistent policy of...	一贯秉持……原则
honest, reliable and best services	真诚待客、信守诺言、服务周到

the best names in products	优质/名牌产品
seek after quality ...products	以生产优质产品为宗旨
make constant endeavors	不断努力
be in line with international standards	达到/符合国际标准
establishment of good reputation	建立良好信誉
be abundant in ... resources...	资源丰富
heavily participate in	积极参与
exert energetic efforts to develop	积极努力发展
utilize the natural advantage of ...	利用……天然优势
promote international trade	促进国际贸易
maintain close contacts with ...	与……保持紧密联系
be elected director/chairman of ...	被推选为……的理事长/主席
fellow traders	同业，同行
conform to the spirit of ...	符合……精神
offer the best services to ...	为……提供精心服务
Quality Primacy, High Reputation.	质量第一，信誉第一
Good Quality, High Efficiency.	优质高效
be awarded the gold prize	获得金奖
qualified enterprise	优质公司
class A enterprise	一级公司
honorable enterprise	荣誉公司
Service Supremacy, Equality and Mutual Benefit.	服务至上，平等互利
Stressing Reputation and Paying Attention to Service.	讲信誉，重服务
ensure a powerful support system	充分发挥辅助作用/形成有力的辅助系统
Unity, Striving, Hardwork, Creation and Dedication.	团结、拼搏、务实、创新、奉献
pass/gain/obtain/be granted the Certificate of ISO9002 International Quality System	通过ISO9002国际质量体系认证

公司宣传材料常用句型

1. be established...	创建于……
2. be founded...	创建于……
3. be incorporated...	合并于……
4. be involved in....	涉及……

5. be listed as the.... 被列入（跻身于）……
6. be located in... 位于（坐落于）……

7. be named one of the World's 100 most recognizable brands in a global name brand list edited by the World Brand Laboratory.

被世界品牌实验室命名为世界最具影响力的 100 个品牌之一。

8. be ranked...which were the top three 跻身前三甲

9. Haier has established 18 design institutes, 10 industrial complexes, 22 overseas production factories and 58,800 sales agents World wide.

海尔已经在全球建立起了 18 个设计院、10 个工业园区、22 个海外工厂以及 58 800 个销售代理。

10. have a general assets of... annual turnover ... and annual trading value

拥有资产总额……，年销量……，年贸易额……

11. manufacture a wide range of... 生产一系列的……

12. The Group has a general assets of 12.1 billion RMB, annual turnover 11.7 billion RMB and annual trading value 3 billion RMB.

该集团现有资产总额 121 亿元、年营业额 117 亿元、年经贸额 30 亿元。

13. In 2002, the group was listed as the 114th of top 500 enterprises in China.

2002 年，该集团公司在中国公司 500 强排序中名列第 114 位。

公司宣传资料各部分常用句式

1. Nature of a Company

... is a specialized corporation engaged in ...

... is a comprehensive business corporation with a legal entity.

... is a specialized foreign trade company directly authorized by ...

... has been ranked one of the top 500 foreign trade companies in China.

...is a joint venture with independent legal person qualification invested (approved) by…

...is a state-owned (private-owned) enterprise

...is a company registered officially in…

...is a legal entity with the authority to handle…

...is one of the national first class enterprises.

2. Scale of a Company

Our corporation has set up branches or joint ventures in ...

We have established steady business relations with clients in more than 50 countries.

...has ... subsidiaries across the country.

...has offices in...

...has been expanding extensively into a ...

3. Principles of a Company

By adhering to and under the guidance of the principle of ... the corporation has been steadily expanding its business lines.

The corporation will provide first rate services.

The guiding principle of our company is...

We aim principally at...

The company will follow its motto...

We will persist in (adhere to) the principle of ...

Following the principle of ... the company will ...

... has adopted a consistent policy of ...

4. Scope of a Company

The scope of our business is as follows:

Our business line covers:

Business scope:

Our company mainly deals in...

Our business scope includes...

Commercial Advertisement

 Warm-up: Have a Try

Try to translate the following advertisements into Chinese

1. We lead, others copy. (理光复印机)
2. Good to the last drop. (麦斯威尔咖啡)
3. Intelligence everywhere. (摩托罗拉手机)
4. The relentless pursuit of perfection. (凌志轿车)
5. Cleans your breath while it cleans your teeth. (高露洁牙膏)
6. Details make delicate lives. (帅康厨房电器)
7. The World is all around you. (中国电信)

8. Create possibilities for your dreams. (蒙牛牛奶)

9. Technology innovator, Medi air-conditioner. (美的空调)

10. Life makes TV plays. (CCTV-8)

11. To me, the past is black and white, but the future is always colorful. (轩尼诗酒)

12. Let's make things better. (飞利浦照明产品)

13. Fresh up with Seven-up. (七喜饮料)

14. Connecting people. (诺基亚通信产品)

15. Breakfast without orange juice is like a day without sunshine. (橘汁)

16. Flowers by Interflora speak from the heart. (鲜花)

17. Once tasted, always loved. (饮料)

18. Big thrills. Small bills. (出租车)

Background: Learn Something About Commercial Advertisements

1. 广告的定义

广告，即广而告知之意。英语广告"advertise"一词源于拉丁语的advertere，意为"唤起大众对某种事物的注意并诱导于一定的方向所使用的一种手段"。(Advertising is the non-personal communication of information usually paid for and usually persuasive in nature about products, services or ideas by identified sponsors through the various media.) 根据这一定义，广告应具备信息功能、诱导功能、美感功能和表情功能。

广义的广告包括非经济广告和经济广告，非经济广告不以营利为目的，如政府行政部门、社会事业单位，乃至个人的各种公告、启事、声明等，主要目的是推广。狭义的广告仅指经济广告，也叫商业广告，指由商品经营者或者服务提供者承担费用，通过一定媒介和形式直接或者间接地介绍自己所推销的商品或者所提供的服务的广告形式。

Advertising is an audio or visual form of marketing communication that employs an openly sponsored, non-personal message to promote or sell a product, service or idea. Advertising is communicated through various mass media or text messages. The actual presentation of the message in a medium is referred to as an advertisement or "ad". Commercial ads often seek to generate increased consumption of their products or services through "branding", which associates a product name or image with certain qualities in the minds of consumers.

2. 汉英广告语言的差异

1) 语音差异

汉语和英语在语音、拟声或用韵方面均有不同特点。在英语广告词中，经常采用头韵（首音节押韵）、元韵（元音节押韵）、后韵（末音节押韵）等方式增加广告词的音韵美，如 Spend a dime, Save you time.（某电器广告），BETA Builds it Better.（家具广告）（头韵），而要在汉语译文中保留这种音乐美是很难做到的。

例1. Hi-fi, Hi-fun, Hi-fashion, only for Sony.（索尼音箱广告）（押韵）

"fi" "fun" 和 "fashion" 三个词押头韵，使广告读起来朗朗上口，富有节奏感，像音乐一样婉转悦耳，很契合产品的特点。但是这种押韵方式很难在保留原文意思的前提下照搬到译文中。

某些广告词语的读音还可能会在目标语言中产生负面印象。例如，日本东芝公司曾在中国使用过一句广告歌词："Toshiba（东芝），Toshiba（东芝），大家的东芝。"被一些年轻人开玩笑地用谐音法念成"偷去吧，偷去吧，大家的东西"。一经引申，这则广告的严肃性就大大降低了。

2）语义差异

汉英词汇的内涵有时大相径庭，如果直接按字面翻译，而不考虑到文化、政治、风俗等其他因素，常会产生贻笑大方的译文，甚至会引起反感和误解。

例如，上海产"白翎"钢笔，如果英译为"White Feather"，在英语国家就会无人问津，因为英语中有句成语"to show the white feather"，意思是"临阵逃脱"。

又如法国某公司在向中国推销男用香水时，将其香水命名为"Opium（鸦片）"，本意是想用"鸦片"一词突出其产品的魅力难挡，结果产品上市后即引起了中国消费者的强烈反感，因其违反中国商标法，1999年被国家工商局撤销其注册商标。这是因为该公司不了解中国人民对鸦片的憎恨心理，无意中挫伤了国人的民族自尊心。

相反，美国女用化妆品牌 Revlon 译为"露华浓"，一看译名便会联想起唐代诗人李白描写杨贵妃花容月貌的著名诗句"云想衣裳花想容，春风拂槛露华浓"，从而引发读者对该产品的美好联想。

另外，由于东西方社会制度不同，一些反映中国特色的政治、经济、社会方面的词语，对不熟悉中国国情的西方人也会造成信息传递障碍。

比如，我们提倡"五讲、四美、三热爱"，有人曾译为"five stresses, four beauties and three lovers"，但是却让以英语为母语的西方人误解为"四个美人和三个情人"。修改后的译文"five stresses, four points of beauty and three aspects of love." 则避免了这种误解。

因此广告翻译中要避免使用政治上有特别含义、容易引起误解的商品名称。比如"大鹏"卷笔刀的英译名就不宜译为"ROC sharpeners"，大鹏是汉民族神话传说中的一种最大的鸟，汉语成语中有"鹏程万里""鲲鹏展翅"之说，具有志存高远、前途无量的褒义。但 ROC 三个大写字母也是常用新闻词语中"中华民国"的英语缩写，这样的英文势必产生误解或不必要的联想，既不利于创立出口商品的良好形象，也不利于维护国家的尊严。

3) 内涵差异

不同国家、民族和地区所用的文字对某些文字的偏好和厌恶可能大相径庭。据调查，日本人最喜欢的汉字为"诚""梦""爱""愁""美"等；根据美国作家 Irving Wallace 选出的最美丽的英文词是：Chime（一串铃）、Golden（金色的）、Lullaby（摇篮曲）、Melody（旋律）、Murmuring（低语）等；中国人喜欢的汉字为"福""寿""喜""乐"等。

因此翻译时要顾及广告词汇的情感意义，最大限度地扩大一个词的愉悦联想。比如"Carrefour"超市和"Cocacola"饮料分别译为"家乐福"和"可口可乐"，满足了中国人"平安是福"和"求吉求利"的心理。再如，以中国药科大学教授命名的"丁家宜"精华护肤霜系列产品的品名，原来是用汉语拼音"Dingjiayi"来表达的，但不如现在改用的"Tjoy"好。因为"Tjoy"不仅在语音上是"丁家宜"的谐音，而且其含义还能让英语国家的消费者产生愉快的联想。其中的 T 可以令人想起服装展示中的 T 型舞台和模特儿的靓丽身影，而且 joy 本身就是一个令人愉悦的词汇。

香港领带品牌 Goldlion 初译为"金狮"，但因"狮"与"死"谐音，有"不吉利"之意而影响销售，后改译为"金利来"，其中的"金"者"利"也，"金利"为意义的重叠，"来"则从 lion 的发音而来。

4) 思维差异

思维方式对文本内容的编排有着很大的影响，它影响着人们在说话和行文时的遣词造句、谋篇布局。西方社会崇尚个人主义，而东方强调集体主义。国内广告常用"×××，用了都说好""我们都喝×××，今天你喝了没有？""部优""省优""中国消费者协会推荐产品"等措辞。而英美等国家的人们追求的是特立独行的个性，他们的广告不会引导和鼓吹从众，更不会迷信和盲从所谓的权威，其广告词体现在文化方面更多的是"个性(Individual/Individuality)""独立(Independent/Independence)""隐私(Private/Privacy)"。因此，汉语有些广告如果直译为英语，就会使英语国家的消费者难以接受。所以英译时要尽量少用"大家都说好""昔日宫廷×，今日×××"等广告词。

例 2. 高档装修——中档价值——星级服务——大众消费——4000 平方米大店气宇非凡，各系列菜一应俱全，正餐、大餐、小吃任君品尝——豪华包间、雅间、大厅由你选择——品尝陶然风味，俯瞰山峡风情。

这则广告的创作意图是宣扬陶然居餐饮店，但广告词的开头只是介绍具体情况，而未点出主题，直到最后点明广告的要点，充分体现了中国人螺旋式的思维方式。然而，英语广告受西方人直线式思维方式的影响，在内容的编排上往往采用直截了当、一目了然的方法。

例 3. 在四川，有一处美丽的去处。它背依岷山主峰雪宝顶，树木苍翠，花香袭人，鸟声婉转，流水潺潺，名胜古迹荟萃。它就是松潘县的黄龙。

参考译文：One of Sichuan's finest spots is Huanglong (Yellow Dragon), which lies in Songpan County just beneath Xuebao, the main peak of Minshan Mountain. Its lush green forests, filled with fragrant flowers, bubbing streams and songbirds, are rich in historical interest as well as natural beauty.

这则汉语旅游广告直到段末才点出最重要的信息"黄龙"二字，而其英译文开篇第一句即将"Huanglong (Yellow Dragon)"译出。

5) 修辞差异

广告语常用修辞手法，其中最难处理的是双关的翻译，要做到两全其美确实很难。

如，我国的"玉兔"商标并不译成"Jade Rabbit"，而是译作"Moon Rabbit"。这是因为玉兔是我国神话中陪伴吴刚生活在月宫桂花树下的兔子，所以它又成为月的代称。"Moon Rabbit"这一译名既体现了我国的古老文化，又避免了误解，使人不会误认为是玉做的兔子。

汉语广告习惯上则偏重使用"四字格"词组（包括成语与非成语），另外，汉语广告常常选择顶级词语，如"第一""最""更""超""大""新""独""全""王""霸"等，还有隐含"第一"与"极致"意义的其他词语，如"品质超群、领袖风范、卓越不凡、无出其右、空调专家、搬运权威、销售冠军、精心杰作、天地精华、唯一推荐、领先潮流、超值享受、尽显风流"等。这些四字格词组使汉语广告相对于英文广告来说，更显典雅简洁，翻译时要依照英语行文特点，采用保留、替代、删减的方法对有关信息进行处理，从而增强广告对不同受众的吸引力和说服力。

例4. 桂林的山，平地拔起，百媚千娇，像高耸云霄的奇花巨葩，盛开在锦绣江南；漓江的水，澄明清澈，晶莹碧绿，恰似翡翠玉带，透迤于奇山秀峰之间。

参考译文：Guilin is surrounded by abrupt rock hills rising straight out of the ground. The hills have a myriad of forms, some graceful, others grotesque. Among them winds the flowing Lijiang River which holds a mirror to them.

6) 习俗差异

任何国家、民族都存在许多忌讳，对于千百年来形成的民族风俗，我们应给予必要的尊重，否则会影响到出口商品的销路问题。例如，英国人不喜欢大象，但很喜欢熊猫；意大利人和西班牙人喜欢玫瑰花，忌用菊花；日本人忌讳荷花、狐狸和獾，而喜欢樱花、乌龟和鸭子；俄罗斯人则认为黄色的蔷薇花意味绝交和不吉利；法国人和比利时人认为核桃、孔雀和菊花是不祥之物；北非一些国家忌讳狗的图案；信奉伊斯兰教的国家忌用猪、狗作商标等。在翻译时，有关颜色的广告词也不可忽视：比利时人最忌蓝色，认为蓝色是不吉利的凶兆；土耳其人绝对禁止用花色物品布置房间和客厅，他们认为花色是凶兆；日本人忌绿色，而印度人却喜爱绿色。

例如，中文的"芳芳"一词作为商标名称，能在中文读者心中产生美好的联想，但如直译为"Fangfang"，在英文读者心中产生的却是恐怖的联想，因为"Fangfang"

一词在英文中的意思是"蛇的毒牙"之意。

又如，英文中的 blue 一词有"蓝色的，忧郁的"意思，但也有"色情的"意思，故"blue disk"翻译成汉语要改译为"黄色光碟"。

中西方在颜色、动物等方面存在较大习俗差异，译者在平时要勤于积累，翻译时对习俗差异要有高度的敏感。

各种禁忌无奇不有，并非三言两语能说清楚，它在民俗学中是一种专门的学问。作为国际广告的翻译工作者，应大力研究。

Discussion: Talk About How to Do the Task Well

广告译文不仅要提供明白易懂的商品信息，而且还要具有原文的感染力，让译文读者也能获得同样的感受。在翻译中最重要的是要实现功能对等，必要时必须打破字面对等的积习，注意不同民族的文化差异。这就是《跨文化翻译》的作者丹尼尔·肖所主张的忠实的翻译。广告翻译常用方法如下。

1) 直译法

直译要求译文和原文的形式、结构尽量一致，从而在有效表达原文意义的同时，反映原文的风格。例如："典雅大方 (elegant and graceful)""畅销全球 (sell well over the World)""汰渍到，污垢逃 (Tide's in, dirt's off)"；"Double delicious, Double your pleasure(双份美味，双份愉悦)""Coca-Cola is it(还是可口可乐好)""My Paris is in a perfume (巴黎恰在香水中)""Kiss your coughs goodbye"(一种新型感冒药的广告，"一吻去感冒")。

2) 音译法

不少商品品名在目的语里找不到对应的词汇来表示。在这种情况下，通常都是采用音译的翻译方法来处理的。如：Pierre Cardin(皮尔·卡丹)、Kodak(柯达彩色胶卷)、Philips(飞利浦电器)、青岛啤酒 (Tsingdao beer) 等。

3) 音意兼译法

音意兼译法是指将一个词分成两部分：一部分音译，另一部分则意译。例如：apple pie 苹果派，其中"苹果"为意译，"派"则是音译。此类译法还有 pizza(比萨饼)、Hamburg(汉堡包)、Budweiser(百威啤酒) 等。

4) 修辞法

如果在同一层次找不到合适的表达方法，也可以跨层次寻找新的表达方法，以求艺术效果的一致。如"We take no pride in prejudice."（《泰晤士报》的广告语），"Pride in Prejudice"运用了仿拟的修辞手法，与英国名著《傲慢与偏见》(Pride and Prejudice) 联系起来；另一种是押头韵 (alliteration)。原文可译为"对于有失偏颇的报道，我们并不引以为豪"。通过这样的翻译，英语的修辞格仿拟 (parody) 和押头韵 (alliteration)

转换成了汉语的修辞格押尾韵 (rhymes)，同样生动地传达了原作的意韵。

在实际的广告翻译实践中，很多情况须采取其他的灵活翻译法，以实现译文与原文有着同等的效果。比如汉语广告中的顶真、回环等的翻译需要变通处理才行。

例5. 输入千言万语，奏出一片深情。(文字处理软件广告语)

参考译文：This word processor plays a tune of deep feeling whenever you are typing.

该句汉语原文蕴含隐喻，对仗工整，相应的英译虽不是对仗工整，但因其主句为隐晦形象的隐喻，加上"feeling"与"typing"押韵，读来生动流畅。此外，"typing"后面的宾语给省略了，整个译句颇为简练。

例6. 皮张之厚无以复加；利润之薄无以复减。(上海鹤鸣皮鞋广告语)

参考译文：The leather shoes made here are thick enough; the profit that's obtained is slight enough.

汉语中一"厚"一"薄"对照鲜明，一"加"一"减"相映成趣。相应的英文译文，虽然未能保留原句的对照辞格和对联形式，但传达了原文的意义，且由于句末重复了"enough"，押了尾韵，读来流畅，给人深刻印象，其功能不亚于原文。

例7. 第一流产品，为足下增光。(红鸟鞋油广告标语)

参考译文：This first-rate shoe polish adds luster to your shoes and honor to you, our friends.

该句汉语含有双关辞格。"足下"同时含有两种意思：一是指搽用红鸟鞋油之后，脚下增加不少光彩；二是对朋友的尊称，"为足下增光"表示为您增添光彩。相应的译文虽然未含双关修辞方法，但揭示了原文双关的双重意义，译得正确、巧妙、深刻。

例8. 世界看中国，中国有先科。(VCD广告标语)

参考译文：As she boasts advanced science, China attracts global eyes.

该句汉语是工整的对偶，节奏感强，并含有顶真修辞方法，突出了产品的先进性和巨大魅力。相应的译句是个表因果关系的复句，虽然失去了原句的辞格，但因为作主语的"中国"在原因状语从句中给拟人化了，谓语动词生动形象，加上"science"与"eyes"有点儿押韵，整个译句充分传达了原句的意义与神韵，与原句功能对等，可与原句媲美。

例9. 甜甜蜜蜜，无限爱恋尽在其中。(饮料广告语)

参考译文：With boundless love in it, the drink is more than sweet.

此句为抒情式广告语，作者把顾客对饮料无比喜欢比作对情人的无限爱恋，产品给拟人化了，极能打动人心。相应的译句译出了拟人辞格，而且押了韵，营造了浓浓的情感氛围，令潜在的消费者怦然心动。

从前面的翻译实例可以看出，在本民族中一则优秀的广告对其他民族的读者来说未必就好。如果片面追求字面上的对等，译文可能达不到原来的效果，因此，广告翻译应允许因语言文化的差异而对原文所涉及的有关语篇功能方面的词句、修辞手法进行有意识的调整。调整的原则必须是以目的语文化为价值取向，充分考虑译文读者的接受心理。

5) 增译与创译

广告语言本身就充满了丰富的想象力和极大的创造性，正如意大利谚语"Tradutori, traditori"（翻译是背叛者所言），在国际广告翻译中要注重创新。增译，就是对原文进行意义的挖掘，将原文的深层意思加以发挥，使译文的意义明显超出原文。创译，就是在原文的基础上创造性地进行翻译。例如，Elegance is an attitude.（优雅态度，真我性格——浪琴表）。Connecting people.（科技以人为本——诺基亚）。从上述例子可以看出，译者很恰当地表达了广告的目的。如果译者不用增译、创译的手法，而用直译的方法，将其译为"优雅是一种态度"和"联系大众"就会让广告大失其色，让消费者不知所云，更不可能激发消费者的购买欲望。

国际广告中的文化及语言差异确实给翻译工作者增加了不少难度，中国的译者肩负着介绍国外商品及其文化的重任，把中国商品及文化介绍给国外的重任也落在中国译者的身上。中国的商品要进入国际市场，就必须得有优秀的广告译文。译者首先应深入地了解所译广告及商品的特点。掌握商品的特征，了解原广告策划创意，了解该广告受众国的文化传统以及消费心理，在翻译的时候才能掌握好广告的重点。

Follow-up: Do It Yourself

Translate the following ad. into Chinese

Keebler Snack Cracker is baked to a secret recipe of specially selected wholesome ingredients. The light and crispy crackers bring you and all your family that uncommonly good taste and freshness as only Keebler knows how.

As an established world leader, we are committed to baking biscuits of the highest quality. Our products are sold in over 90 countries around the world.

Homework: Practice Makes Perfect

1.Translate the following ad. into Chinese

The First Ever, The Last You'll Ever Need.

The first and only quartz watch to generate and store electrical energy through nature human movement.

Needs no battery. Perpetually accurate, totally reliable. Environment friendly. Exclusive from Seiko.

Seiko Kinetic. Someday all watches will be made this way.

2.Translate the following ad. into English

热烈祝贺奥林巴斯青春系列相机产品销量突破 2000 万！促销期间，每购买一台指定的奥林巴斯相机或数码录音笔，均可免费获得由香港独家代理商提供的特别礼品一份，千万别错过哦！

Extend Your Eyes

广告常用英语词汇

above-the-line advertising	线上广告
account executive(AE)	客户经理
account service	客户服务
advertising agency	广告代理商（习惯上称为"广告公司"）
advertising campaign	广告活动
advertising department	广告部
airport advertising	机场广告
appeal	诉求
area sampling	区域抽样
audience	受众
bus stop pillar advertising	站牌广告
bus stop shelter advertising	候车亭广告
clicks	点击次数
cost per thousand impression(CPM)	千人成本
demands	需求
demonstration	演示
direct mail(DM)	直接邮递广告
direct-response advertising	直接反应广告
direct response advertising agency	直接反应（直效）广告代理商
off-the-page offer	报纸夹页广告
discount	折扣
domestic market	国内市场
duplicated audience	重复受众（或称 overlapping audience 重叠受众）
exchange advertising	交换广告
export advertising	出口广告
magazine advertising	杂志广告

mail order advertising	邮购广告
mail survey	邮寄调查
mailing list	邮件列表
maintenance advertising	维持性广告
margin	页边空白
market research	市场调查
market segmentation	市场细分化
media buying	媒介购买
media department	媒介部门
media evaluation	媒介评价
media mix	媒介组合
media objectives	媒介目标
frequency	广告出现的频率
media recommendations	媒介介绍
media research	媒介调查
media service	媒介服务

Press Release

Warm-up: Have a Try

1. Try to translate the following passage into Chinese

I would like to begin by expressing, on behalf of the World Tourism Organization, our congratulations to the grand inauguration of the festival and promotion conference. It is also a great pleasure for me to take the privilege of participating in the Guangdong International Tourism and Culture Festival, and in particular in today's Tourism Promotion Conference. This event is a proof of the dynamism and importance of China, and Guangdong in particular, in today's world tourism.

......

I am sure that this forum will contribute to further develop the tourism industry in China and in Guangdong in particular. I would like to finalize by wishing the forum a complete success. Thank you, ladies and gentlemen!

2. Try to translate the following passage into English

尊敬的各位领导，各位来宾，朋友们，女士们，先生们：今天我们很高兴在这里欢聚一堂，在金秋十月美丽的天津参加这次庆典活动。我谨代表我公司全体同仁向华美广告公司成立十周年表示最热烈的祝贺。同时，我也想对华美公司对我方的邀请表示衷心的感谢。很高兴有机会在这里与不远万里参加此次活动的尊贵的来宾和朋友相聚。

Background: Learn Something About Business Conference

商务会议是指带有商业性质的会议形式。一般包括：新产品宣传推广会、大型的培训沟通会议、上市公司年会、招股说明会、项目竞标会、跨国公司年会、集团公司年会、行业峰会、企业庆典、新闻发布会、巡回展示会、答谢宴会、商业论坛、项目说明会、项目发布会等。

飞速发展的中国经济促使国际的商业合作日益频繁，在相互之间的合作中经常会有一些商务会议需要召开，这些跨国跨地区的商务会议都需要配备专业的会议翻译。商务会议翻译不仅仅关系着公司的前途，同时也关系着国家的形象，要做好商务会议翻译，译员必须同时是一名专才也是一名通才，除了掌握一定的翻译理论知识和技能外，还必须熟悉商务会议中要翻译的行业的相关专业知识，务必专业、准确、流畅地翻译出会议发言人所传达的信息。

会议准备阶段的一个重要工作就是专业词汇的准备。2008 年 6 月在北京新闻中心举行了奥运交通保障新闻发布会，讨论有关奥运期间北京车辆单双号限行措施的有关问题，"限行"这一关键词的翻译，译员可以预先通过搜索国外媒体，寻找有关的说法。通过搜索，发现对北京单双号限行的有关报道中，《纽约时报》(*New York Times*) 的报道是：More than millions of vehicles are ordered to be off the roads of Beijing...；《金融时报》(*Financial Times*) 的报道是：Beijing's removal of millions of vehicles off the road proves to be successful；《南华早报》则写的是：Beijing declared its 4-day car-ban trial a success.

译员在选择某种表达方式的时候，一定要确定其感情色彩，看其是否带有偏见。因为北京市是通过倡议书形式实行单双号政策，西方报道中用的 order the vehicles off the road 不适合中方的立场，最终译员选择了 remove 一词。

译员在接到翻译任务后，要提前准备有关组织公司、新闻发布人、发布信息、媒体信息及专业词汇等材料。通常在会议伊始，主持人一般会向媒体介绍此发布会要发布的内容，并介绍与会者。虽然内容比较简单，但是准确的翻译可以保证会议的开头流利、顺畅。

Discussion: Talk About How to Do the Task Well

商务会议翻译的基本原则如下。

1. "名从主人"的原则

译员在某种程度上,就是发言人本身,翻译时要遵守"名从主人"的原则,不能根据自己的理解去解释发言人的讲话,在意思上不能有任何遗漏或任意发挥。例如,当发言人以第一人称发言时,译员也要用第一人称,而不能翻译成"他认为这是个有用的意见……",男译员要能用非常自然和有说服力的口吻说"作为一个已怀过四次孕的女人,我要说……"。

在记者见面会的提问环节中,媒体名称的翻译尤其要遵守"名从主人"的原则,例如,中国香港的《大公报》译为"Takung Pao";北京的《新京报》译为"Beijing News",而不是根据字面意思翻译为"New Beijing News";《财经》杂志的英文是"Cai Jing",而不是"Financial Magazine"。另外,还要注意准确地将英文的媒体名称翻译成中文,尤其是大家都熟悉的国外媒体。比如大家都熟悉的CNN,其完整的中文译名是"美国有线电视新闻网"。

2. 主语确定原则

由于英语是主语突出型语言 (subject-prominent language),强调主谓结构 (subject-predicate structure),主语决定了整句话的句法结构;而汉语是话题突出型语言 (topic-prominent language),句子属于话题—评论结构 (topic-comment sentence Structure),其中主语的重要性相对较低,无主语的现象比比皆是,所以在汉英转化中最重要的就是确定主语。请看以下例句中英语主语的选择。

例1. 这一目标的实现,最直接的应该是老百姓住得更宽敞了,更舒服了。

参考译文:The citizens will live more spaciously and comfortably, benefiting most directly from achieving the goal. (使用源语主语)

例2. The idea of a national ID, however, was locked out of earlier drafts of legislation by a coalition of civil rights and ethnic groups.

参考译文:然而,持自由论观点的民众和少数民族结成联盟,推翻了立法的最初几次草案中关于实施全国统一身份证的主张。(重新确定主语)

例3. 但是中美之间的关系也不能幻想从此就会一帆风顺。

参考译文:But we cannot have the illusion that Sino-US relations will be free from troubles from now on. (增补主语)

3. 动宾连接原则

在英语中,不同成分的宾语决定了谓语的使用,因此在翻译动宾短语的时候,应先考虑宾语的成分。

例 4. 中国人民始终希望天下太平，希望各国人民友好相处。

参考译文 1：The Chinese people are always looking forward to global peace and friendship among all nations.

参考译文 2：The Chinese people are always hoping that the World is at peace and people of all nations will coexist on friendly terms.

以上例子中"希望"的选择面很大，既可以用 hope 连接句子，也可以用 hope for, look forward to 等连接名词词组，只有先考虑宾语，才能更容易选择谓语。

英译汉时，对于英语中较长的宾语，一般有两种处理方式：一是把谓语变成直接能够接宾语的表达形式，如例 5 中的 react to 不必翻译成"对……做出反应"，可译为"面对……"；二是把宾语先译出，然后再译出主谓，如例 5，或使用谓语的相反含义，再接上原主语，如例 6，sustain 表示"决定了"，那反义短语就是"取决于"。

例 5. The rest of the World will have to react to this millennial economic shift to Asia, and to the rising power of China.

参考译文：在新千年，经济重心将向亚洲转移，中国将迅速崛起，世界其他地区将不得不对此做出反应。

例 6. The annual budget sustains both the existence of R&D section and the fiscal solvency of the company.

参考译文：研发部的存在，公司的资金偿还能力，这些都取决于年度预算。

4. 谓语最小化原则

英语属于静态型语言，其动词使用的频率远远低于汉语，因此，在汉译英中，要尽量减少动词的使用，可以有意识地将动词转换为其他词性。

例 7. 今年的亚太经济贸易合作组织会议将主要侧重两个方面：一是加强亚太经合组织成员之间的合作，共同应对可能出现的经济衰退，重树信心；二是继续推进亚太经合组织贸易投资自由化进程，推动世界贸易组织尽早开始新一轮谈判。

参考译文：The APEC meeting in this year will focus mainly on two aspects: one is on strengthening the cooperation among all APEC members to cope with the possible economic recession with rebuilt-up confidence; the other is on promoting the liberalization of trade and investment among all APEC members for the start of a new round of negotiations by WTO.

以上例句在汉语原文中共有 7 个动词，翻译为英语后只保留了 4 个动词。

5. 连接原则

英语重形合，汉语重意合，汉译英的难点之一就是处理句群关系，要多加连词，两三句之内就要考虑句群的逻辑关系，抓住主要谓语，选择合适的连接方式，适当合句或换序。

例 8. 中国加入世界贸易组织的谈判已经进行了 15 年了。中国的立场始终如一。

参考译文：China has been engaged in the talks for entry into the WTO for 15 years with its consistent stance.

例 9. 经过二十多年的快速发展，中国西部地区已奠定了一定的物质技术基础，社会保持稳定，市场经济体制正在逐步建立和完善，为西部经济持续快速增长创造了有利的市场环境。

参考译文：Thanks to the rapid development in the past 20-plus years, a relatively solid foundation in terms of material wealth and technology has been laid in the western region of China.

6. 减少 of 原则

汉语中"……的"不仅表达所属关系，也表达包含关系等，翻译时不要一见到"……的"就翻译为"of ..."，可以把一些非定语关系的 of 架构转化为其他成分。

例 10. 中国的富强和发展不会对任何国家构成威胁。

参考译文：A strong, prosperous and developed China will pose no threat to any countries.

例 11. 我们之间关系的发展，使我们不仅成为亲密的朋友，而且成为兄弟。

参考译文：Our relations have so grown that bind us not only as close friends but also as brothers.

7. 名词词组与分句互译原则

汉语中的宾语和定语地位较低，在英译汉中，较长的宾语从句常常会转化为名词词组，比如例 12 句中的"how"如果翻译为"如何花去税款"这个宾语从句，在汉语中就显得不伦不类。此外，对于英语中修饰语较多的名词性短语，汉语也不喜欢用定语进行堆砌，而偏向于使用简单的主谓短语，如例 13 中没有把"the most skeptical Gates"翻译成"一个持怀疑态度的盖茨"，而是译为主谓短语"盖茨对此持怀疑态度"。

例 12. They provide a means by which wealthy people and corporations can in effect decide how their tax payments will be spent.

参考译文：基金会提供了一种方式，可以让有钱人和大公司能实际支配花去税款的方式。

例 13. But the most skeptical Gates of the new millennium is someone who evinces a passion for giving and government aid.

参考译文：但新千年盖茨对此持怀疑态度，热衷于施舍和政府援助。

Follow-up: Do It Yourself

1. Translate the following sentences and paragraphs into English

(1) 值此中国进出口商品交易会隆重开幕之际，我代表本公司向交易会表示热烈的祝贺。

(2) 我们祝贺大会胜利召开，并借此机会向东道主为大会所做的努力表示感谢。

(3) 能在这次活动上发表讲话，我感到十分高兴和愉快。

(4) 我们怀着愉快的心情，向光临本次交易会的全体来宾表示热烈欢迎。我对我们在贸易合作中发展起来的友谊和建立起来的信任是非常珍视的。我确信，这次交易会将会进一步加强我们之间的关系，直接对扩大我们之间互利贸易做出贡献。

(5) 我能在这次国际会议上讲话，感到十分荣幸和愉快。这次会议是在中华人民共和国首都召开，并受到了中国商务部的大力支持。我相信我们共同的努力必将富有成果并为大会成功做出贡献。

2. Translate the following sentences and paragraphs into Chinese

(1) We have only been in Beijing for ten days, but have already been impressed by the careful planning and organizing that have obviously gone into the meeting.

(2) The conclusion of the agreement between our company and China Machinery Company indicates that the future is even brighter.

(3) I also take this opportunity to express my heartfelt thanks to all the organizers and staff, for their outstanding contribution in preparing the celebration ceremony.

(4) As president of the Exhibition, I should like to convey warm greetings to all our visitors to the Exhibition. I believe they will find much of interest. We welcome the opportunity for cooperation and trade which this Exhibition will provide. We look forward to playing an increased part in the building of stronger ties between the two countries.

(5) On behalf of the delegates from 28 different countries representing all regions of the World, I am happy to have the honor of replying to Mrs. Chairman's gracious words of welcome. I wish to thank the Organizing Committee for the inviting all of us and for all the hard work and thought they have given to the arrangements for this meeting.

Homework: Practice Makes Perfect

Translate the the following speech (abridged) into English

尊敬的施瓦布主席(Klaus Schwab)，尊敬的各位政府首脑，尊敬的各位贵宾，女士们，先生们：很高兴与大家在天津再次相聚。首先，我代表中国政府，对夏季达沃斯论坛的召开，表示热烈祝贺！对各位远道而来的嘉宾和媒体界的朋友，表示诚挚欢迎！

……

天津是一个世界大港，从这里可以走向浩瀚的海洋。巨轮远航，需要持久强劲的动力。我们愿与世界各国一道，紧紧抓住新一轮科技和工业革命的机遇，共同打造经济增长新的发动机,推动世界经济在转型升级中实现稳定复苏,共创人类社会发展更加美好的明天!

预祝本届论坛圆满成功!

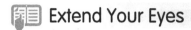 Extend Your Eyes

商务会议常用词汇与句型

1. (致) 欢迎 / 开幕 / 闭幕词 (make/deliver) welcome/opening/closing speech
2. 揭幕仪式 unveiling ceremony
3. 宣布……开幕 / 结束 declare the commencement/closing of
4. 为展览会揭幕 inaugurate an exhibition
5. 答谢宴会 return banquet
6. 晚宴 evening reception/dinner
7. 招待会 / 宴会 reception
8. 签字仪式 signing ceremony
9. 剪彩仪式 ribbon-cutting ceremony
10. 就职仪式 inauguration ceremony
11. 颁奖仪式 prize giving ceremony/award ceremony
12. 全球庆典 global celebration ceremony
13. 友好访问 goodwill visit
14. 良辰佳时 a wonderful time
15. 宣布……闭幕 declare...the conclusion/closing of...
16. 发表热情友好的讲话 make a warm and friendly speech
17. 热情洋溢的欢迎词 gracious speech of welcome
18. 阁下 Your/His/Her Honor/Excellency
19. 尊敬的市长先生 Respected/respectable/honorable Mr. Mayor
20. 远道而来的朋友 friends coming from afar/coming all the way
21. 来自大洋彼岸的朋友 friends coming from the other side of the Pacific/ocean
22. 商界的朋友们 friends from the business community
23. 媒体的朋友们 media members
24. 嘉宾 distinguished/honorable guests
25. 全体同仁 all my colleges
26. 东道国 host country
27. 主办单位 sponsor

28. 承办单位 organizer
29. 组委会 the organizing committee
30. 大会主题 theme of the conference/meeting/forum/summit
31. 作为友好使者 as an envoy of friendship
32. 值此……之际 ...on the occasion
33. 以……的名义 in the name of
34. 本着……精神 in the spirit of
35. 主持讨论会 chair a discussion/seminar
36. 请……发言 give the floor to
37. 我很荣幸 It is a great pleasure for me to
38. 请……颁奖 Let's invite...to present the award
39. 承蒙/应……的盛情邀请 at the gracious invitation of
40. 对……表示衷心祝贺 extend our sincere congratulations on
41. 以掌声对……表示的最热烈的欢迎 propose the warmest applause to
42. 荣幸地答谢您给予我们的热情招待 have the honor of reciprocating your warm reception
43. 寄希望于本届大会 place our hopes on the current conference
44. 使……取得预期效果 attain the results expected
45. 结交新朋 establish new contacts
46. 友好款待 gracious hospitality
47. 增进理解 promote understanding
48. 相互促进 mutual promotion
49. 促进友好合作关系 advance our friendly relations of cooperation
50. 进行真诚有效的合作 carry out sincere and rewarding cooperation
51. 符合双方共同利益 accord with our common interests
52. 保持良好的贸易伙伴关系 keep a good trading partnership with
53. 携手合作 make joint efforts/make concerted efforts
54. 祝愿来访富有成果 hope your visit will be rewarding
55. 预祝……圆满成功 wish...a complete success
56. 共同举杯 join us in a toast to
57. 为友谊/合作/健康干杯 propose a toast to our friendship/cooperation/health
58. 我愿借此机会…… I would like to take this opportunity to...
59. 出席今天招待会的有 We have with us at the reception...
60. 有朋自远方来，不亦乐乎。 It's a delight to have friends coming from afar.

Reference Version

Module 1 Merchant/Investment Inviting

Task 1 Name Card 名片

Warm-up

1. Put the following Chinese into English.

ZHONGDE (CHINA) ENVIRONMENTAL PROTECTION CO., LTD.

Wang Lantian

General Manager

Mobile: 136********

E-mail: xiaobin2288@126.com

Add: 5F. Huayi Commercial Capital South Building, Zhongshan Road, Wuhu City, 241000

---

2. Put the following English into Chinese.

新泽西大学

唐纳德·范德格里夫特 博士

商学院经济学教授

地址：美国新泽西州尤因城 7718 信箱

电话：609-771-2294

邮箱：vandedon@tcnj.edu

Follow-up

1. Translate the following English into Chinese.

(1) 助理工程师

(2) 培训主管

(3) 销售代表

(4) 企划部

(5) 伦敦圣约翰路 145-157 号 304 房　　邮编：EC1V 4PY

(6) 纽约市布鲁克林区 54 大街 770 号 邮编：11220

2. Translate the following Chinese into English.

(1) Purchasing Department

(2) Marketing Department

(3) Senior Clerk

(4) Secretary

(5) No.2 North Xisanhuan Road, Haidian District, Beijing, 100089

(6) Room 601, No. 34 Long Chang Li, Xiamen, Fujian

Homework

1. Put the following name card into Chinese.

> 菲尔蒙五金产品公司
> 约翰・泰勒
> 销售经理
> 加州圣迭戈市
> 橡园大街 725 号 FHI 大厦
> 邮编：91023
> 电话：2976 3322
> 传真：2976 3366
> 电子信箱：johntaylor@fhi.com

2. Design a name card according to the following information and then translate it into English.

> INNER MONGOLIA MENGNIU DAIRY (GROUP) CO., LTD
> Zhang Dacheng
> Brand Director
> Brand Management Center
> Add: No.1, Area 1, Food Industrial Area, Tongzhou, Beijing, 101107
> Tel: 133********
> Fax: 010 61526245
> E-mail: luan4u@126.com

Task 2 Business Exhibition 商务展览

Warm-up

1. Put the following passage into Chinese.

世界博览会是全球大型的非商业性博览会，主要参展者为各国政府和国际组织。世博会是展示世界各国社会、经济文化、科技成就和发展前景的舞台，是各国人民交流经验、相互学习、开展合作的盛会。因此，世博会享有"经济、科技、文化领域内的奥林匹克盛会"之美誉。

2. Put the following passage into English.

Expo 2010 Shanghai is the first registered World Expo hosted by a developing country. It is an opportunity for China and also for the World. In the coming six months, focusing on the theme Better City, Better Life, the Expo will offer a platform for all countries and regions to fully exhibit their achievements in urban civilization, share best practices and spread advanced ideas on urban development. We will learn from each other, draw on each other's strengths and explore new models of housing, living and working for mankind in the new century.

Follow-up

1. Translate the following passage into Chinese.

国内外专家们信心十足、意志坚定，他们从来不会拖着犹豫不决的脚步或抱着摇摆不定的决心组织这样盛大的展会，因而保证了"纽约美容保健品展会"的品质和成功，同时也给展会带来了浪漫的色彩和诱人的魅力。

2. Translate the following passage into English.

Guangzhou Fair is a significant initiative through which newly-founded China has explored different ways to expand foreign trade and open wider to the outside World. Now the Fair has developed into a bridge between Chinese enterprises and global market, a window for the World to know about China as well as a platform of international cooperation. Known as the "weather-vane" of China's foreign trade, Guangzhou Fair plays an indispensable role in promoting Chinese trade development. It is thus honored as "Route of Friendship and Bridge of Trade".

Homework

1. Try to find the English versions of the following MICE names on the Internet.

(1) 2016 China (Tianjin) Trade & Investment Fair and PECC Int'l Trade & Investment Expo

(2) 2016 Tianjin-World Famous Brand of Global Entrepreneurs Expo

(3) The 12th Western China International Fair

(4) Food & Drink Technology Africa 2016

(5) China Beijing International Wedding Expo 2016
(6) ISPO Beijing
(7) 2016 the 8th China International Low Carbon Industry Exhibition
(8) The 14th China International Scientific Instrument and Laboratory Equipment Exhibition
(9) China International Occupational Safety & Health Exhibition
(10) Chinese International Pension Service Industry Expo

2. Translate the following passage into Chinese.

有些策划单位赠送宣传小册子、研讨会的详细介绍、讲员介绍、娱乐演员、演示人员、会场地图和方向以及菜单。参展商和销售商的宣传资料必须包括展区地图、展位空间、展览时间、展台搭建与拆卸时间以及提前装船信息。

3. Translate the following passage into English.

Tianjin Meijiang Convention&Exhibition Center(MJCEC) is located in Tianjin Ecological Living Region near Meijiang scenic area. With beautiful surroundings and convenient transportation links, the total land area is 356,200 square meters, with a construction area of 100,000 square meters, 50,000 square meters of indoor exhibition space and 30,000 square meters of outdoor exhibition space. Facilities include 7,000 square meters of conference rooms and a superior banquet hall that can accommodate 2,000.

Task 3 Bidding Documents 招标文件

Warm-up

Try to translate the following document into Chinese.

招标合同

日期：
标号：
一、中华人民共和国从世界银行申请贷款，用于支付_____项目的费用。部分贷款将用于支付工程建筑、_____等各种合同。所有依世界银行指导原则具有资格的国家，都可参加招标。

二、中国_____公司（以下简称A公司）邀请具有资格的投标者提供密封的标书，提供完成合同工程所需的劳力、材料、设备和服务。

三、具有资格的投标者可从以下地址_____获得更多的信息，或参看招标文件：_____。

四、每一位具有资格的投标者在交纳_____美元（或人民币），并提交书面申请后，均可从上述地址获得招标文件。

五、每一份标书都要附一份投标保证书，且应不迟于_____（时间）提交给 A 公司。

六、所有标书将在_____（时间）当着投标者代表的面开标。

七、如果具有资格的国外投标者希望与一位中国国内的承包人组建合资公司，需在投标截止日期前 30 天提出要求。业主有权决定是否同意选定的国内承包人。

八、标前会议将在_____（时间）_____（地址）召开。

Follow-up

Translate the following sentences.

(1) 投标人应提交金额不少于投标报价总价 2% 的投标保证金，并作为其投标的一部分。

(2) 本合同应按照中华人民共和国的法律进行解释。

(3) 投标人提供的货物和服务用美元货币报价。

(4) All tenders must be received at the following address on or before the due date.

(5) The Bidder shall prepare one(1) original and six(6) copies of the set of documents comprising the tender.

Homework

Translate the following paragraph into English.

Instructions to Tenderers

1. Description of Works (sketch)

2. Source of Funds

The People's Republic of China has applied for a loan and credit from the World Bank (hereinafter referred to as the IFI) towards the cost of _____ Project, and intends to apply a portion of the proceeds of the loan and credit to eligible payments under the Contract for which these documents are issued. Payment by the IFI will be made only at the request of the Chinese Government and upon approval by the IFI and will be subject in all respects to the terms and conditions of the Loan Agreement. No party other than the People's Republic of China shall derive any rights from the Loan Agreement or have any claim to the loan proceeds.

3. Eligibility and Qualification Requirements

3.1 This tender is open to all pre-qualified tenderers from eligible source countries as defined under the "Guidelines for Procurement" of the World Bank.

3.2 All goods and services to be supplied under this Contract shall have their origin in eligible source countries, and all expenditures made under the Contract will be limited to such goods and services.

3.3 The origin of goods and services is distinct from the nationality of the tenderer.

3.4 To be eligible for award of contract, tenderers shall have provided evidence satisfactory to the Employer of their eligibility under clause 3.1 above, and of their capability and adequacy of resources to effectively carry out the Contract. To this end, the Employer and_____company may, at any time prior to award of contract, request tenderers to amplify or update previously submitted prequalification data.

3.5 For the purposes of sub-clause 3.4, tenderers who have been pre-qualified may update and augment the information supplied with their applicatio for pre-qualification, and, in particular, shall give particulars of work in hand at the date of tendering.

4. Cost of Tendering

The tenderer shall bear all costs associated with the preparation and submission of his tender and neither the Employer nor his agent_____ Company will in any way be responsible or liable for those costs, regardless of the outcome of the tendering process.

5. Site Visit

The tenderer is advised to visit and examine the Site of the Works and the surroundings and to obtain for himself on his own responsibility, all information that may be necessary for preparing the tender and entering into a contract. The costs of visiting the site shall be at the tenderer's own expense.

Module 2 Foreign Trade Operations

Task 4 Business Correspondence 商务信函

Warm-up

Try to translate the following counter offer into Chinese.

敬启者：

你方 4 月 23 日函悉。

十分抱歉，由于我方疏忽，所开信用证有误。该证修改已相应办理，并通知银行电传发出，现一切办妥。鉴于我方急需此货，务请及早装运。

敬请放心，若此批货到后令我方客户满意，他们有可能大量续订。

谨启

Follow-up

1. Translate the following sentences into English.

(1) comply with your request

(2) take effect

(3) place a large order with you

(4) have confidence in; It would be appreciated

(5) In view of our long friendly relations

2. Translate the following business letter into Chinese.

敬启者：

兹证实收到你方 8 月 16 日来函，并注意到你方电汇付款的建议。

很高兴地告知，我们同意你方上述建议。然而我们认为还是明确一下为好，对于日后的交易，电汇付款仅适用于每笔金额不超过 10,000 美元的交易，若金额超过这个数字，要求采用信用证支付。

谨启

汤姆·怀特

Homework

1. Translate the following Chinese sentences into English.

(1) We are interested in all kinds of Chinese Bicycles. Please send us your price list covering these articles.

(2) Your price is too high, and we can hardly sell your products.

(3) Please inform us whether you'd like us to furnish any further information.

(4) We look forward to receiving the samples and price list stated in your letter.

(5) We are informed that you are a state-operated corporation handling chemical.

(6) We will, however, revert to this matter and contact you by email, once the supply position improves.

(7) As the stock is light with active demand, we would like to increase our order to 1000 sets.

(8) We will reserve the right to cancel this order or reject the goods for any delay in shipment.

(9) We do not deny that the quality of Japanese products is superior to that of Chinese make, but the difference in price should in no case be as big as 50%.

(10) Information indicates that some parcels of similar quality from other sources are being sold at a level about 10% lower than yours.

2. Translate the following business letter into Chinese.

敬启者：

我们从瑞典驻华大使馆商务参赞处了解到贵公司的名称和地址，承蒙参赞处告知贵公司打算购买中国制造的自行车。

我们愿借此机会与贵公司联系，以期与你方建立贸易关系。

我们是一家经营中国自行车出口业务的公司，为了使你方了解我们的业务范围，我们随函附去一份关于目前可以获得的主要商品的出口清单。

如果你方对其中任何的商品感兴趣，请告知我方，收到贵公司具体要求后，我方将乐于向你方报最低价格。

期待早日收到你方的询盘。

谨启
汤姆·怀特

Task 5 Instruction Manual 产品说明书

Warm-up

1. Put the following English into Chinese.

乐 口 福

乐口福系采用麦精、牛乳、可可粉、鲜黄油、鲜鸡蛋等上等原料，以科学的方法精制而成，含有丰富的维生素 A、B、D 及天然有机磷质，具有提神醒脑、增强体质之功效，特别适用于用脑过度、神经衰弱的患者。常饮本品，可以增强肌体的免疫力。本品适宜于四季饮用，是老少皆宜的营养饮料，也是馈赠亲友之佳品。

饮用方法如下。

热饮：取乐口福两至三茶匙，然后倒入适量开水，搅拌至完全融化为止。加入适量的牛奶和糖，味道更佳。

冷饮：取乐口福两至三茶匙，然后倒入适量冷开水，搅拌至完全融化为止。可再加入适量的鲜牛奶或炼乳，是夏季消暑保健之佳品。

2. Put the following Chinese into English.

To obtain the best performance and ensure years of trouble-free use, please read this instruction manual carefully.

When operating the monitor, don't put any drink or food beside the keyboard in case you might accidentally knock it / them over, resulting in a short circuit.

Should some problems occur, please refer to this troubleshooting guide prior to calling the helpdesk.

Follow-up

1. Put the following English into Chinese.

(1) 煎炒时，小心食油着火。

(2) 经常擦用本品，可增强皮肤细胞活力，促进新陈代谢，保持皮肤洁白、红润，延缓衰老。

(3) 此外，它可以与任何电话线相连，用来发送电子邮件、传真或上网。

(4) 将视频电缆的蓝色插头连接到计算机后面的蓝色视频插口上。

(5) 室温干燥处，避光，密封保存。

2. Put the following Chinese into English.

(1) Rich in whitening and nourishing plant essences, this mask removes flecks and makes your skin fair and soft.

(2) These pills are yellow sugar-coated, but are brown without the sugar-coat, and taste bitter.

(3) When making the electrical connections, check that the current socket has a ground connection and that the voltage values correspond to those indicated on the data plate inside the appliance itself.

(4) Never leave the socket or the plug wet or damp in case of leakage; never submerge the kettle in water.

(5) Suggested drinking method: make 3-5 Chrysanthemum flowers into tea with boiled water and add other ingredients according to individual taste.

Homework

1. Translate the following product instruction into Chinese.

防玷污银器上光布

此银器上光布由高支全棉制成，布内含有洗涤剂和防污剂。

日常使用可去除轻污的银器、包银器具，使器具表面保持光亮，长期防污。避免水洗，清洁布将保持长期有效。

德国技术

2. Translate the following product instruction manual into Chinese.

使用产品前，请仔细阅读使用说明书，同时妥善保管以备将来参考。

- 产品连接电源前，请检查产品上标示的电压是否与当地电源电压相符。
- 定期检查电源线。如果产品的插销、电源线或者产品本身已经损坏，请不要使用。
- 如果电源软线损坏，为避免危险，必须由制造厂家或其维修部门或类似的专职人员来更换。
- 请不要让此产品与水接触！不要在盛水的浴池、浴盆或其他容器附近使用电吹风。
- 在浴室使用时，使用后请拔下电源插头，因为即使在吹风机关闭的情况下，靠近水也可能存在危险。
- 有关其他保护措施，建议在供电的电路中安装额定剩余工作电流不超过 30 毫安的漏电保护器 (RCD)。有关建议，请咨询安装人员。
- 不要让儿童接触此产品。
- 不可阻塞电吹风风口。
- 如果产品过热，它将自动关闭电源。拔下产品电源并使其冷却几分钟。再次打开电源前，请检查出风口，确保没有绒毛、头发等杂物将其堵塞。

- 即使仅将产品放下一会儿,也应始终关闭其电源。
- 使用后一定要拔下产品的插头。
- 不要将电源线缠绕在产品上。

Task 6　Business Documents　商务单证

Warm-up

Try to translate the following sentences into Chinese.

(1) 第三方单证可以接受。

(2) 有关单证备妥后当即寄上。

(3) 若单证不符,一个不符点扣15美元手续费。

(4) 空运费用包括机场理货费、空港费、文件单证费。

(5) 我们的付款通常采用不可撤销的信用证,凭单证议付。

(6) 所有单证装成一个袋,一次性用DHL发给开证行。

(7) 备货、制单证、订舱位……所有这些都要花时间。

(8) 海关凭口岸动植物检疫机关签发的检疫单证或者在报单上加盖的印章验放。

(9) 办理出境检疫手续时,须向检验检疫机关出示所购食品、饮用水清单等有关单证。

(10) 在我行柜面收到与信用证相符合的单证即视为我们获得指示可以汇款。

Follow-up

Translate the following sentences and paragraphs into English or Chinese.

(1) 信用证是银行代表买方向卖方支付信用证规定金额的书面承诺,这意味着如果受益人提交的单据构成相符提示,开证行将取代买方对卖方承担第一付款责任。

(2) 提单是一种货权单据,意味着提单的合法拥有者就是货物的合法拥有者。承运人仅凭所提交的正本提单放货。当提单转移的时候,货物的拥有权也同时转移。

(3) 显然单据代表着货物,可以证明贸易商的执行情况,它成为国际贸易结算中进行支付的基础。同时,对于贸易商来说,确保单据与信用证的条款条件完全相符是非常必要的。

(4) Upon presentation of the documents strictly complied with all credit terms, we authorize you to draw on our H/O reimbursement a/c value five working days later under authenticated SWIFT advice to us without any charges on our part.

(5) The shipper shall be liable for any damage to the interest of the carrier resulting from the inadequacy or inaccuracy or delay in delivery of such documents.

(6) Signed commercial invoice in five fold certifying that goods are as per Contract No.12345 of March 11th, 2004 quoting L/C Number BTN/HS NO. and showing original invoice and a copy to accompany original set of document.

Homework

Translate the following document into Chinese.

1. 不可撤销的 45 天远期信用证。

信用证编号：96/0500-FTC

货物描述：288 箱 CHAMPION 品牌的篮球（注：其他描述见信用证，此处翻译省略。）

金额：数字显示的是 USD117,227.52(大写文字显示的是 USD53,570)

注意：两个金额不一致

有效期：1996 年 6 月 15 日在中国有效

2. 启运港：上海。

目的港：纽约

最迟装运期：1996 年 6 月 30 日（注意：最迟装运期晚于信用证有效期！）

不允许分批、转船

3. 单据要求：

(1) 签字盖章的商业发票 (3 份正本，3 份副本 (复印件))

(2) 装箱单 (3 正 3 副)：注明单个包装的重量、体积

(3) 商会出具的原产地证 (1 正 3 副)

(4) 全套正本提单（一般可以做成 3 正 3 副）：注明运费预付

Consignee 写：TO ORDER OF CATHAY BANK 777 N.BROADWAY, NEWYORK, USA

通知人写信用证申请人

(5) 保险：根据 1982 年 1 月 1 日 ICC(国际商会) 条款，按照发票金额的 130% 投保

(6) 受益人出具的证明每一件商品都印有 "MADE IN CHINA" 字样的证明

4. 特殊说明：美国以外的银行费用由受益人承担。

(1) 所有货物必须装在 1 个 20 尺长的集装箱里，以 CY-CY(港到港) 方式运输；

(2) 提单上注明运费预付；

(3) 单证相符，否则一个不符点扣 35 美元。

另外，此信用证适用 UCP500 条款。

Task 7　Business Contract 商务合同

Warm-up

Try to translate the following contract into Chinese.

出 口 合 同

编号：

签约地点：

卖方：

地址：

电话：

传真：

电子邮箱：

买方：

地址：

电话：

传真：

电子邮箱：

买卖双方经协商同意按下列条款成交：

1. 货物名称、规格和质量

2. 数量

3. 单价及价格条款

（除非另有规定，"FOB""CFR"和"CIF"均应依照国际商会制定的《2000年国际贸易术语解释通则》(INCOTERMS 2000)办理。）

4. 总价

5. 允许溢短装：____%

6. 装运期限

收到可以转船及分批装运之信用证____天内装运。

7. 付款条件

买方须于____前将保兑的、不可撤销的、可转让的、可分割的即期付款信用证开到卖方，该信用证的有效期延至装运期后____天在中国到期，并必须注明允许分批装运和转船。

买方未在规定的时间内开出信用证，卖方有权发出通知取消本合同，或接受买方对本合同未执行的全部或部分，或对因此遭受的损失提出索赔。

8. 包装

9. 保险

按发票金额的_____%投保_____险，由_____负责投保。

10．品质/数量异议

如买方提出索赔，凡属品质异议须于货到目的口岸之日起30天内提出，凡属数量异议须于货到目的口岸之日起15天内提出，对所装货物所提任何异议于保险公司、轮船公司、其他有关运输机构或邮递机构所负责者，卖方不负任何责任。

11．由于发生人力不可抗拒的原因，致使本合约不能履行，部分或全部商品延误交货，卖方概不负责。本合同所指的不可抗力系指不可干预、不能避免且不能克服的客观情况。

12．争议的解决

凡因本合同引起的或与本合同有关的任何争议，均应提交中国国际经济贸易仲裁委员会，按照申请仲裁时该会现行有效的仲裁规则在南京进行仲裁。仲裁裁决是终局的，对双方均有约束力。

13．通知：

所有通知用_____文写成，并按照如下地址用传真/电子邮件/快件送达各方。如果地址有变更，一方应在变更后_____日内书面通知另一方。

14．本合同为中英文两种文本，两种文本具有同等效力。本合同一式_____份。自双方签字(盖章)之日起生效。

卖方签字：　　　　　　　　　　　买方签字：

Follow-up

Translate the following sentences into Chinese or English.

(1) 承包商应负责按工程师书面提交的有关点、线和水平面的原始参数如实准确地进行工程放线，且如上所述，负责校准工程各部分的方位、水平、尺寸和定线，并负责提供一切必要的相关仪器、装置和劳力。

(2) 一旦顺利完成这些测试，买方须签署一张工厂验收证，证明测试已经完成，并列出将由CAE在买方同意的期限内校正的任何经认可的缺陷。

(3) 买方须随时能对专利软件的复制做出解释，拷贝的目的只在于提高其预期功能的使用效力。

(4) After friendly consultations conducted in accordance with the principles of equality and mutual benefit, the Parties have agreed to enter into a distributorship relationship in accordance with the applicable laws and the provisions of this Contract.

(5) The Distributor shall store and transport the products in conditions that will preserve the products in good condition and will comply with any reasonable requests made by the Supplier concerning the conditions in which the products are to be stored or transported.

Homework

1. Translate the following contract into Chinese.

商务合同

合同编号：005327

签订日期：2002 年 5 月 18 日

买方：皮特有限公司（英国伦敦林肯街 18 号）

卖方：约翰·海得有限公司（美国纽约市梅顿巷 20 号）

本合同系买卖双方共同订立。据此，买方同意购买，卖方同意出售符合下列条款的商品。

货物名称：印花棉布

产品规格：标号：127

纱支：30's × 30's，68 × 60

宽度：35.36 英寸

长度：每匹 40 码

质量要求：以买方 2002 年 3 月 9 日所寄样品为准。

订购数量：40,000 码

产品价格：伦敦到岸价每码 6.6 美元

总金额：264,000 美元（二十六万四千美元）

装运：2002 年 6 月上旬装运。不得分批发运。

目的地：英国伦敦

支付条款：买方见票后，将委托伦敦银行开立全额贷款的信用证。

本合同一式两份，双方各保存一份，并在双方代表签字后生效。

买方：皮特有限公司　　　　　卖方：约翰·海得有限公司

签字：（经理）　　　　　　　签字：（经理）

2. Translate the following contract into English.

Sales Contract

Contract No:

Signed at:

Date:

The Buyers:

The Sellers:

The Buyers agree to buy and the Sellers agree to sell the following goods on terms and conditions as set forth below:

(1) Name of Commodity, Specifications and Packing	(2) Quantity	(3) Unit Price	(4) Total Value
	(Shipment Quantity %more or less allowed)		

(5) Time of Shipment:

(6) Port of Loading:

(7) Port of Destination:

(8) Insurance: To be covered by the _____ for 110% of the invoice value against _____ .

(9) Terms of Payment: By a confirmed, irrevocable, transferable and divisible letter of credit in favor of _____ payable on sight with TF reimbursement clause/ _____ days'/sight/date allowing partial shipment and transshipment. The covering Letter of Credit must reach the Sellers before _____ and is to remain valid in _____ , China until the 15th day after the aforementioned time of shipment, falling which the Sellers reserve the right to cancel this Sales Contract without further notice and to claim from the Buyers the resulting losses.

(10) Inspection: The Inspection Certificate of Quality/Quantity/Weight/Packing/Sanitation issued by _____ of China shall be regarded as evidence of the Sellers' delivery.

(11) Shipping Marks:

(12) OTHER TERMS:

a) Discrepancy: In case of quality discrepancy, claim should be lodged by the Buyers within 30 days after the arrival of the goods at the port of destination, while for quantity discrepancy, claim should be lodged by the Buyers within 15 days after the arrival of the goods at the port of destination. In all cases, claims must be accompanied by Survey Reports of Recognized Public Surveyors agreed to by the Sellers. Should the responsibility of the subject under claim be found to rest on the part of the Sellers, the Sellers shall, within 20 days after receipt of the claim, send their reply to the Buyers together with suggestion for settlement.

b) The covering Letter of Credit shall stipulate the Sellers' option of shipping the indicated percentage more or less than the quantity hereby contracted and be negotiated for the amount covering the value of quantity actually shipped. (The Buyers are requested to establish the L/C in amount with the indicated percentage over the total value of the order as per this Sales Contract.)

c) The contents of the covering Letter of Credit shall be in strict conformity with the stipulations of the Sales Contract. In case of any variation there of necessitating amendment of the L/C, the Buyers shall bear the expenses for effecting the amendment. The Sellers shall not be held responsible for possible delay of shipment resulting from awaiting the amendment of the L/C and reserve the right to claim from the Buyers for the losses resulting there from.

d) Except in cases where the insurance is covered by the Buyers as arranged, insurance is to be covered by the Sellers with a Chinese insurance company. If insurance for additional amount and/or for other insurance terms is required by the Buyers, prior notice to this effect must reach the Sellers before shipment and is subject to the Sellers' agreement, and the extra insurance premium shall be for the Buyers' account.

e) The Sellers shall not be held responsible if they fail, owing to force majeure cause or causes, to make delivery within the time stipulated in this Sales Contract or cannot deliver the goods. However, the Sellers shall immediately inform the Buyers by cable. The Sellers shall deliver to the Buyers by registered letter, if it is requested by the Buyers, a certificate issued by the China Council for the Promotion of International Trade or by any competent authorities, attesting to the existence of the said cause or causes. The Buyers' failure to obtain the relative Import License is not to be treated as force majeure.

f) Arbitration: All disputes arising in connection with this Sales Contract or the execution thereof shall be settled by way of amicable negotiation. In case no settlement can be reached, the case at issue shall then be submitted for arbitration to the China International Economic and Trade Arbitration Commission in accordance with the provisions of said Commission. The award by said Commission shall be deemed as final and binding upon both parties.

g) Supplementary Condition(s): Should the articles stipulated in this Contract be in conflict with the following supplementary condition(s), the supplementary condition(s) should be taken as valid and binding.

Sellers: Buyers:

Module 3 Routine Activities

Task 8 Meeting Minutes 会议记录

Warm-up

Try to translate the following Meeting Minute into Chinese.

参考译文：

2010年4月8日

题目：国内市场销售人员例会

出席：……

主持人：詹姆斯·王

秘书：简·李

请假缺席者：……

讨论内容：

通过上次会议纪要，参加会议者继续讨论下列问题。

1. 约翰逊·王介绍市场调查报告

王先生报告了上次会议期间出现的生产问题的调查。他说这些问题现在已全部解决，并称目前生产已恢复到预期水平。

2. 其他事务

韩先生报告说地方消防官在更换安全执照前还要进行一次检查。

决定：夏洛特·孙先生在秘书协助下负责使各处都达到要求。

3. 给沙利文先生的信

决定：由秘书代表全体人员致信沙利文先生，对他身体欠佳表示问候，并祝他早日康复。

4. 下次会议时间

如不出现其他问题，下次会议将于5月11日（星期二）举行。

11:30 会议结束。

签名：

Follow-up

1. Translate the following words into Chinese.

(1) 宣布开会　　(2) 休会　　(3) 主持　　(4)（在会议上）正式支持

(5) 决议　　　(6) 议程　　(7) 会议记录　(8) 主席

(9) 出席　　　(10) 缺席

2. Translate the following sentences.

(1) 上次会议的会议记录已事先传阅，该会议记录已被确认通过并由主席签字。

(2) 与会者一致提议从加拿大聘请专家为公司全体员工开设培训课程。

(3) 张经理自愿安排人员就修理费用做出估价并在下次会议上汇报有关情况。

(4) 晚上8点45分休会。

(5) 没有其他事项，主席宣布会议结束。

(6) Apologies for Mr. Chen Mingqiang, the manager of HR.

(7) The minutes were then approved as a correct record and signed by the chairman.

(8) It was agreed that the next meeting will be held on 1st July, 2009, at 10:00 a.m. in the conference room.

(9) The Chairman pointed out that it was not within the Committee's power to make such a decision.

(10) A meeting was held at 2:30 p.m. today in the Union Hall to discuss problems arising from domestic sales.

Homework

Write a meeting minutes with the following information.

Minutes of the monthly meeting of the Labor Grievances Committee

The Slate and Johnson Luggage Company

Employees'canteen, September 23, 2003

Presiding:Mr.Falk/Chairing:Mr.Falk

Present: Mr.Baum

   Ms.Dulugatz

   Mr.Fenster

   Ms.Liu

   Ms.Sun

Absent: Ms.Penn

The chairman called the meeting to order at 4:00 p.m.

As the first item on the agenda, the minutes of the previous meeting(August 21) was read by the Secretary Ms.Liu.

Then Mr.Falk corrected a mistake made in the minutes that it was Ms.Dulugatz, not Ms.Penn to conduct a study of the employee washroom in the warehouse.

The correction was approved by all present.

Mr.Fenster summarized the results of a survey of office employees.

He was going to write a report on this and present it to the Board of Directors.

The next meeting will be held at the same time and place on October 22, 2003.

The meeting adjourned at 5:15 p.m.

Prepared by:Liu Xiaoyun,Committee Secretary

Task 9 Application Documents for Going Abroad 出国文书

Warm-up

Try to translate the following recommendation letter into Chinese.

敬启者：

  我是财经大学会计学院的博士生导师，盛桦是我校会计专业辅修课学生，我曾担任该学生的审计学老师和实习指导老师。她上课很用心，我讲过的很多案例，在她参与资信评估的实习时，都能得到运用。

  实习期间，盛桦给我留下了非常好的印象。为了能学习更多的评估专业知识，她主动承担了更多的工作，像正式员工一样主动留下来加班。并且不论工作难度高低，她都能尽心尽力地做好，这样的敬业精神实属难得。她会计基础牢固，核心课程平均成绩 85 分，加之学习能力较强，因此实习期间她已能较好地掌握评估的一些基本业务，而这又进一步使她对会计有了更深的领悟。25 天工作日，她共参与调研了国内外的 15 家公司。在参与撰写评估报告时，她思路清晰、有较强的逻辑性；在独立完成一部分工作的同时，能较好地与老师沟通、合作，并能提一些有深度的问题，得到了大家的一致好评。

  此致

    敬礼

×××

Follow-up

Translate the following recommendation letter.

推荐信

陈加里
首席执行官
中国北京 ××× 数字有限公司
电话：+8613921298225
电子邮箱：garychen@digi100.cn

敬启者：

  2005 年至 2007 年，与市场计划经理沈灵小姐一起工作真是非常愉快的经历。

  作为市场计划经理，沈小姐负责多项工作，从推广产品到与潜在客户发展建立业务关系。

  除了具有出色的团队精神，沈小姐还表现出相当出色的首创精神，并能周到灵活地完成工作。她的时间管理能力和工作安排能力令人印象深刻。同时她还具有很强的承担额外工作的能力。

  总之，沈灵是非常出色的员工，我会毫不犹豫地向您推荐她。如果您需要她的其他信息，我很愿意继续与您保持联系。

  此致

    敬礼

陈加里

Homework

1. Translate the following Curriculum Vitae into Chinese.

个人简历

个人信息

姓名：×××

年龄：40 岁

婚否：已婚

性别：男

出生日期：1970 年 2 月 13 日

原所在国：马来西亚

地址（家庭）：

个人邮箱：peterchang@yaho.com

教育背景：

学校名称	资质	在校时间
abc 大学	学位	1989—1992 年
雅思	英语测试	1989 年
xyz 学院	学历	1985—1988 年

工作经历

工作单位	职位	在职时间
123 公司	高级市场经理	2006 年至今
KKK 公司（上海）	销售经理	2002—2006 年
333 公司	行政主管	1997—2002 年

工作经历：

1) 123 公司：拓展新市场和新业务；负责在现有公司体系中建立新部门；建立与当地大学的合作联系并在中国创立新公司。

2) KKK 公司：在中国管理 22 个中心和 2 个相关附属部门；成功改组歇业公司并使营业额取得 1560 万的增长；使公司取得 1250 万的潜在营业额的增长。

3) TTT 公司：负责日常管理。

2. Translate the following passage into English.

It is with great pleasure and confidence that I take this opportunity to recommend one of my favorite students Li Xia to you. Li Xia has been studying in our university for almost four years under my supervision. With my experience of teaching, dealing with students and understanding of different kinds of students, I can say with certainty and delight that she has been one of the strongest and most industrious students I have ever met.

I started to know Li Xia and notice her soon after she entered into our university. Her being enthusiastic in learning, dynamic in team leadership, creative in problem–solving, strong in logical thinking and English-oriented attitude impressed me and her other teachers immediately and deeply. Not only has she been performing really well in each class, but also she took part in a certain amount of extracurricular activities. Being open-minded, friendly and always accommodating, she is well liked by both her classmates and staff in our university.

In addition to being a top student in our university, Li Xia has also worked as the student leader of the Literature League of our Student Union. She is quite forward-thinking and can take initiatives. With her strong communication and public relationship building skills, she co-organized several literature events which enriched the students' school life a lot.

Li Xia intends to learn business abroad and I recommend her as a student. She would be a proud addition to any institution for learning. I feel confident that, should she be offered the opportunity to study at your institution, she would cope well due to her personalities and overall level of fluency and accuracy in English.

Please feel free to contact me at your convenience if you would like any further information regarding Li Xia.

Task 10　Business Travel 商务旅行

Warm-up

Try to translate the following passage into Chinese.

旅行一直都是商务活动的重要组成部分。从列车之旅到商务航班，人们早已了解旅行对于结交新客户的重要性。改变的，不过是旅行的方式而已。随着科技的发展，世界变得更加紧密互联，全球的商务旅行正变得越来越普遍。这对于旅客而言，有利有弊。一部手机就可以满载安全旅行所需的全部信息，那么万一忘带充电器就会引发一场灾难。所有这些都要归结于细节问题，因此，当涉及商务旅行时，一个全面的行程计划表比以往任何时候都更重要。

Follow-up

1. Translate the following sentences into Chinese.

(1) 如果贵公司在我们酒店有企业优选账户的话，请在这里输入账户号码，我们将据此为您提供您的公司可享受的优选价格。

(2) 请将您随身携带的所有金属物品，如硬币、手机、口香糖（盒），香烟以及带锡纸的物品等放置在篮子里。

(3) 很遗憾地告诉您，这是易燃品，不能随身带上飞机。

(4) 行李一直是您自己保管的吗？

(5) 您要接受额外抽查。

(6) 今晚 8 点恒天然公司邀请您参加在奥克兰皇冠假日酒店举行的欢迎宴会。

(7) 让我向您介绍马克·席勒先生，我公司市场部经理。

(8) 让我把您介绍给我公司总经理李先生。

(9) 史密斯先生，这位是我公司总经理郑先生，这位是市场部主任林先生，这位是研发部经理王先生。

(10) 要是我没认错的话，您是来自法国的陈小姐吧？

(11) 您还记得我吗？我是 PVC 公司市场部的小刘。我们几年前见过面。

(12) 还有没介绍到的吗？/ 我还忘了介绍哪位吗？

(13) 很高兴和您谈话。

(14) 这是我的名片。/ 我能给您留张名片吗？

(15) 我能向您要张名片吗？/ 您能给我一张名片吗？

2. Translate the following passage into Chinese.

(1) 对于送洗的衣物，本酒店将会做小心适当的处理，如有任何发生于洗烫过程中的损坏或丢失（如纽扣或饰物损坏或丢失），本酒店概不负责。任何衣物的损坏或丢失，其赔偿将不超过洗烫费的五倍。所有投诉，必须在送还后 24 小时内提出。请客人在数量栏内填写衣物的数量，如没有填写，将以酒店数字为准，在数量出现误差的情况下，我们将尽快与您联系。如您不在，则以酒店点数为准。在没有特别要求下，男士衬衫和女士衬衫均挂架送回。

(2) 房价是每个房间每入住一晚的价格，具体内容根据酒店的情况而定。优惠价包括两个成人和一个孩子的住宿，入住 2 晚及以上的宾客还可享受免费的自助早餐。加床依据酒店的情况而定。如果您预订了 2 个房间，酒店将尽力提供毗邻的房间（视情况而定）。此价格有资格获得洲际酒店集团优悦会的奖励积分。个别酒店可能提供当地景点的门票，并可能会有所不同。如需当地景点的额外门票，可从酒店购买。请注意奥克兰随上随下的观光车并不包含进入任何景点的费用，这些费用将由乘车者自行承担。

Homework

1. Translate the following dialogue into Chinese.

有预订情况下的入住：

Johnson：晚上好，我有预订，名字是 Johnson。

服务员：好，我找到了。是 27 日退房吗？

Johnson：没错。

服务员：我能用您的信用卡扣划押金吗？

Johnson：当然可以。另外，请给我一间无烟房间。

服务员：当然可以，先生。这是您的房间钥匙。您的房间在 7 层左侧，房间号码 8781。退房需要在中午 12 点之前。

无预订情况下的入住：

Johnson：你好，我想入住贵酒店。

服务员：当然可以，能把姓名给我吗？

Johnson：约翰逊先生。

服务员：好的，您是明天退房吗？

Johnson：是的，没错，是明天退房。

服务员：先生您需要唤醒服务吗？

Johnson：是的，请在早上 6:30 唤醒我。

服务员：好的。您的房间号码是五层的 8502 房间。早餐是早晨 6:30 到 9:00。祝您入住愉快。

Johnson：谢谢你。

2. Translate the following dialogue into English.

W: Mr. Sun, I'd like you to meet Mr. William Johnson, sales manager from Lanston of Canada.

(Sun extends hand first; Sun and Johnson shake hands) Mr. Johnson, Mr. Steven Sun, general manager of Cast Trading.

S: It's very nice to finally meet you, Mr. Johnson, after so many phone calls and faxes. (offers his business card first) I'd like you to have my business card.

J: Thanks very much, Mr. Sun. Please accept mine. (offers his own card) And please, call me William. (Both of them look at cards for a few seconds, then put them in wallets-not pockets.)

J: Wang appears to be a top-notch young man, Mr. Sun. Talent and enthusiasm like that is hard to find.

S: He's doing a great job for us. And please, call me Steven.

J: Steven, can you tell me in a nutshell what the retail market is like in Tianjin?

S: Well, as per capita income goes up and up, the growth sector seems to be going upscale.

J: Retail is going upscale here? Tianjin is certainly growing more quickly than I had imagined.

S: Yes. Things certainly have changed since I was a boy. We've developed very quickly.

J: Do you think the trend will continue?

S: I don't see why not. We do have some problems, but we are still willing to work hard—and wages aren't too high at this point.

J: Everything I've seen so far is very impressive. Very impressive indeed.

Task 11 Business Report 商务报告

Warm-up

Try to translate the following business report into Chinese.

关于本年度巴黎服装展的总结报告

交与：约翰·布朗总经理

提交人：丽莉·乔恩斯，营销部门

日期：2009年4月14日

导言

本年度服装展于2009年4月6日至12日在巴黎国际展览中心举行。为期一周的展会吸引了来自世界各地的8000多名展商参展。其中，我们是来自中国的在环保织物方面首屈一指的公司。能看到那么多著名的服装品牌，我们感到非常兴奋，但同时激烈的竞争也让我们备感压力。

发现

由于是第一次参加这种大型的高级别的服装展，我们发现有很多地方有待改进。

＊我们的口号缺少创意，也不够新颖，无法在众多原创的、有吸引力的大小品牌中彰显个性。

＊宣传诉求不符合我们的产品；环保的主题未能显现。

结论

通过这次展会，我们发觉参加这样的展出是至关重要的，既能了解行业的最新动态，又能从对其他服装品牌的学习中有所收获。

建议

基于这次展会的体会，我们提出如下建议：

＊改换口号。我们应提出一个新的、更适合的口号，既体现创造性又很新颖，这样才能从其他类似品牌中脱颖而出。

＊改变营销策略。宣传活动应突出产品环保的主题，如在新产品设计中增加绿色系列的比重等。

Follow-up

Translate the following business report into Chinese.

(1) 根据您的指示，我们对上海分部销售下滑的原因作了调查。

(2) 这份报告将提供针对我们新系列产品的改进而搜集的一些资料。

(3) 因此我提出以下建议供您参考。

(4) A thorough comparison promoted a decision on the third program.

(5) I have chosen the third among the twelve because it's more feasible.

(6) In this report I present the information you wanted to have before deciding whether or not to invest in ABC Company.

Homework

Translate the following English passage into Chinese.

参考译文：

主题：关于本年度利润再投资的可行性报告

引言

本报告旨在审核本年度利润再投资的可行性。

考虑之列的再投资项目

本报告列入再投资考虑范围的项目为：

1. 购买新计算机
2. 提供外语培训课程
3. 发放特别奖金

评估

1. 购买新计算机

本公司的大多数计算机都尚属新品，完全可以胜任日常工作之需。因此购买新计算机不足为取。

2. 外语培训课程

公司有意增加出口，尤其是增加对法国和西班牙出口业务，因此举办外语培训班对在海外有业务伙伴和客户的员工来说非常有益。（另一方面，培训课程也有助于提高士气——员工不仅对课程感兴趣，还会认为公司愿意为他们投资。因此，提供外语课程是可取的。）

3. 发放特别奖金

尽管发放特别奖金会有利于提高士气，但对公司运作并不产生直接作用。另一方面，挑选合格员工为本年度和今后特别奖金发放对象会引起问题。因此，发放特别奖金不足为取。

结论

1. 目前并无购买新计算机的必要。
2. 发放特别奖金极可能引发问题。
3. 提供外语培训课程对公司运作和提高士气均有利。

建议

综上所述，对公司和员工都有利的方案是投资于提供外语培训课程。建议公司组织法语和西班牙语培训课程。与业务伙伴有联系的员工应优先考虑，其他有兴趣的员工也可参加。

Module 4 Corporate Campaign

Task 12 Corporate Profile 企业形象

Warm-up

Try to translate the following company introduction.

1. Put the following Chinese into English.

Founded in 1966 by Mr. Pierre Bellon, Sodexho made an initial public offering of shares on the Paris Bourse in 1983 and on New York Stock Exchange in 2000 and set up its global headquarter in Paris, France.

Today, with more than 40 years of rich experience and successful operations on the five continents, Sodexho has grown into the largest multinational corporation in catering and facility management around the World. As a global Fortune 500 company with more than 324,000 employees, Sodexho has established more than 24,000 contract operations in 76 countries by the end of 2005.

2. Put the following English into Chinese.

海尔集团成立于1984年，总部设在山东省青岛市。成立之初，海尔只生产单一型号的冰箱，如今的海尔已经成为世界领先的白色家电制造商。海尔集团已经生产出96个领域一万五千多个不同规格的家电。海尔产品现在销售于世界一百多个国家。海尔旗下拥有240多家法人单位、110个设计中心和贸易公司，全球员工总数超过5万人。重点发展科技、工业、贸易、金融四大支柱产业。海尔产品范畴广，包括冰箱、冰柜、空调、洗衣机、电视机、手机、家庭影院、电脑、热水器、DVD等，其中9类产品在我国市场遥遥领先，3类产品位居世界第三。

Follow-up

Translate the following sentences and paragraphs into English / Chinese.

(1) 在产品更新、产品质量、产品设计和产品价值等方面我公司已建立很高的知名度。

(2) 我们的品牌知名度和新产品研发能力在全球范围内享有极高的声誉。

(3) 目前，在世界100多个国家里，我公司提供专业化的销售及市场服务。在世界11个国家设有专业化的生产商，包括在中国的3个生产商。

(4) 百得公司是世界上在电动工具、金属配件、家用小电器、管道设备及建筑用产品方面最大的市场占有者及生产商之一，所生产的产品广泛运用于家用及商业领域。

(5) 2009年10月，顶新国际集团偕同日本早稻田大学宣布共同投入2640万美元，以高额奖学金资助中国优秀学生到世界名校深造。

(6) A fortune 100 company with global presence and impact, Motorola had sales of US$35.3 billion in 2005.

(7) For three consecutive years since 1990, our company has been listed as one of the top 30 enterprises among China's 500 largest foreign trade companies in import-export volumes.

(8) Boasting tremendous technological strength, this Company owns a well-qualified management and staff. It has also established close cooperative relationships with several research organizations at home.

(9) For more than 10 years, this Company has built an excellent reputation among customers at home and abroad for its quality products and superior services.

(10) Approved by Zhuhai Council of Foreign Economic Relations and Trade, Zhuhai Dement Trading Co., Ltd. is a foreign trade enterprise possessing the state of legal body.

Homework

1. Translate the following paragraph into Chinese.

联合利华在中国资助建立了9所希望小学；在高校开展"联合利华希望之星"项目，为200个贫困学生提供4年的大学费用；公司还在复旦大学设立奖学金，奖励品学兼优的学生。从1996年开始，公司还在全国范围开展护齿宣传的系列活动。2000年，联合利华在中国十几个省开展了植树活动，旨在提高人们的环保意识。

2. Translate the following paragraph into Chinese.

摩托罗拉公司一直是全球电子通信领域研发的领导者。摩托罗拉在中国的研发投资达6亿美元，在北京、天津、上海、南京、成都和杭州6个城市建立了17个研发中心和实验室，研发人员约3000人。摩托罗拉中国研究院已经成为摩托罗拉的全球研发基地之一，也是跨国公司在中国建立的最大的研发机构。

3. Translate the following paragraph into English.

China Golddeal has a progressive and visionary staff always ready to devote themselves to creation and design, to the maintaining of cultural tradition and the promotion of economic development. It is them who have created the legend of three years of rapid development of China Golddeal.

4. Translate the following paragraph into English.

Tianjin Foreign Enterprises & Experts Service Co., Ltd. (TJFESCO) provides human resources service for representative offices of overseas enterprises in Tianjin, foreign-funded enterprises, state-owned enterprises and private enterprises. TJFESCO plays an important role in Tianjin human resources service market and wins the title of Tianjin Excellent Enterprise in 2003 and 2004.

Task 13 Commercial Advertisement 商业广告

Warm-up

Try to translate the following advertisements into Chinese.
(1) 我们领先，他人复制。(理光复印机)
(2) 滴滴香浓，回味无穷。(麦斯威尔咖啡)
(3) 智慧演绎，无处不在。(摩托罗拉手机)
(4) 不懈追求完美。(凌志轿车)
(5) 牙齿清洁，口气清新。(高露洁牙膏)
(6) 精致生活，源自细节。(帅康厨房电器)
(7) 世界触手可及。(中国电信)
(8) 为梦想创造可能。(蒙牛牛奶)
(9) 创新科技，美的空调。(美的空调)
(10) 生活就是一部电视剧。(CCTV-8)
(11) 对我而言，过去平淡无奇；而未来，却绚丽多彩。(轩尼诗酒)
(12) 没有最佳，但求更好。(飞利浦照明产品)
(13) 君饮"七喜"，醒脑提神。(七喜饮料)
(14) (科技) 以人为本。(诺基亚通信产品)
(15) 没有橘汁的早餐犹如没有阳光的日子。(橘汁)
(16) 英特拂劳拉的鲜花倾诉衷肠。(鲜花)
(17) 一次品尝，永远喜欢。(饮料)
(18) 莫大的激动，微小的费用。(出租车)

Follow-up

Translate the following ad. into Chinese.

奇宝巧克力选用上乘原料，采用独特秘方精制而成。轻巧松脆，让您的全家体验到奇宝特有的新鲜美味。

全球饼干及零食领袖——联合饼干集团专注于烘制最优质的饼干及零食，产品遍及全球90多个国家。

Homework

1. Translate the following ad. into Chinese.

一旦拥有，别无他求。精工液晶表将是您的第一也是您的唯一。
日常活动即可充电，无须电池。环保材料制造，走时准确，性能可靠。
精工特别奉献。
Kinetic 精工制造，引领表业新潮流。

2. Translate the following ad. into English.

Congratulations! Olympus youth series has reached 20 million cameras sold. Within the promotion period, get a special free gift with every purchase of selected Olympus cameras or digital recorders. Distributed by the Hong Kong sole agent. Don't miss it!

Task 14 Press Release 新闻发布

Warm-up

1. Try to translate the following passage into Chinese.

首先，我谨代表世界旅游组织向这次文化节和招商会的开幕致以诚挚的祝贺。我非常荣幸来参加广东国际旅游文化节，特别是今天的旅游招商会。这次活动见证了中国的活力与重要性，尤其是广东，在世界旅游业中的活力与重要性。

……

我敢肯定这次招商会将进一步促进旅游业在中国，尤其是在广东的发展。最后，我祝愿这次会议圆满成功。谢谢大家！

2. Try to translate the following passage into English.

Honorable heads, distinguished guests, dear friends, ladies and gentlemen,

It is a good pleasure to join you all today. The beautiful city Tianjin is very lucky to be able to host the celebration during this golden month of October. On behalf of all the staff of our company, I would firstly like to extend my warmest congratulations to the 10th Anniversary of Huamei Advertising Co. At the same time, I would also like to express my sincere thanks to the invitation from Huamei Corporation. It is such an exciting experience to be together with honorable guests and friends who have traveled so far to come to this celebration.

Follow-up

1. Translate the following sentences and paragraphs into English.

(1) On the occasion of the opening of the Chinese Import and Export Commodities Fair, I'd like, on behalf of our Company, to extend our warm congratulations.

(2) I wish the congress every success, and I would like to take this opportunity to extend our thanks to the government of our host country, for the great efforts it has made for the convening of the current congress.

(3) It is truly a privilege and a pleasure for me to address this activity.

(4) I am delighted to send this personal message of welcome to all visitors to the Trade Fair. I greatly value the friendship and confidence that we enjoy as trading partners. I am certain the Fair will strengthen our relationship and contribute directly to further trade expansion to the benefit of our countries.

(5) It is indeed a privilege and a pleasure for me to address this International Conference, convened in the capital of the People's Republic of China with the substantial

support from the Ministry of Commerce. I believe our cooperative efforts are sure to be productive and will contribute to the success of the Conference.

2. Translate the following sentences and paragraphs into Chinese.

(1) 我们到北京仅 10 天，但会议周密的计划与组织工作已给我们留下了深刻的印象。

(2) 这次我公司与中国机械公司达成协议说明我们的前景更加光明。

(3) 我还要借此机会，对所有组织者和工作人员在筹备庆典活动中所做出的杰出贡献，表示衷心的感谢。

(4) 本人作为这次展览会的主席，对所有前来参观的来宾表示热烈的欢迎。我相信他们将会对这个展览会产生很大兴趣。我们期望这个展览会能为两国间的合作提供更多机会，并期望它能在加强两国关系方面发挥更大的作用。

(5) 我十分荣幸和愉快地代表来自世界各地区的 28 个不同国家的代表团，感谢主席先生刚才热情洋溢的欢迎词。我们还要感谢组织委员会邀请我们来这里参加会议，并感谢他们为这次会议的安排所付出的辛勤劳动和心血。

Homework

Translate the the following speech (abridged) into English.

Professor Klaus Schwab, Distinguished Heads of Government, Distinguished Guests, Ladies and Gentlemen, It's a great pleasure to meet you again in Tianjin. At the outset, I wish to congratulate, on behalf of the Chinese government, the opening of the Annual Meeting of the New Champions, and extend sincere welcome to all our guests coming from afar and friends from the press.

……

Tianjin is a big port in the World, where people could start a voyage to sail to the vast ocean. For a giant ship to sail far, sustained and strong driving force is needed. China will work with other countries to seize the opportunities brought by the new round of technological and industrial revolution. Together, we will build new engines of economic growth, promote steady recovery of the World economy through transformation and upgrading, and jointly usher in a better future for the development of mankind.

I wish this forum a full success !

Bibliography

[1] 陈准民，陈建平.商务英语翻译.北京：高等教育出版社，2007

[2] 丁衡祁.对外宣传中的英语质量亟待提高.北京：中国翻译，2002(4)

[3] 蒋磊.英汉文化差异与广告的语用翻译.北京：中国翻译，2002(3)

[4] 李波阳.商务英语汉英翻译教程.北京：中国商务出版社，2005

[5] 李明.商务英语翻译（汉译英）.北京：高等教育出版社，2007

[6] 李运兴.汉英翻译教程.北京：新华出版社，2006

[7] 梅德明.新编商务英语翻译.北京：高等教育出版社，2005

[8] 潘红.商务英语英汉翻译教程.北京：中国商务出版社，2004

[9] 潘月洲.商务英语翻译教程.北京：北京交通大学出版社，2008

[10] 谭卫国.英汉广告修辞的翻译.北京：中国翻译，2002(2)

[11] 王恩冕.如何翻译英语报刊经济文章.北京：对外经济贸易大学出版社，2005

[12] 许建平.英汉互译实践与技巧.3版.北京：清华大学出版社，2007

[13] 余富林等.商务英语翻译（英译汉）.北京：中国商务出版社，2003

[14] 张新红、李明.商务英语翻译（英译汉）.北京：高等教育出版社，2003

[15] 邹力.商务英语翻译教程（笔译）.北京：中国水利水电出版社，2005

[16] 杨自力.会展英语翻译.大连：大连理工大学出版社，2008

[17] 宿荣江，曹珊珊，周媛.会展实用英语.北京：中国人民大学出版社，2008

[18] 董晓波.实用经贸文体翻译.北京：对外经济贸易大学出版社，2013

[19] 陈可培，边立红.应用文体翻译教程.北京：对外经济贸易大学出版社，2012

[20] 袁洪，王济华.商务翻译实务.北京：北京对外经济贸易大学出版社，2011

[21] 刘作永.试谈招投标文件的语言特点.北京：中国翻译，2001(2)

[22] 何晓琴. 英汉语招投标文件的语言特点及翻译技巧. 江西: 科技师范大学学报, 2002 (6)

[23] 杨跃. 实用科技英语翻译研究. 西安：西安交通大学出版社，2008

[24] https://www.airnewzealand.co.nz/

[25] https://www.crowneplaza.com/

[26] http://www.chinadaily.com/

[27] https://www.tac-online.org.cn/

[28] https://www.catti.net.cn/